SERIAL KILLERS

SERIAL KILLERS

Issues Explored Through the Green River Murders

Tomás Guillén
Seattle University

PEARSON
Prentice
Hall

Upper Saddle River, New Jersey 07458

Library of Congress Cataloging-in-Publication Data

Guillén, Tomás.
 Serial killers : issues explored through the Green River murders / Tomás Guillén.
  p. cm.
 Includes bibliographical references and index.
 ISBN 0-13-152966-8
1. Serial murders—Washington (State)—Green River Region (King County)—Case studies.
2. Serial murder investigation—Washington (State)—Green River Region (King County) 3.
Ridgway, Gary Leon, I. Title.

 HV6533.W2G85 2006
 364.152'30979777—dc22

2005026911

Executive Editor: Frank Mortimer, Jr.
Assistant Editor: Mayda Bosco
Marketing Manager: Adam Kloza
Editorial Assistant: Kelly Krug
Production Editor: Jessica Balch, Pine Tree
 Composition
Production Liaison: Barbara Marttine
 Cappuccio
Director of Manufacturing and Production:
 Bruce Johnson
Managing Editor: Mary Carnis

Manufacturing Manager: Ilene Sanford
Manufacturing Buyer: Cathleen Petersen
Senior Design Coordinator: Mary Siener
Cover Designer: Michael L. Ginsberg
Cover Image: Natalie G. Guillén
Manager of Media Production: Amy Peltier
Media Project Manager: Lisa Rinaldi
Media Development Editor: John J. Jordan
Formatting and Interior Design: Pine Tree
 Composition
Printing and Binding: Courier Stoughton

Pearson Education, Ltd., *London*
Pearson Education Australia Pty. Limited, *Sydney*
Pearson Education Singapore, Pte. Ltd.
Pearson Education North Asia Ltd., *Hong Kong*
Pearson Education Canada, Ltd., *Toronto*
Pearson Education de Mexico, S.A. de C.V.
Pearson Education—Japan, *Tokyo*
Pearson Education Malaysia, Pte. Ltd.
Pearson Education, Upper Saddle River, *New Jersey*

10 9 8 7 6 5 4 3 2 1
ISBN 0-13-152966-8

Dedicated to my family: Susan, Anne, Phillip, and Natalie.
For 23 long years, they have endured
my physical and psychological absence
as I was consumed by the Green River Murders.
May this book bring closure for us all.

CONTENTS

PREFACE

The torturous dream came in black and white as I slept in a serene bed-and-breakfast far away from the sleepless streets of Seattle. In the dream I sat fidgeting on a sandy beach watching the angry waves of a turbulent river reach out to thick, gray fog. Suddenly, someone rushed up behind me, yelling at me to get up, help!

"There's a woman buried in the sand," said the voice. "We have to get her out!"

The voice persisted as it ran with me toward a raised bed of sand. Reaching the raised bed, I dropped to my knees and frantically started digging with my hands.

"We have to get her out! We have to get her out!" my mind kept screaming. "We have to get her out!"

I dug and dug, but I couldn't find her. I knew she was in there! I could hear her gasps for air inside the sand.

"My God, where is she? Help me find her!" I yelled. The wind carried my words downstream with the river. "We have to get her out! We have to get her out!"

My arms became so tired from clawing at the wet, rough sand that my head bumped the bed of sand with every breath I took. Large drops of sweat created shallow holes in the sand as quickly as I shoved sand away.

All of a sudden, the gasps became louder, clearer, and I could see the tip of her chin and lips. I dug faster and her entire face appeared. She had blond hair combed back and she was alive. Yes, very alive!

I awoke sweaty and breathing heavily. I couldn't get the gasping woman out of my mind. Thank God she lived.

It was no mystery to me why my mind concocted the dream: That night I had read the "Summary of Evidence" against a man dubbed the Green River Killer. Most of the women who crossed his path died. He choked over 60 women, and on the day of my dream, I had read every merciless detail of how the killer murdered the women, and then returned to the corpses days later to satisfy his voracious, distorted, sexual appetite.

How did I come to read that depressing "Summary of Evidence"? How did the victims of the Green River Killer come to embed themselves in my psyche? How did they end up weighing heavy on my heart like the big rocks used to weigh several victims down in the Green River?

I was at the Green River just south of Seattle, Washington, in 1982, shortly after the first victims of the most prolific serial killer in the history of this nation were discovered. I was dispatched there as a journalist by *The Seattle Times* to report on the grisly discoveries and keep track of the police investigation. Little did I know then that the assignment would span more than two decades. For years I stood along rural highways waiting for skeletal remains to be carted out; interviewed heartbroken parents and siblings who may never find closure; harassed police administrators into releasing more information; analyzed the strategies and missteps of investigators; passed the time away with prostitutes on the street and pimps in jail; stayed up nights talking with Green River suspects; traveled around the country studying serial murder cases; relished assignations in out-of-the-way restaurants with Green River Task Force detectives; and sat in dark, wooded, body dump sites to visualize the killer with his victims.

Often it feels like only yesterday that the first bodies were fished out of the Green River. Sometimes it seems like the slayings never happened. Initially the 1982 river murders appeared unrelated to each other. By the time King County Police investigators realized the four women in the river and the one left on the bank of the river were the work of a serial killer, the perpetrator had moved to depositing the results of his murderous misdeeds in rural, wooded areas. When mushroom hunters and hikers began stumbling across skeletal remains throughout King County, police administrators and politicians in charge of resources finally realized that a massive effort needed to be launched to identify and capture the killer.

It was not until 1984 that the Green River Task Force was formed. It consisted of over 50 investigators from several law enforcement jurisdictions, including the Federal Bureau of Investigation. The task force did a superb job infiltrating the streets and reconstructing the ebb and flow of life on the prostitution strip, where the killer preyed on women and girls. But it was all for naught; the task force could find no trace of the killer. Eventually the clock ran out. Politicians decided they had spent enough time, money, and resources on the hunt. "Sorry," they seemed to say. "We tried! We have to move on. . . ." By 1990, the Green River Task Force was no more. A single detective was left to babysit the case and answer the never-ending telephone calls from misfits, dissatisfied parents of the victims, and out-of-state police officers investigating a serial case in their city. The killer appeared to have won!

Throughout the decades, hundred of suspects were investigated and interviewed. In fact, the Green River Killer case proved difficult to solve because there were *too many* good suspects. There were too many men— lawyers, priests, engineers, husbands, politicians, landscapers, journalists, hamburger flippers—obsessed with women and sex. They regularly ventured to the seedy streets to find instant gratification with a prostitute. Wives and girl-friends and neighbors were sure they knew who the Green River Killer was.

It was while examining this sea of perverts that the Green River Task Force came across an Auburn, Washington, truck painter by the name of Gary Leon Ridgway. Investigators subjected him to a polygraph, pried into his life and family, and searched his home, but they failed to find the evidence to charge him with the murders. In investigating Ridgway in 1987, however, detectives routinely had him suck on a cloth swab for a saliva sample. Such a sample, back then, could only provide a person's blood type. That, in turn, could be compared with the blood type of semen or other body fluids found at crime scenes. DNA technology became so refined by the early 2000s that investigators were able to compare the DNA in the saliva sample with DNA in semen found in several of the Green River victims. And in 2001 Ridgway was arrested again, but this time he was charged with a handful of the slayings.

When King County Sheriff David Reichert suggested that investigators finally had caught him, Ridgway teased: "No, what got me caught was technology."

Ridgway surprised everyone by opting to confess to killing over 60 women, the latest in 1998. He told investigators he may have killed as recently as 2001, but he couldn't remember. His confession spanned six months. Beginning on June 13, 2003, investigators interviewed Ridgway almost daily to determine the extent of his killings and to identify his victims. He was interviewed primarily by four King County Police detectives and four psychologists. The detectives were Tom Jensen, Randy Mullinax, Sue Peters, and Jon Mattsen. The psychologists were Dr. Robert Wheeler, Dr. Christian Harris, Dr. Mary Ellen O'Toole, of the FBI's National Center for the Analysis of Violent Crime; and Dr. Judith V. Becker. The confession ended December 16, 2003.

It was Ridgway's confession that spawned the "Summary of Evidence" and my torturous dream. When Ridgway came up for sentencing eight days before Christmas in 2003, I took a seat in the courtroom less then ten yards from him and his team of attorneys.

In exchange for Ridgway pleading guilty, the state promised not to seek the death penalty. Although Ridgway's fate was known—life in prison without the possibility of parole—relatives and friends of the killer's many victims asked to address Ridgway in open court during the sentencing. A few relatives dug deep into their soul to forgive. Most could not.

"Gary Loser Ridgway . . . I will never forgive you . . . I'm angry; I will always be angry," shouted Jose Malvar, Jr., whose sister was killed by Ridgway.

Nearly every major newspaper, broadcast station, and news website carried extensive coverage of the details in the "Summary of Evidence" and the emotional sentencing. Those events monopolized the news nationally, as the Green River Murders had done since 1982. The investigation and the case-ending sentencing particularly commanded the attention of *The New York Times*, *People* magazine, A&E, *Time* magazine, the History Channel, and international news outlets in such countries as Germany and England. And by the year 2005, several books had been penned about the infamous Green River Murders.

Much has been written about the Green River mystery and the horrid deaths of the many women. However, little has been said about the plethora of challenging issues that permeated the massive investigation. The intent of this book is to provide a collection of essays that focus on some of those rich issues. Taken as a whole, the essays offer an interdisciplinary perspective of the Green River Murders and the turbulent relationship of the many people it touched for over two decades. Although the essays revolve around the Green River Murders, the issues that are identified and explored are relevant to any in-depth discussion of such controversial topics as murder investigations, justice, victimology, interrogation techniques, media coverage of crime, the public's role in criminal investigations, and grief. Readers will find the details in the essays particularly valuable as they ponder theories that apply to criminal justice, law enforcement, sociology, political science, communication, persuasion, and psychology.

The issues in the essays are presented in a chronological fashion, in the order that they surfaced in the Green River Murders investigation. As readers discover the complexity of this serial killer mystery, they will better comprehend the impact of the issues throughout the case.

Gary Leon Ridgway's own words will be used extensively to convey the perpetrator's unique point of view regarding the issues. At times, his description of a kill will be graphic and unsettling, but it will help readers grasp his inhumanity and disdain for women. Particularly revealing will be his reluctant confession, in which investigators interrogated him for months to better understand the troubling questions and psychological trauma that arise from such serial crimes. To allow the reader to fully comprehend the deviant mind of a serial killer, this book includes a CD with video of Ridgway's confession and acrimonious relationship with his nemeses.

Tomás Guillén

ACKNOWLEDGMENTS

There are many individuals who should be thanked for their valuable contribution to making this interdisciplinary book possible. They provided the varied support critical to successfully completing scholarly work amid a hectic and rigorous academic setting.

Funds are always necessary in an undertaking as massive as this. Analysis of the numerous issues could not have been possible without the collection of over 100 DVDs that contained the killer's confession and the tens of thousands of investigative documents. Several academic entities and individuals helped defray the cost of the expensive DVDs, including Seattle University College of Arts and Sciences Dean Wallace Loh and Manager of Budget and Operations Kojay Pan; Communication Department Chair Jeffrey Philpott; and Center for the Study of Justice in Society Director Jeanette Rodriguez, PhD. Chameleon Data Corporation, the Seattle company that produced the DVDs for the King County Prosecutor's Office and King County Police, worked closely with researchers to ensure quality DVD video, audio, and text.

If the lack of funds can hamper projects, the lack of research assistance can cripple it. Several students helped research some of the theories related to the issues in this book. Seattle University English Department Associate Professor Mary-Antoinette Smith facilitated the search for researchers Antonietta Lincoln, Kelly Francis, Cody Goins, Michelle Molina, and Katrina Titchenal. They were diligent and punctual. Other Seattle University students helped, too, in informal ways. During classes or campus conversations, these students inspired new thoughts on the issues: Kista Koster, John Misko, Celina Santi, and Vlad Shegnagaev.

Seattle University's Office of Information Technology provided frequent assistance on this project. My special thanks to IT technical consultants Bill Hill, Charles Thompson, Brandy Long, and Sommar Kramer. Susan Cole of Reprographic and Mailing Services also contributed greatly. Administrative and moral support came from Seattle University Communication Department Administrative Assistant Lauren St. Pierre.

With any project of this magnitude, there are always legal questions. I am indebted to several individuals for supplying useful legal insights throughout the years: U.S. District Court Judge Robert Lasnick, King

County Superior Court Judge William Downing, and Gregory Silverman, Associate Professor in the Seattle University School of Law.

Of course, no book ever becomes a reality without an editor having faith in the project. Pearson Education Executive Editor Frank I. Mortimer, Jr., supported it wholeheartedly. Throughout the lengthy process, he received support from John Jordan and Joe Saba of Zaza Interactive. They helped complement the book with video vignettes of the lengthy confession by the Green River Killer. Mayda Bosco of Prentice Hall helped shepherd the entire project.

I would also like to thank the following people who reviewed the book: Professor Charisse T. M. Coston, University of North Carolina, Charlotte, NC; Professor Steven Christiansen, Green River Community College, Auburn, WA; and Professor Dwayne Smith, University of South Florida, Tampa, FL.

Finally, and most important, I owe my deepest gratitude to the families of the Green River victims who welcomed me into their homes at a time of great strife in their lives. They were patient and encouraged me to seek the truth from all sides. I very much appreciated their hospitality and understanding.

Tomás Guillén

SERIAL KILLERS

KING COUNTY DEPARTMENT OF PUBLIC SAFETY

MISSING PERSON REPORT

Patrol District **G2**

SECTION A

ORIGINAL REPORT ☒ (Sec. A;B;C;D;) — JUVENILE RUNAWAY ☒ — JUVENILE ESCAPE ☐
LOCATED REPORT ☐ (Sec. A;C;E;) — JUVENILE MISSING ☐ — ADULT MISSING ☐

Case Number **84-02236 5**

Date Report Taken **2/2/84** Time **1545**

IF LOCATED REPORT ORIGINAL REPORT DATE:

614 "F-O"

VICTIM — NAME (Last-First-Middle) **ESTES, DEBRA LORRAINE** — Age **16** — Res. Phone **834-4864** — Bus. Phone

SECTION B

Address **4203 So 297 PL** — City **AUBURN** — State **WA** — Zip **98001** — Occupation

Rac **W** | Sex **F** | D.O.S. **9-7-67** | Height **5-2** | Weight **120** | Hair **BLO** | Eyes **BLU** | Comp. **FAIR** | Student at ☒ — Employed at ☐ **KILO JR HI**

Wearing

VSM **TATOO OF HEART ON ONE SHOULDER** — AKA **MUFFIN : DEBBIE** — Glasses Yes ☐ No ☒ Type

Single ☒ — Married ☐ — Separated ☒ — Divorced ☐ — Widowed ☐

Has Serious Medical Problem? YES ☐ NO ☒ Type — Requires Medication? Yes ☐ No ☒

Last Seen Date **7/4/82** Day of Wk. **SU** Time **0300** Where **HOME**

By Whom: R/P ☒ Other ☐

Relationship

Address — State — Zip — PHP — PBP **SAME**

May Be With/At Suspected Reason for Leaving **RENEWAL OF 82-132639/82-220503/83-2293**

SUBJ IS 10-62 IN WACIC. ~~~~ **NO INFO ON ASSOCIATES,**

MOTHER WILL FURNISH PHOTO. DENTAL CHARTS ON FILE

Has Left/Escaped/Ran Before: Yes ☒ No ☐ When Last: — How Long: **2 WEEKS**

Was Located Where: **HARBORVIEW HOSP** — With Whom: **UNKNOWN**

Vehicle Involved: **NONE** | LIC | LIS | VYR | VMA | VMO | VST | VCO

If R/P Other Than Parent's Name:
Parent's Address — City — State — Zip — PHP — PBP

SEC. C

R.P. — Relationship — PHP — PBP

Address **SAME** — City — State — Zip — Occupation — Sex **F**

SECTION D

Patrol Follow-Up Yes ☐ No ☐ UNIT _____ — Teletype Sent Yes ☐ No ☐ — SAR Notified Yes ☐ No ☐

Check (Computers) Time _____ OP # _____ CCN _____ — Enter Time _____ OP # _____

Report taken By **DET T. R. JENSSN** — Unit # **0804** — Supervisor Reviewing — PERS# — Date & Time Signed

SECTION E

DISPOSITION

Returned Home ☐ Other _____ — Located Where _____

Date Located/Returned _____ Time Loc/Ret _____ Date R/C _____ Time R/C _____

Check (Computers) Time _____ OP # _____ CCN _____ Clear Time _____ OP # _____

Report taken By _____ Unit # _____ Supervisor Reviewing _____ PERS # _____ Date & Time Signed _____

C.I.D. Screener _____ Off./ Invest. Assigned _____

PAGE **1** OF **1**

KCDPS C-109 (1/81)

CHAPTER

Marginalizing the Missing

I know they didn't do a good job in our case. Debbie slipped through the system more than once.

Carol Estes[1]

Tom and Carol Estes knew their teenage daughter needed help, but they did not know how to help her. Debbie was headstrong and made friends with older girls as early as junior high. She was 12 going on 20, her mother often said. And, in fact, Debbie first ran away from home at the age of 12. Several times her parents found her and brought her back home. Making matters worse was the parents' penchant for working long hours to make ends meet. The Esteses realized they had a bigger problem when they discovered that a pro-choice organization provided their young daughter with birth control pills. It seemed inevitable that Debbie would end up on the street with the wrong crowd. Eventually Tom and Carol sought help from police when they could not find their daughter. Since police seemed indifferent to looking for her as a runaway, the Esteses filed a petty theft report against their daughter to force King County Police into action.[2] When Debbie snuck out of the house on July 3, 1982, she had taken $280 from her mother's purse. That day would be the last time they would see her alive. The Esteses cared little about the money. They simply sought help from police or any government or private group in handling and protecting their daughter. However, even the theft report failed to prompt police to respond.

A petty theft report or a runaway/missing person report on a teenager in 1982 was too low on a law enforcement agency's priority list in the Seattle, Washington, metropolitan area. In retrospect, the police handling of runaway/missing person reports and society's unsympathetic sentiments toward troubled teenagers contributed heavily to providing Green River Killer Gary Leon Ridgway with an abundance of victims to choose from between 1982 and when he was arrested in 2003. By the time investigators realized the link between runaway or missing teenagers, Ridgway had abducted and murdered most of his victims.

Tom and Carol Estes were only two of thousands of parents rebuffed by law enforcement procedures and attitudes, but their case best exemplifies the frustration most of the victims' parents were forced to endure. By the summer of 1982, Debbie—using the name Betty Lorraine Jones—had been arrested twice for prostitution by the Seattle Police Department and twice by the King County Police vice squad. When the first five victims in the Green River Murders case were found in the Green River in July and August 1982 and police were attempting to identify them, the Esteses contacted investigators. Carol feared her daughter was one of the unidentified girls in the river. After examining dental records, police determined Debbie was not one of the river victims and informed the Esteses that they had no record of a Debbie Estes being involved in prostitution. Debbie, in fact, had been arrested four times, but under the alias Betty Lorraine Jones. King County Police did know where Betty Jones was, but the Esteses were neither aware of her using the alias or that police knew the whereabouts of Betty Jones. How did police come to know a woman named Betty Jones? Toward the end of August 1982, Betty Jones accepted a ride from a man who forced her to have sex at gunpoint. A King County Police detective interviewed Betty Jones, then provided detectives working the Green River case a copy of the report. When Betty Jones failed to appear in court to testify against the rapist, the detective filed a missing person report that indicated she was last seen in the latter part of September 1982. In the meantime, Tom and Carol cruised the highways frequented by prostitutes looking for their daughter. They were joined by Rebecca Marrero, the mother of another missing teenager. Rebecca also had been battling to get police to look for her daughter. She last saw her 20-year-old daughter, Becky Marrero, leaving home in December 1982 following a phone call. Becky asked her mother to take care of her child and hurried out. Unbeknownst to Rebecca and the Esteses, the parents of Marie M. Malvar also were spending their spare time cruising the same prostitution strip in hopes of finding their 18-year-old daughter. Marie vanished in the latter part of April 1983 after getting into a pickup truck for a "date." In the end, all three girls became victims of the Green River Killer.

In 1984, King County Police finally created a multi-agency group dubbed the Green River Task Force, whose mission it was to determine the magnitude of the killings and identify the perpetrator. Soon after the task force was formed, the Esteses appealed to the investigative group for help in finding their daughter. Again, they were rebuffed. They were told there was no evidence Debbie had been a prostitute, and the task force was mostly charged with finding missing prostitutes who might be victims of the

Green River Killer. In desperation, Tom and Carol visited the Seattle Police Department vice squad and convinced a detective to allow them to look through photographs of known prostitutes. There they found a photograph of their daughter with dyed black hair and using the name Betty Lorraine Jones. The couple immediately took a copy of the photograph to task force headquarters, where they found an identical photograph on a wall with photographs of other possible Green River missing persons.

"Had they done their job, Debbie would be alive now," said Carol. "Police don't care. They don't care if a girl is 12 years old. But let it be their daughter. The system and police killed my daughter because of their I-don't-care attitude."[3]

Why were runaway youth and missing teenagers low priority among law enforcement agencies in Seattle and King County in the 1980s? To a large extent, police lacked the resources. They did not have enough police officers to look for the hundreds to thousands of teenagers reported as runaways or missing. Often police, too, grew tired of finding a runaway/missing teenager only to have the same teenager turn up missing again in a matter of days. Police also tended to drag their feet when it came to handling runaway/missing teens who had a history of prostitution. To police, the teenagers probably were simply traveling the prostitution circuit down the coast from Washington to Oregon to California. Police especially were dubious about taking a missing person report when a "pimp/boyfriend" called to report a prostitute missing, as was the case in the disappearance of several Green River victims. James Michael Tindal and Gisele Lovvorn fit in that category. A day after 19-year-old Lovvorn disappeared while working the prostitution strip in mid-July 1982, Tindal tried but could not file a missing person report. A day or so later police finally took a report when he became angry. The general feeling among police: they'll turn up one of these days. Lovvorn did turn up on September 25, 1982—dead in a wooded area south of the Seattle-Tacoma International Airport. She was another victim of the Green River Killer.

At times, sheer incompetence resulted in police taking no report, as Shirley Bonner found out when she went to the Tacoma Police Department on July 30, 1982, to file a missing persons report on her daughter, Debra L. Bonner, 23. Police would not take one, even after Shirley told an officer about a threatening note her daughter received. When King County Police made some inquiries about Debra and a possible connection to the Green River investigation, Tacoma police filled out a missing persons report and backdated it to the day Shirley attempted to file her report. Tacoma police had been reluctant to fill out a report because officers did not believe Debra was missing. Tacoma's report ended with: "advised Mrs. Bonner that she should report Debra missing with Seattle P.D., if that's where Debra had been living."[4] The officer's final notation in the report pointed to another problem that caused the victims' parents frustration and made it difficult to alert police something was amiss on the prostitution strip. Shirley, like many parents of Green River victims, was unsure where her daughter disappeared from. If a parent seemed unsure, police often refused to take a police report and asked the parent to contact a different agency. Some parents were bounced from one police department to another and back again.

Dysfunctional families, ineptness, police indifference, and the lack of manpower contributed to the number of potential Green River victims on the streets. But those factors did not appear to have as much impact on teenage waywardness as a Washington law that in effect legalized the right of children to run away. The law equated a teenager's right to an adult's rights, hence police regularly told parents they could not force their teenager to return home. All police could do was tell the runaway that their parents would like a call home. Consequently the names of teen runaways would be entered into a police computer, which routinely purged the names from the system after 30 days. Parents wise to the process filed runaway or missing person reports often to keep their teens' cases in the computer system.

The end result was hundreds of teenage girls frequenting the prostitution streets and seedy hotels in Seattle and King County during the 1980s. Daily, the girls went looking for change to buy food or alcohol or drugs. The girls became easy prey for pimps itching to use them to make money. After pumping them full of booze and drugs, the pimps easily convinced many of the girls to become streetwalkers. Once the girls were hooked on the street life, they rarely returned home to parents with abstinence and curfews on their minds. Hence, the prostitution problem in the 1980s in Seattle and King County was tremendous. At busy intersections near the airport girls routinely pursed their lips as they sat on the hood of vehicles stopped at a red light. It was nearly impossible to travel a block in some areas of the airport without being propositioned by several prostitutes.

"I'm angry at the way she was exploited and used," said Carol Estes. "The guys that picked her up. The pimps."[5]

Men simply saw the girls as objects to be used. Business owners along the airport prostitution strip tended to marginalize the victims, too, by seeing them only as a detriment to business. The businessmen and women complained bitterly to the politicians, who controlled the purse strings of the law enforcement agencies. The politicians, in turn, complained to the King County sheriff, who then ordered his men to organize a special effort to clean up the strip. For two months during the summer of 1983, police harassed the pimps and prostitutes. Some patrol cars were even stationed in motel parking lots with their lights flashing. Prostitution arrests went from 23 in June 1983 to 62 in September 1983. The emphasis patrol could quantitatively claim success, but it did little to abate the prostitution problem; it only forced the women to relocate in the city of Seattle.

The arrest and judicial process also reflected how law enforcement and society considered the missing women-turned-prostitutes as throwaway kids. After being arrested, the women spent the night in jail and were bailed out the next morning. The process repeated itself again in a few days or weeks in Seattle, King County, or in another city. It was not uncommon for women to use several aliases. When the women failed to appear in court for a trial on prostitution charges, a "Failure to Appear" warrant for their arrest was issued. Since prostitution was a misdemeanor, police gave low priority to serving the warrants, arresting these women only if they were questioned for another crime. And if the warrants had not been served within three years, they were recalled and stamped "Unable to Locate." It was as if the women and arrests had never occurred. Little was done by police or the judicial system to ascertain who the women really were and what might have thrust them into the clutches of greedy pimps. Were the women victims of rape? Domestic violence? Few people seemed to care. And when someone tried, the girls rebuffed the help. Police and judges simply went along with the women's game of charades. This process would later create havoc for Green River Task Force detectives attempting to learn when the victims were last seen alive, an important key to identifying witnesses and evaluating suspects.

Streetwalkers liked to tell journalists that police would never solve the Green River Murders because they did not care about prostitutes. Throughout the investigation, police would staunchly deny they cared less for murder victims who were prostitutes.

"Bullshit!" King County Police Captain Bob Evans would yell every time police were accused of indifference. "The problem that existed at times was that when the few vocal people that got up and said, 'The Seattle community doesn't care because they're prostitutes or the police don't care,' some dickhead media person who had too little to do that day would capitalize on that aspect of it, and I think unfairly."[6]

Feminists criticized police, too, for moving too slow to muster up the resources needed to investigate such a massive case. During one protest several hundred women marched through downtown Seattle with candles. The protestors chastised the news media, as well, for writing primarily about the criminal past of the women, even though the bulk of the crimes were petty and unworthy of defining individuals in society.

From the beginning of the murders and the investigation, the parents of the Green River victims were bewildered with society's fixation on the label "prostitute." Society's tunnel vision seemed to prevent people from seeing the runaways-turned-missing-turned prostitutes as human beings. Residents living along streets adjacent to the prostitution strip pointed out that the prostitutes and pimps constantly subjected their children to indecent behavior. Residents, too, were tired of finding condoms, hypodermic needles, and beer cans along their roads. Churchgoers liked to remind everyone that prostitution was a sin and prostitutes preyed on family men. They pointed to such passages as Proverbs 7:10–14:

Then out came a woman to meet him, dressed like a prostitute and with crafty intent. (She is loud and defiant, her feet never stay at home; now in the street, now in the squares, at every corner she lurks.) She took hold of him and kissed him and with a brazen face she said: "I have fellowship offerings at home."[7]

To the victims' parents, the so-called prostitutes in Seattle and King County were not like the hard women described in the Bible. In fact, they were not even grown women. They were girls, barely out of puberty. Society failed to see, it seemed to many of the families, the broader sociological problem. This was not just a parent problem. There were too many troubled kids out on the streets. Communities should try to help families when parental resources are lacking or when a family becomes so dysfunctional it is unable to assist a child to grow up to be productive. Why only blame the parents? And in blaming the parents, society tended to be judgmental. Bad seeds come from bad seeds, people appeared to think, which translated into indifference for the victims and their families. Certainly some of the victims' families did a poor job of being responsible role models, but many were hardworking and tried to do their best. More important, society failed to realize that the parents and the surviving siblings were victims of the Green River Killer as well.

The extent of the trauma brought on the families by the disappearances and murders and lengthy investigation came to light only after Ridgway confessed to the murders and the families were given a chance to speak publicly in court. The families spoke up during the sentencing phase of a plea agreement that spared Ridgway his life if he led investigators to the remains of missing victims.

One family after another walked to the podium in King County Superior Court in Seattle on December 18, 2003, to release emotions bottled up for over 20 years. Stated Helen Dexter, mother of victim Constance E. Naon, 20, who disappeared during the summer of 1983:

> Our lives have been run havoc through the news media . . . we've been maligned. We've been referred to as low class, uneducated people. I, for one, resent that. They have no respect. They twist the facts. I have not read a newspaper since 1983 for that reason . . . we were victimized. Her six brothers chose not to come today, the pain was too great for them. I don't know how to describe the pain. It's inside. There are no words for it.[8]

Mary B. Meehan was nine months pregnant when she vanished in 1982 while taking a walk on the prostitution strip she frequented. Her body was found a year later buried in the woods. Said Tim Meehan of his sister:

> I truly believe, if we had had the chance to be more proactive in our sisters' and our daughters' lives as they were growing up, that the possibility of us being here today would be not. I'm glad you choked my sister from behind, that's right, I am glad you choked her from behind . . . the reasons why? At least I know, as she took her last breath, and closed her eyes, I know her last visual memory wasn't of you, the real garbage in our society.[9]

Patricia Barczak's family left everyone with one of the most painfully vivid images. A family representative explained that so little of 19-year-old Barczak was found in the woods that she had to be buried in an infant's casket.

Last to open their hearts was the family of Patricia Yellowrobe, 38, the last-known victim of the Green River Killer. She died in 1998. "I heard that she struggled for her life," cried Rona Walsh, one of Yellowrobe's sisters. "How am I supposed to go through this life knowing that in my mind . . . that she was fighting for her life."[10]

In the end, many of the families felt their lives and the lives of their daughters had been marginalized by police, judges, pimps, the men who paid for sex, the hotel owners who turned the other way when men rented a room for an hour, and journalists.

To the families, one of the greatest travesties in the case was the fact that police made it extremely difficult for parents to file a runaway/missing person report, and when the families finally were able to do so, police often failed to look for their daughter or dragged their feet until it was too late. Although the Green River Killer investigation highlighted the runaway/ missing person reporting problem through out the 1980s, little seemed to change into the 1990s and beyond. An investigation of Washington state's official list of 2,000 runaway/missing people revealed in 1993 that the computerized files were riddled with dated and unworked cases. In brief, missing persons were lost in the shuffle, again.[11] In 2003, the *Seattle Post-Intelligencer* published a 10-part series of in-depth stories examining how law enforcement handled the missing. The year-long investigation found that because of the lack of knowledge, indifference, or poor training, police officers in Washington failed to conduct routine follow-ups when handling missing person reports.[12]

In reality, Green River Killer Gary Leon Ridgway marginalized the victims, too, since he was mimicking society in his murderous series. During his confession in the summer of 2003, he was asked why he decided to pick prostitutes to kill:

RIDGWAY: Because she's a prostitute and not worth anything. Nobody would look for her.
DET. RANDY MULLINAX: Nobody would look for her?
RIDGWAY: Nobody would . . . you wouldn't . . . an officer would not . . . that would be second after looking after an ordinary woman.[13]

In response to another question, Ridgway stated, "They were prostitutes and nobody would be looking for them. They'd be expendable."[14]

Gary Leon Ridgway mused to investigators that there were so many girls strolling the prostitution strip in Seattle and King County that abducting and killing them was like picking candy out of a bowl.

BULLETIN # 85-1

SPECIAL  BULLETIN

DATE: 29 APRIL 1985   TELEPHONE: (206) 433-2013

KING COUNTY POLICE
GREEN RIVER TASK FORCE

THESE TWO COLORS ARE VERY SIMILAR TO THE COLOR OF THE PICKUP.

WHITE MALE, LATE 20'S OR EARLY 30's, CURLY LIGHT BROWN, OR DISHWATER BLONDE HAIR -- POSSIBLY THINNING IN FRONT AND ON TOP, AND CLEAN SHAVEN. LIKELY WEARING A FLANNEL SHIRT. DESCRIBED AS LOOKING LIKE AN "OUTDOORS" TYPE PERSON.

THIS PICKUP IS SIMILAR IN APPEARANCE TO THE VEHICLE BEING DESCRIBED BY THE WITNESS: LATE 60'S OR MID 70'S FORD, CAB HIGH (OR SLIGHTLY HIGHER) CANOPY, NUMEROUS CIRCULAR GRAY PRIMER SPOTS ON THE PASSENGER SIDE, COLOR DESCRIBED AS AQUA OR BLUE. CANOPY MOST LIKELY HAD A HORIZONTAL REAR DOOR.

GAIL MATHEWS WAS LAST SEEN WITH THE ABOVE DESCRIBED MAN AT SOUTH 216 AND PACIFIC HIGHWAY SOUTH SOMETIME DURING APRIL, 1983. MATHEWS' SKELETAL REMAINS WERE FOUND AT 51 AVENUE SOUTH AND SOUTH STAR LAKE ROAD ON SEPTEMBER 18, 1983.

A WITNESS WAS WITH MATHEWS AT A LOCAL TAVERN AT APPROXIMATELY 1800 HOURS ON AN UNDETERMINED DAY IN APRIL, 1983. THE WITNESS LEFT THE TAVERN ALONE AND WALKED TO SOUTH 216 AND PACIFIC HIGHWAY SOUTH. WHILE STANDING ON THE WEST SIDE OF THE HIGHWAY THE WITNESS SAW MATHEWS INSIDE THE TRUCK. THE TRUCK WAS STOPPED IN THE SOUTHBOUND LEFT TURN LANE WAITING TO TURN EASTBOUND ON TO SOUTH 216. ALTHOUGH THE WITNESS ATTEMPTED TO ATTRACT MATHEWS' ATTENTION, SHE WOULD NOT ACKNOWLEDGE HIS GESTURES. THE WITNESS WATCHED THE TRUCK TURN ONTO SOUTH 216 AND DRIVE AWAY. THE WITNESS, WHO WAS LIVING WITH MATHEWS AT A LOCAL MOTEL, NEVER SAW HER AGAIN.

PLEASE STOP ANY SIMILAR PICKUPS AND IDENTIFY THE OCCUPANTS. ASCERTAIN IF THE REGISTERED OWNER WAS THE SAME IN 1983. IF THE OWNER HAS CHANGED SINCE 1983, ATTEMPT TO LEARN WHO OWNED THE PICKUP PREVIOUSLY.

FORWARD ALL F.I.R.S., OFFICER'S REPORTS, ETC., TO: DET. RANDY MULLINAX OR
                                                          SERGEANT FRANK ATCHLEY
                                                          GREEN RIVER TASK FORCE
                                                          14905 - 6TH AVENUE SOUTHWEST
CONFIDENTIAL   POLICE OFFICERS ONLY   SEATTLE, WASHINGTON 98166
NO FURTHER DISSEMINATION WITHOUT PERMISSION

CHAPTER

Science
of Preying

2

Ridgway acknowledged that he devoted considerable time and effort to finding appropriate victims. He would spend hours before work and after, driving through areas of prostitution.

King County Prosecutor's Summary of Evidence[1]

One of the deepest mysteries shrouding the everlasting Green River Murders revolved around the disappearance of the victims. How could the killer abduct so many women? Why seemingly no witnesses? Someone must have seen something? How could over 60 women vanish along a strip known for its hustle and bustle? The streets never seemed to sleep along the Sea-Tac Strip south of Seattle, Washington, let alone nod off long enough for someone to snatch a prostitute against her will.

Denise D. Bush vanished in a matter of minutes. The 23-year-old and her "boyfriend" were staying at a seedy motel on the strip on October 8, 1982, when they discovered they ran out of cigarettes.[2] The two flipped a coin and Bush lost. At 12:30 P.M., during a break in the soap operas, Bush hurried to a convenience store across the street from the hotel on Pacific Highway South near South 144th Street. She was never seen alive again. It would be three years before a few fragments of her bones would be found on Bull Mountain south of Portland, Oregon. Later, more of her skeletal remains would be discovered at the base of a wooded hill just blocks from where she disappeared south of Seattle.

It was the same scenario with Maureen S. Feeney, a smiley 19-year-old who had studied to be a daycare worker at a community college. In trying to become independent from her family, she rented an apartment in a Seattle neighborhood known as Capital Hill. The apartment sat at the edge of an area with a "dope stroll." Day and night men and women hooked on

11

drugs, alcohol, and the underside of life gravitated to the area to get their fix of whatever controlled them. It was inevitable that Feeney would bump into people who would push her toward prostitution. Feeney had not left her family's home long when she ventured out of her apartment on September 28, 1983, about noon to look for a job at a preschool.[3] Across the street from her apartment was a convenience store similar to the one Bush had walked to in search of cigarettes. Feeney disappeared that day. Her skeletal remains were found May 2, 1986, in a wooded area about half an hour east of Seattle near Highway 18.

For years the mystery of the disappearances haunted residents of the Pacific Northwest and investigators and criminologists nationwide. How was the killer abducting the women without a trace? Prostitutes get feisty if taken too far from the strip. Was the killer using a gun to control them? Perhaps he pressed a rag with chloroform to their noses and mouths to render them unconscious? Some detectives speculated that the killer used a vehicle without passenger-door handles inside the vehicle, which would prevent the victims from getting out of the vehicle as it sped away to a secluded area. Maybe the killer was taking his prey to a motel? Every time the question of an abduction came up, the overriding image that surfaced depicted violence. The women had been taken against their will so there had to be some kind of violence in the initial abduction, investigators often thought. Relatives and friends of the victims were certain, in their own mind, that their loved one resisted violently and caused a commotion for someone to witness. Surely, many thought, the victims could sense the killer's motive and tried to get away. How could so many women not know they were in danger? Didn't the killer look crazy? Why were there no reports of women bolting from the killer's vehicle or hotel room?

The answers to those questions and overall mystery did not come until the summer of 2003 when Gary Leon Ridgway opted to confess to avoid the death penalty. Throughout his six-month confession, he described how he turned his sexual fetish into a "career"[4] and became a "killing machine."[5] How was Ridgway so successful at abducting women without causing a public scene or leaving behind witnesses? He duped the women, he tricked them, he conned them into letting down their defenses. Chicanery proved to be Ridgway's key to success. Ridgway had a knack for reading/sensing the women's emotions and needs. It is clear from a detailed examination of the confession, however, that Ridgway's talent for being deceitfully glib took some time to develop. He refined his techniques with every victim he killed, with every passing year he went uncaught. Also clear throughout the confession is how Ridgway's relationship with family and friends strongly affected his urge to kill and hunting patterns.

EXPERIMENTING

Gary Leon Ridgway started experimenting with murderous behavior as a young boy, long before the Green River would be infamously associated with the nation's biggest serial murder case. There was little doubt in the minds of the many investigators and psychologists who interrogated Ridgway that his urge to harm and likely kill people surfaced early. A deep-seeded anger manifested itself in a variety of deviant behavior, although Ridgway was unaware of its significance then. Ridgway admitted during his confession that his pattern of stalking prostitutes actually began in junior high school. Experts call this "practice behavior."

DR. ROBERT WHEELER: You started stalking people, following people didn't ya?

RIDGWAY: I started following a few, I mean it wasn't . . . you know, it wasn't a . . . a . . .[6]

WHEELER: I want some details now.

RIDGWAY: That started when I was, ah, in . . . in, ah, probably junior high. I was following a . . . a . . . a girl home that lived in the same area, not goin' way outta the area, but just following her and . . . and, ah, seeing what it . . . it was like. I didn't never think it was called, you know, stalking, just . . . just following her and curiosity where she'd go and what kinda reaction when I'm, you know, when I'm . . . I'm following her and. . . .

WHEELER: Where did you follow her to?

RIDGWAY: I just followed her up the hill towards where I lived and was the way . . . one of the ways I'd go. . . . She looked like a nice, ah, nice, ah, girl and. . . .

WHEELER: So you were attracted to her.

RIDGWAY: I was attracted to her.

WHEELER: And what was your attraction? Describe the attraction.

RIDGWAY: Well she was, ah, I knew she was fourteen or fifteen or sixteen or somethin' like that, ah, well proportioned, ah, young . . . young woman. Ah, and she just, ah, ah, somebody, you know, wanted to . . . you might wanna talk to some time or. . . . And that was just about it. I think I did it about twice and, ah, . . .

WHEELER: And then she confronted you?

RIDGWAY: She confronted me on the . . . maybe on the first time, but after I told her I live over here on the other side of that tower, she didn't think anything of it.

WHEELER: Did you go home and masturbate thinking about her?

RIDGWAY: No. I didn't . . . didn't masturbate about her.

WHEELER: How do you know you didn't?

RIDGWAY: Cause I don't think I did. I mighta just picked up . . . if I did I
 probably just picked up a Play . . . Playboy and looked at it and. . . .
WHEELER: And maybe imagined that she was the person in the Playboy?[7]
RIDGWAY: Maybe . . . maybe once or twice I might have, I don't know[8]

About the same time in his life, Ridgway experimented with using a
knife to take out his anger out on people. At the time, he was a sixth grader.
In talking with FBI Profilist Mary Ellen O'Toole, Ridgway blurted out:

RIDGWAY: Um, I stabbed a kid one time.
O'TOOLE: Tell me about that.
RIDGWAY: Uh, it was down by uh, Chinook where I used to go to school, and
 a boy was playin'. I stabbed him in the side and . . . uh, didn't kill him. And
 uh, I, I was about um, sixth grade, or I think it was, go . . . it was seventh
 grade, and I, I uh, that was at the same time I was, you know, breaking out
 windows, throwin', was throwin' rocks at windows at school, but . . .[9]

The victim ran home, bleeding profusely, but he survived. His assailant
remained unknown until Ridgway detailed his involvement.

That episode and Ridgway's habit of getting nosebleeds convinced
Ridgway that he lacked the appetite for seeing or shedding blood when he
felt the need to kill to lessen his anger.

During the confession Ridgway revealed a third major incident that illustrated his drive to harm people. He confessed to trying to drown a boy
who kept splashing him.

At one point during the interrogation, O'Toole stated

All of those are behaviors now that you're carrying into your . . . you
know, 16–17 year old time frame. . . . I mean can we safely say at that
point, Mr. Ridgway, that um, these are behaviors that have followed you
until, 'til the time you're 54 years old—the enjoyment of the watching and
the following and the control and getting somebody into your comfort
zone, and you know in your head what you're gonna do to them and they
don't have any idea. That's kind of exciting for you.[10] Um, you're not
going back to being um, um, you know, a "Leave It To Beaver" type young
man. That's just not happening. So as, as this, as you develop and you get
older um, you brought all these behaviors with you and, in fact, you carried them into um, you know, your forties and your fifties. Am I right?

RIDGWAY: Yeah . . .
O'TOOLE: I mean that's just, that's the anatomy of this thing.[11]

Indeed it was. Eventually, Ridgway settled on the type of victim on
whom he would mercilessly inflict his vengeful anger. And he made that
decision in a very premeditated fashion. Ridgway told Dr. O'Toole:

Well low risk victims would be, ah, ah, prostitutes who eagerly get in your car for . . . for money, and they wouldn't be missed. Where the high risk victim would be like somebody at a college. . . . They would be more of a . . . of a risk of . . . of, ah, people caring more about 'em, and friends asking questions . . . low risk prostitutes they're not . . . they're not as valued as much as a college person . . . or a business person.[12]

Victims of opportunity became Ridgway's mainstay. But when Ridgway first decided to prey on prostitutes, he was tentative. Several times he began choking them, then released them. Luckily for him, no one turned him in. Occasionally, he considered using other methods to disable and kill the women. One elaborate scheme involved creating his own mini-electric chair:

You put on the hot wire and you—you hold this to the ground and then you turn on the ignition and it goes on a little bit and comes up. Well, I thought about taking the hot wire off the coil, running it over under the dash with some kind of wire, just thinkin' of running it to the seats—the passenger seat of the vehicle and making some kind of a grate or something so that she sits on it. And then make sure she's touchin' some metal or a door handle and switch it, you know. Hittin' the switch (unintelligible—over talking) like a little electric chair.[13]

In the end, Ridgway thought the scheme too complicated and abandoned it.

Most nights, Ridgway left his small, rambler house in a cul-de-sac south of Seattle and cruised the Sea-Tac Strip, a road crowded with motels, fast-food restaurants, and heavy traffic leading to the Seattle-Tacoma International Airport. In 1982, the strip constantly was full of streetwalkers who sashayed in high heels. For Ridgway, it was a perfect hunting ground. He liked to say that his victims underestimated him.

I look like an ordinary person. . . . I was shakin' but I, ah, I . . . I played into it. Ah, I, ah, acted in a way with the . . . prostitutes to make 'em feel more comfortable . . . got in their comfort zone . . . here's a guy . . . he's not really muscle bound, he's not, ah, look like a . . . a fighter, just an ordinary john, and yet that was their downfall . . . my appearance was different from what I really was. I was able to dupe them.[14]

Ridgway picked up women and killed them with ease and impunity. He'd been right, no one seemed to miss *these* victims. He'd offer them a few bucks and drive his pickup a block or two away from the strip into dark residential neighborhoods. To convince the women to get in the back of the truck under a canopy, he liked to carry a spare tire in the cab to make it too crowded to engage in sex. "We can't date in the front, I've got this tire," Ridgway told investigators. "And so that was a ploy to get them in the back or out in the field. So I always had a tire in there or tools or something or a bunch of clothes."[15] Once the women were in the back of the truck, Ridgway jumped behind them and used a choke hold with his arm to kill them. Most of the women were dead within minutes of climbing into the pickup. Ridgway's first victim in the summer of 1982, Wendy L. Coffield, 16, was dumped in the Green River southeast of Seattle. That summer four more women, including Debra L. Bonner, ended up in or on the bank of the river. Some of the women in the river were weighted down with heavy rocks. Small rocks were inserted in the vagina of two of the river victims.

Amid the slaying of the river victims, Ridgway preyed on Gisele A. Lovvorn, 19, and hid her body in the woods. Her abduction revealed to what lengths Ridgway was willing to go to psychologically disarm a potential victim. At the time, Ridgway was twice divorced. He and his second wife had a son, Matthew, who was at that time 8 years old. On the night of July 17, 1982, Ridgway had his son with him when he desired to kill a prostitute. Ridgway told investigators:

> I took her there with, ah, Matthew in the car. She was next to Matthew, I picked her up some place. Either before, ah, from my parents to that site or from my house to . . . it had to a been from my . . . from my parents house to the site where I . . . I killed her. Ah, I . . . I took her in, we walked into . . . a space where we couldn't see the truck.

When Ridgway was behind the woman, he tricked her into raising her head by saying his son was coming into the woods. When Lovvorn raised her head, Ridgway choked her with his arm, then a pair of black socks tied together.[16] Asked what he told his son about the woman leaving, Ridgway said, "She wanted to walk home. She only lives a close distance."[17] Since Ridgway needed to attend to his son and leave the area, he returned the following day to better hide the body, but not before having intercourse with the corpse.

Ridgway considered taking his first victims to his home, but at that time he was renting out his house to help pay the mortgage. While a family with children lived in the home, Ridgway slept in the garage of the house located adjacent to Military Road. The morning after a kill, Ridgway always felt nervous, but by the time he left work that afternoon, he looked forward to outsmarting another woman during the hunt.

Those first few weeks the preying did not always go smoothly. Sometimes a prostitute wanted too much money or seemed too cocky for Ridgway. How did Ridgway get rid of her?

> I'd just drop her off at a, a block away from where the uh, bank was, and I would use that ploy. Or, or uh, "Here's," you know, "I'll go up to the bank and here's five dollars. I need a, I have to have sex with a rubber," so she'd

get five dollars and go into the store for a rubber, and then I would take off and f-forget about her.[18]

Sometimes, however, Ridgway would forget who he tricked into getting out of his pickup and he would pick up the same woman again another night. Ridgway re-created a heated conversation that followed:

> "You picked me up the other day and you, you . . . you dropped me off at the uh, the damned store and, 'cause you didn't have uh, didn't have e-enough money for me. Uh, I been with you three times now. I been, three, three times you haven't dated me and I'm getting a little bit pissed off at you pickin' me up. Don't ever pick me up again." And, 'cause each time I picked her up there was some'n wrong and, and she's, she was a, a bitch that I didn't wanna date, but here I go, and she's dressed up different, and now I pick her up and I says, Oh, my God, I got this bitch out here that I don't wanna date, uh, because she's . . . some'n . . . I, I screwed up her on the last two times, now I got her back in the car and we're gonna go through this shit again, and I just got to get rid a this, this woman. And, and I, you know, I lied to her two times before and now I got to lie to her again, uh, about some'n. And then she, she jumps down my throat, "Next time I see ya, I'll have my boyfriend uh, you don't do that with women out here on the street."[19]

IN THE GROOVE

Although Gary Ridgway never did well in school, he turned out to be an exceptional student of the street. It did not take him long to learn the ways of the prostitutes and their pimps. He particularly proved an astute student of the little clues that give away a person's thoughts. Through trial and error, he honed his skills at taking advantage of a twitch in a prostitute's eye or a teenager's yearning for a donut. In academic terms, he was a quick study. During those years, Ridgway "always wanted to date,"[20] and he quickly developed a hunting routine. He'd get off of work, stop and have a beer, grab a burger or fried chicken at a fast-food restaurant with a cup or two of coffee, and then start cruising for prostitutes.

> If I found a, a lady to date, I'd drive by and uh, check out anything, you know, anybody watching her or anything like this, or . . . and uh, then I'd go pull in a alley, or come back and pull in an alley and wave to her or, and I'd drive around the block and wave to her and if she sees me again, I, the woman, I, I'd pick her up and go date.[21]

Often, to grab a prostitute's attention, Ridgway waved money at them as he drove by. Once the women jumped into the cab of his truck, the psychological game began. Some women suggested they go to a motel room acquired by the prostitute prior to the pair meeting. Ridgway would make up an excuse not to go to the room. Sometimes he said he had a sister who worked at that motel. "I had a lot'a different lines, and I used every one of 'em to my advantage."[22] If a woman asked for more money than Ridgway carried that night, he would drive to a cash bank machine. As the prostitute stood near by, Ridgway withdrew the amount the woman demanded. That exercise turned out to be just another Ridgway ruse since the money he would pay the prostitute would end up back in Ridgway's wallet after he killed her. To disarm the most leery women and convince them he was not a cop, he regularly carried beer in his truck. Or he would expose himself. Ridgway stopped at nothing to get the women from "bein' afraid."[23] He knew many of the women needed money and always sought small jobs to make ends meet. As he cruised the strip, Ridgway made it a point to find "help wanted" signs. After picking up a prostitute, Ridgway managed to introduce jobs into the conversation. Soon, Ridgway would be driving the prostitute to fast-food businesses and hotels for the woman to pick up applications for cleaning or maintenance openings. Then he'd take the woman out on the date.

> No, I didn't help them to fill it out. I'd just be kinda, you know, anxious with them, "I'm glad you're getting a job so close by here that we can get together and have, have dates," and uh, you know, "Because it's so close to where I live, or so close where I can help ya, help ya out." . . . I'd have sex with 'em, and . . . they would be uh, thinkin' I'm gonna . . . drop 'em back off at hotel or some'n like that . . . and ninety percent a the time you'd never see the woman again.[24]

Ridgway even offered his car to teenagers to con them into cooperating.

> I was tryin' to talk to one of 'em, if they wanna be a regular I'll give ya' my car keys to the car and you, you supply the gas and, and you can have the car to drive around, but I, I killed her. . . . I didn't have to go through with the promise.[25]

Even though Ridgway sometimes did not have time to abduct a prostitute, kill her, and then dispose of her body, he still cruised and picked them up on his way to a union meeting or work. It was time well invested, in his mind. He was always trying to get the confidence of potential victims so he enjoyed picking up young girls and buying them donuts, coffee, or beer. His benevolence also was intended to debunk any possible talk on the street that he might be the Green River Killer. He succeeded in having street-walkers think: "You seem like a safe guy."[26]

On at least one occasion, however, Ridgway lost track of time and gave in to his strong desire to kill.

There was another time I killed a woman . . . in the back of my truck there. And I left her in there. Um, uh . . . drove to work and killed her. So I must've killed her in the morning. Left in there, work all day. Went out and uh, made sure . . . made sure she was dead. It was all locked up and covered up. Um, and I went back up to her at lunchtime, now I remember, and pulled in the parking lot and had sex with her again after she was dead. . . . Uh, I finished my job . . . wasn't worried at all about . . . just take my time. I'm always late getting out anyway.[27]

Despite his many ruses, Ridgway failed to abduct and kill some of the women he picked up. The ones who were lucky enough to get away were older, more experienced. Ridgway referred to them as hardcore.

There's a few of them that were just too tough to kill. Too uh . . . too um, mean . . . mean lookin'. And hardcore. . . . Yeah, I had conversation with 'em and, and then I'd uh, drop 'em off and tell 'em I'd pick 'em up later and never would.[28] . . . had one woman, I don't know what the reason was, I acted insane with her. I picked her up. She got mad at me for something and she wanted . . . she wanted $20 so I took the truck and I speed up and I said, "you're not going to get no money from me. We're going to go down here and run into that telephone pole." She said, "I want the fuck out." I threw on the brake, she hit the dash and opened the door and told her to "get the fuck out. You're not going to get anything from me." She slams the door and almost breaks the window.[29]

Ninety-nine percent of the time, Ridgway found it easy to catch his prey, even without having to drive around. He liked parking his pickup truck at convenience stores and raising the hood to pretend he was troubleshooting a mechanical problem. When a woman passed by on her way into the store, Ridgway enticed her into his truck with serious money. That appears to have happened to Denise D. Bush and Maureen S. Feency, who vanished in 1982 and 1983, respectively. Even Ridgway can't be 100 percent sure that is how he abducted Bush and Feeney. Why? He preyed on so many women the actual details of many of the abductions and the women's faces have become a blur.

Many of Ridgway's victims were dead within 20 minutes of losing the cat-and-mouse game with their abductor. The rest appear to have died within an hour of getting into Ridgway's pickup truck. Ridgway claimed he cried "a lot" as his rage subsided after each kill and then he drove randomly to secluded wooded areas to deposit the bodies.[30] Frequently, he gravitated toward roads he'd driven while visiting his two former wives and former girlfriends. Ridgway was as cunning in discarding his victims as he was in abducting them. When he found a dark, secluded road, he would pull off the road near the guard rail, pull the woman out of the truck, and lay her down just off the side of the road. He would then drive a short distance down the road, park, and return to the body to move it farther into the woods to hide it. Why this routine? Ridgway sought to distance his vehicle from the corpse in case a law enforcement officer happened on his vehicle.

To the many psychologists and investigators who listened to Ridgway for months detail his many ruses to kill women, there was only one way to describe him: *a chameleon*. Ridgway possessed an innate ability to adopt to endless scenarios on the street. He could think on his feet as the situation and environment changed.

LIKE A MACHINE

Ridgway had a voracious appetite for sex. He desired it four or five times a week. During his most prolific killing years in the early 1980s, he had a steady girlfriend he met at a Parents Without Partners gathering. They liked going out for drinks and dancing. Their sexual and social relationship, however, flourished mostly on weekends since she was a single parent and had children to care for. Ridgway, too, seemed to want to limit their days together because he believed his girlfriend was a bit on the heavy side and unattractive. He rationalized that he needed weekdays to date thin, young, pretty, sexy girls who walked the streets. Toward that end, Ridgway constantly connived to refine his techniques of preying. Hence, he created what FBI Profilist O'Toole dubbed the "Ridgway Code."[31] The code consisted of a combination of telephone numbers, grocery list, names, merchandise receipts, and paint codes, the type Ridgway used as a truck painter at a Seattle-area truck company. When Ridgway met a prostitute he wished to date a second time or to set up to kill at a later date, he would write down her first name in a booklet. Next to the name he wrote the name of a male. Reason? To make it seem the notation pertained to a couple. If the booklet fell into the wrong hands—police or one of his girl-friends—the names would not arouse suspicion. Next to the woman's name Ridgway cryptically wrote "black car" if the woman was African American or "white house" if the woman was Caucasian. If Ridgway had paid the prostitute $20, next to the woman's name he'd write $20.75 and "price for the clutch."[32] Anyone reading the information would think Ridgway purchased a clutch for $20.75. Often Ridgway would combine the woman's home telephone number with numbers used to designate a paint color. Adjacent to some names Ridgway wrote "maid," meaning the woman once talked about trying to get a job as a maid. This tidbit of information proved valuable to recontact the woman for an assignation, which ended in a date or the woman being murdered. Ridgway described to investigators the typical phone call he made to some of the women's homes: "This is John from so and so motel. Alicia put an application in last week and we'd like to talk to her."[33] Sometimes Ridgway would speak to the woman's father or mother. Ridgway claimed to have 50 phone numbers in his book, which he said he destroyed long before being arrested.

One of Ridgway's most successful ruses to abduct women called for using his son's toys and elementary school picture. To allay the fear of potential victims, Ridgway took to putting toys on the dashboard of his truck. There was nothing better to get the women to trust Ridgway and think of him as a family man, not a killer. If they were still leery after getting into the truck, he would pull out his wallet to show identification and give his victims a glimpse of his son.

> So I whip out my ID and with my ID would be my, I'd put my finger over my driver's license to hide my name . . . but on the opposite side was um, pictures . . . and uh, picture of my son . . . and then she'd uh, see my son and they would know I was prob'ly a normal person.[34]

Perhaps the most significant event that transformed Ridgway from a random serial killer to a systematic serial killer involved his house. For some time Ridgway had been living in his garage while renters occupied his home. He eventually grew tired of the rent coming in late and the renters abusing the house. When Ridgway kicked them out, the horrific deviant behavior began that would make him this country's most prolific serial killer. Woman after woman would be brought to the house to meet their death. In the end, most of Ridgway's victims would die in that house.

How did Ridgway convince so many woman to enter his home? For Ridgway, it was simple: *money*. All Ridgway had to do was drive up to his house and open his wallet.

> I'd get 'em close to the house. I says, "Well, here's ten dollars . . . I can take you back to where I, I wasted your time if you don't wanna go in the house." But they were wanting that forty dollars, so they'd, every one of 'em I used that ploy as a, a way of getting 'em into the house.[35]

Once in the house, Ridgway encouraged them to look around.

> That was to give them the security that nobody else is around. . . . You had to get their defenses down. . . . They look around and everything, they're getting more secure as you go. They look in the bedrooms, nobody's in there, nothin's, you know, there's my son's room, hey, this guy has got a son, he's not gonna hurt anybody. His name's written on the door and it's empty and it's got his bunk bed there, toys on the floor. They look in the master bedroom, there's nothin'. Then we go in the bathroom and, uh, I go to the bathroom if I need to go. She goes to the bathroom, washes up a little bit.[36]

And before they knew it, he was behind them, choking them. Many of the women fought. One even made it to the front door before Ridgway caught up to her. To get a woman to stop struggling, Ridgway would say, "Calm down. I'll let you go if you quit fighting."

O'TOOLE: And did they?
RIDGWAY: They calmed down and. . . .
O'TOOLE: You killed them.
RIDGWAY: I killed them.[37]

Just another Ridgway ruse!

One of the women who fought the hardest was Marie M. Malvar, who was picked up by Ridgway on the strip a short distance from where Ridgway lived. She used her long fingernails to scratch her assailant. She left deep gashes in Ridgway's arm. After that challenging encounter, Ridgway used a ligature—a towel or extension cord—to strangle women who had long fingernails.

Once the women were dead, Ridgway took their clothes and jewelry, dragged them to the front door, and, in the dark of night, put them in the back of his pickup truck. As he drove along secluded highways, he tossed out the victims' clothing. Some he deposited in Goodwill bins. The jewelry he kept for a short time before he hid it in several outdoor locations away from his home.

While in the beginning of his killing series Ridgway deposited his victims in random locations, he soon developed a propensity for grouping bodies. During the lengthy investigation, detectives dubbed the body sites "clusters." And for over two decades they wondered why the victims had been left in clusters. As many as six women were deposited at one location. It was not until Ridgway confessed that investigators learned the answer. Ridgway clustered his victims to better remember where he left them. Why did Ridgway need to recall the dump sites? To return to the scene to have intercourse with the victims after death. Sometimes, Ridgway visited a corpse long after maggots had formed.

In his own twisted thinking, Ridgway thought he would have brought fewer women to his home had he had an attractive women in his life. "If I had a better looking woman. Um, she was the key if, if, uh, that would have been a hell of a lot less people dying if I had a, a nice woman to go home, go home to." Incredulous, King County Detective Randy Mullinax asked, rhetorically: "So are you telling me that you killed all these women because you had a fat girlfriend, Gary?"[38]

RETIRING FROM KILLING

At the height of his murderous series, Ridgway was slaying four to five women a month. And it seemed nothing could abate his urge to be with prostitutes or to kill them if he was so inclined. Ridgway's name had been turned in as a suspect, but he was one of thousands of deviant men confounding investigators.

Unbeknownst to anyone, though, there was a mild-mannered woman with back problems who was beginning to have a profound effect on his preying. Her name was Judith and Ridgway had fallen in love with her in 1985. They would eventually marry. When Judith entered the picture, suddenly Ridgway appeared to have little time to hunt. Being a devoted boyfriend, and then husband, meant being accountable to Judith.

The Green River Murders case experienced its most profound change in years when Judith moved in with Ridgway at the Military Road home that Ridgway used to kill young prostitutes. Gone now was Ridgway's chamber of horrors. Judith roped Ridgway into selling Amway with her. Before long, the couple was attending an Amway conference and a Christian Faith Center operated by Amway. Ridgway was meeting so many new people through Amway he was fearful of coming across a customer while preying on the strip. During the week Ridgway had to be mindful that Judith expected him home shortly after Ridgway got off work. And on weekends, Judith and Ridgway frequented swap meets. In short, Judith served as a restraint on Ridgway's activities, no doubt saving the lives of many young ladies during the late 1980s and 1990s.

But it was Ridgway's nature to visit prostitutes, and eventually he began giving in to the urges. "Still had a craving for a prostitute. I wanted sex. I'd have sex at night, and I'd want it again. I didn't wanna w-wear out Judith."[39] Soon, Ridgway began finding ways to prey. Sometimes he stopped at his parents' home for a cup of coffee after work, which was acceptable to Judith. He'd make time on the way home, however, to pick up a prostitute for "a fast one."[40] On those occasions, Ridgway had no time to kill the women. To create time to kill a prostitute, Ridgway liked to offer to work overtime on Saturdays. He would go in and work a couple of hours and on the way home pick up a prostitute to kill. Even when Ridgway managed to create time to hunt, he found he had little money since Judith kept a tight hold on the family finances. Ridgway could not simply spend any amount he wanted like in the early 1980s.

> So if I got one for tw . . . less than twenty dollars, that would be fine. A lot
> 'a times I'd get 'em for, "if you take me down to Kent I'll, I'll do you, I'll
> do you for twenty, twenty dollars. . . . You take me into Seattle, I'll, I'll do it
> for twenty dollars, or I'd do it for free."[41]

Ridgway always found ways to acquire a few extra dollars. It was not unusual for him to sneak some of the proceeds from a garage sale or a swap meet deal. Some of the spare change would go for buying condoms, which he hid in various locations. Some went underneath a rug on the floor, some underneath the dashboard of the truck, and some in the wheel well of the driver's side. Ridgway even hid condoms underneath rocks behind a popular department story. Even though Ridgway managed to abduct and kill prostitutes, he felt "ashamed of getting off the wagon."[42]

He did not feel good about lying to Judith and feared he would stumble and get caught.

> I had, uh, everything paid for. . . . And a, a nice house and everything. . . . I guess told myself that, you know, don't . . . don't, uh, screw anything up by killing any prostitutes, because, uh, you're gonna lose everything.[43] I was . . . in a way getting scott free, and I didn't want to, um, ruin it.[44]

Somehow Ridgway managed to have sexual intercourse with a number of prostitutes during the late 1980s and 1990s and not kill them. Still, the rage he possessed when he killed with impunity in the early 1980s continued to simmer in him. And when he least expected it, it boiled over, and he found himself choking another woman. Those were unplanned kills and they caused him to panic. He thought he was much more in control of his rage, but he wasn't. Ridgway recalled a 1998 murder:

> She was a hard core, ah, prostitute. I mean she wasn't one that just started, she was in her twenties and . . . and she was arrested many, many times. But she just didn't . . . gave her the thirty, twenty bucks . . . she's not willing to take five more minutes for me to . . . to have a climax. You know, screw her. . . . Your time is up. She gets up and gets her clothes on. I started to get mad, and get madder and madder, and soon as I get her outta the car, put the tailgate up, open the truck . . . truck door on the passenger side, I reached around and grabbed her and, ah, started chokin' her and she died within, ah, she passed out within ten seconds I think it was.[45] In the late '90's, it was I'd kill 'em and uh, panic and leave 'em there . . . the one I can remember, I, I, I panicked and uh, just left her there instead of putting her in the truck and transporting her someplace where she wouldn't be found . . . she was fully clothed, and uh, I just left her there and pushed her up by, so nobody could see her, and then I got in the truck and uh, got the heck out 'a there. And uh, didn't want to re-member about killing her 'cause I, I, I thought I was th-through killing. And this wasn't a, a pl-planned kill and I wasn't in that mode.[46] I was trying to quit. And to, uh, uh, eventually, uh, uh, in the '80's I, uh, semi re-tired, in a way. In the '90, or in the '90s I was semi-retired. In the 2000s, I was planning on being, not, uh, being around it. And, um, move to some-place where I wouldn't be around them. And, and there's my . . . the Green River Killer's still up in Washington and here I am in, let's say, Oregon. Free, uh, free from all that, um, the dreams, memories of the killings.[47]

Instead, Ridgway "was more of an amateur."[48] Ridgway, in fact, lost his edge in managing to cut down on his killings to please Judith.

And in the end he tried minimizing his vicious preying. He told his in-terrogators:

I was doing you guys a favor, killing, killing prostitutes, here you guys can't control them, but I can.[49] I mean if its illegal aliens, you can take 'em to the border and fly 'em back out 'a there. But if it's a prostitute, you'd arrest 'em, they were back on the street as soon as they get bail and change their uh, name, and you guys, you guys had the problem. . . . I had the answer.[50]

Green River Victims	Disappearance Date	Found Date
Wendy L. Coffield	July 8, 1982	July 15, 1982
Gisele A. Lovvorn	July 17, 1982	Sept. 25, 1982
Debra L. Bonner	July 25, 1982	Aug. 12, 1982
Marcia F. Chapman	Aug. 1, 1982	Aug. 15, 1982
Cynthia J. Hinds	Aug. 11, 1982	Aug. 15, 1982
Opal C. Mills	Aug. 12, 1982	Aug. 15, 1982
Terry R. Milligan	Aug. 29, 1982	April 1, 1984
Mary B. Meehan	Sept. 15, 1982	Nov. 13, 1983
Debra L. Estes	Sept. 20, 1982	May 30, 1988
Linda Rule	Sept. 26, 1982	Sept. 31, 1983
Denise D. Bush	Oct. 8, 1982	June 12, 1985
Shawnda L. Summers	Oct. 9, 1982	Aug. 11, 1983
Shirley M. Sherrill	Oct. 20–Nov. 7, 1982	June 12, 1985
Colleen R. Brockman	Dec. 24, 1982	May 26, 1984
Alma A. Smith	March 3, 1983	April 24, 1984
Delores L. Williams	March 8–March 17, 1983	March 31, 1984
Gail L. Mathews	April 10, 1983	Sept. 18, 1983
Andrea Childers	April 14, 1983	Oct. 11, 1989
Sandra K. Gabbert	April 17, 1983	April 1, 1984
Kimi-Kai Pitsor	April 17, 1983	Dec. 15, 1983
Marie J. Malvar	April 30, 1983	Sept. 28, 2003
Carol A. Christensen	May 3, 1983	May 8, 1983
Martina T. Authorlee	May 22–May 23, 1983	Nov. 14, 1984
Cheryl L. Wims	May 23, 1983	March 22, 1984
Yvonne S. Antosh	May 31, 1983	Oct. 15, 1983
Carrie A. Rois	May 31–June 13, 1983	March 10, 1985
Constance E. Naon	June 8, 1983	Oct. 27, 1983
Kelly M. Ware	July 19, 1983	Oct. 29, 1983
Tina M. Thompson	July 25, 1983	April 20, 1984
April D. Buttram	Aug. 18–Sept. 1, 1983	Aug. 30, 2003
Debbie M. Abernathy	Sept. 5, 1983	March 31, 1984
Tracy A. Winston	Sept. 12, 1983	March 27, 1986
Maureen S. Feeney	Sept. 28, 1983	May 2, 1986
Mary S. Bello	Oct. 11, 1983	Oct. 12, 1984
Pammy A. Avent	Oct. 26, 1983	Aug. 18, 2003
Delise L. Plager	Oct. 30, 1983	Feb. 14, 1984
Kim L. Nelson	Nov. 1, 1983	June 13, 1986
Lisa L. Yates	Dec. 23, 1983	March 13, 1984
Mary E. West	Feb. 6, 1984	Sept. 8, 1985
Cindy Smith	March 21, 1984	June 27, 1987
Patricia Barczak	Oct. 11, 1986	Feb. 3, 1993
Roberta Hays	February 1987	Sept. 11, 1991
Marta Reeves	March 5, 1990	Sept. 20, 1990
Patricia Ann Yellowrobe	August 1998	Aug. 16, 1998
Jane Doe Bones 10		March 21, 1984
Jane Doe Bones 16		Dec. 30, 1985
Jane Doe Bones 17		Jan. 2, 1986
Jane Doe Bones 20		Aug. 21, 2003
Unofficial Victims		
Amina Agisheff	July 7, 1982	April 18, 1984
Kase A. Lee	Aug. 28, 1982	Missing
Becky Marrero	Dec. 3, 1982	Missing
Tammie Liles	June 9, 1983	April 23, 1985
Keli McGinness	June 28, 1983	Missing
Patricia Osborn	Oct. 20, 1983	Missing
Jane Doe Oregon Bones 1 (Later Lost)		April 22, 1985

CHAPTER

Privacy Amid the Media

3

To the media, you cannot conceive the damage you have inflicted upon my family.

Victim Kimi-Kai Pitsor
Family Letter[1]

Journalists often pride themselves on seeking out victims of crime to tell their story of misfortune and tragedy. Day in and day out reporters and editors of print, broadcast, and digital news organizations make it a priority to contact crime victims to ensure their side of the story is prominently included in crime stories. Regularly, several short crime stories are compiled into a seemingly unimportant "police blotter." Still, reporters are instructed to make an effort to represent the victim in the articles. Just as often, high-profile crimes dominate the front page. It is for those lengthy articles that journalists go to extra efforts to locate and interview victims and their relatives. "Police Beat" reporters, especially, have become literary experts at crafting narratives that capture the emotion of the moment or the depth of the pain. They are revered in the journalism world for writing what is known as a ten-hanky story, a journalism piece that touches the reader so deeply that the reader needs 10 hankies to wipe away the tears. Those narratives are what elicit sympathy and empathy from the public. And if it were not for such stories—heavy on a victim's pain, tears, and travesties—society would care much less about crime and those who commit it. So journalists for years have seen themselves as advocates of crime victims, ensuring that they are not left by the wayside while the public's fascination with the perpetrator steals the day.

Journalists, in fact, deserve praise for emphasizing the plight of crime victims for decades. However, experts who routinely care for victims believe

27

journalists also deserve harsh criticism for adding to the trauma experienced by victims and those close to them. As journalists have gone about their daily job covering crime, few appear to be aware of the pain their aggressive reporting inflicts. And in no place is that more evident than in the Green River Murders case. This massive case—in which the killer murdered over 60 girls and women—sheds light into how the news media handle the private lives of crime victims and their relatives, especially in a high-profile criminal investigation. Serial killer cases add a unique twist to privacy issues in crime since the investigations run for years, or even decades. A serial killer is perhaps the most disruptive criminal to enter the jurisdiction of a law enforcement agency. Serial killers are virtually impossible to catch, and their presence creates hysteria in a community. The crisis atmosphere prompts law enforcement to cloak the entire case with secrecy and the media to seek extraordinary access. In this setting arises some of the greatest friction between media practice and individual privacy. Media coverage in serial killer cases epitomizes journalism practices born in the mid-1880s. During the Industrial Revolution, "news" shifted from political and shipping events to an emphasis on society, crime, and the private lives of individuals. Crime news revolving around individuals has been an integral part of the mass media for decades, and today it permeates this country's culture. To many, the heavy focus on crime victims tends to adversely affect the victims' private lives and lead to more crime-related trauma.

For over two decades journalists pounced on every twist and turn of the Green River Murders case. Every time a new name was added to the list of missing women and possible victims, journalists wrote a profile. Every time skeletal remains were found in the woods, dozens of journalists inundated the area for days in hopes investigators would provide new details. Every time a grieving parent felt compelled to comment on the investigation, journalists listened and conveyed their comments to the public. The primary news media were *The Seattle Times,* the *Seattle Post-Intelligencer,* the Tacoma *News Tribune,* KIRO Television/Channel 7, KOMO TV 4, and KING 5 Television. Those Seattle-area news organizations made the case a priority in their daily coverage. At times the slayings and investigation received attention from such national organizations as the *New York Post, Los Angeles Times, People* magazine, *The New York Times, Time* magazine, *NBC Nightly News,* and CNN. Lengthy special programs were produced for the History Channel and Court TV. Few of the local and national journalists ever wrote a story about the Green River case or did a broadcast stand-up without a segment that included information on one of the Green River victims. Invariably, the journalists sought photographs and memories of the victims and interviews with relatives.

An analysis of media coverage from 1982 to 2004 reveals flagrant intrusion into the private lives of the victims and their relatives. While journalists viewed their actions as innocuous and claimed they were simply doing their job, those on the receiving end of their endless questions felt victimized all over again. A pattern of journalistic behavior emerged through the years and that behavior can be grouped into four categories: *Intrusion during Grief, Psychological Intrusion, Character Intrusion,* and *Wanton Intrusion.* Together, the intrusions created a phenomenon that can be described as *Privacy in Limbo.*

INTRUSION DURING GRIEF

The media's overtures toward relatives shortly after death notification amounted to intrusion. The families of the murder victims felt the grieving process was private. In following routine journalistic practices, journalists physically intruded by visiting a family residence or telephoning relatives of the victim. This was never a "one-time" occurrence, instead repeating itself many times.

To surviving relatives, the journalists' transgressions were exacerbated by the fact that relatives were traumatized when asked for interviews. The death of a daughter, mother, or wife plunged survivors into a numbing grief that caused them to be dysfunctional for weeks, months, and even years. Suzanne Villamin, whose daughter Mary Sue Bello was murdered by the Green River Killer in 1983, intimated in 1988 that something inside her died, too, when her daughter was murdered and sometimes she wished she could die to be with her.[2] For years Villamin carried her daughter's remains in a tin box in her purse. Said Nancy Gabbert, mother of slain Green River victim Sandra K. Gabbert, "For a period after that (notification of death) I was . . . not keeping track of time. If it was daylight I knew that it was day time and if it was dark outside I knew it was night outside."[3]

Gabbert did not want reporters going to her home after her daughter was found. Tom Estes, father of victim Debra L. Estes, felt the same way: "Give the family time to bury their children. Right after Debbie was found . . . they (journalists) wanted to come to the house, right then and there. No time for grief."[4]

In April 1984, the remains of Terry Rene Milligan were found. Milligan's mother, Mary, telephoned Linda Barker, a Seattle victim advocate who worked with many of the Green River victims' families. Milligan asked Barker to help her write a statement for the media.

> I went over there and one television station was driving around. In fact (they) set up their camera in a field next to the house and started filming the house and I just went around and closed the curtains so that they couldn't film into the house.[5]

Telephone calls from journalists were just as disruptive during grieving. Barker said, "A lot of the time reporters are calling when they're (parents) trying to call their family members and tell them what happened. That's stressful for them (families)."[6]

The *Seattle Post-Intelligencer* went beyond contacting families at home for personal details. *Post-Intelligencer* reporter George Foster attended the eulogy at a funeral chapel for victim Opal Mills in 1982.[7] After the service, Foster interviewed friends of the family.

The heartbreaking news articles on the emotional funerals and memorials for many of the victims were published or broadcast nationally. Most likely, readers and viewers of the news reacted with sympathy, but relatives of the victims were horrified with the reporting of every facet of a family's life, the good and the bad. Every family decision seemed open for scrutiny in public. One of the families most affected by the intense news media coverage was the Pitsors. Kimi-Kai Pitsor, a 16-year-old who chronically ran away from home, was seen last in mid-April 1983 in Seattle.[8] About a week before Christmas of the same year, her skull was found on the side of a rural road near a cemetery. Media coverage of the Green River case and the discovery of Pitsor's skeletal remains caused the Pitsors to flee the Seattle area. They dreaded having their life thrown out for grabs in the public arena, for everyone to pick at and judge. When it came time in 2003 for Ridgway to be sentenced for killing Pitsor and dozens more young women, the Pitsor family sent a letter to be read in open court. A King County Prosecuting Attorney's Office lawyer read the letter in open court. In part, it said:

> To the media, you cannot conceive the damage you have inflicted upon my family. Your jackal-like behavior forced our removal from the city that we loved . . . as we hid from your constant invasion. After witnessing the circus atmosphere of other families, attempts at funerals and memorial services, we were forced to forgo any funeral services and had to bury a beloved child far away from her home, where she lies in an unmarked grave, lest it too be used to feed your frenzy.[9]

PSYCHOLOGICAL INTRUSION

Relatives of the Green River victims were a captive audience when it came to media coverage. Their stake was so great they felt compelled to follow every twist and turn in the press, on the radio, on television, and in cyberspace. They needed to follow the case for any hint on the welfare of their loved one. As Barker put it, "When your child is missing, you focus on where are they? You go on a roller coaster ride of emotion. Are they dead? Are they alive? Are they hurt? Are they crying for me? Are they hungry?"[10] As the families sought to find closure, they became unwilling readers, listeners, and viewers of excruciating images. The relatives never knew when something offensive or personally painful would appear.

The picture that epitomizes years of psychological intrusion shows Wendy L. Coffield being carried out of the Green River in a body bag in 1982. Often broadcast stories introduced updates on the case with a film clip of Coffield's removal. A photographer for the *Valley Daily News* in Kent took the same shot. In 1991, New American Library chose that photograph for the cover of the book *The Search for the Green River Killer.*[11] That disturbing image became one of many as still photographers and television camera crews captured investigators unceremoniously carrying sagging body bags out of the woods. While officials in Washington tried to limit the filming of such removals, officials in Oregon did not. In 1985, the media in Washington and Oregon were ecstatic when Portland-area investigators allowed photographers to take close-up shots of the excavation of newly discovered skeletal remains related to the Green River Murders case. For months the public saw close-up shots of a Portland medical examiner picking up the skull of a Green River victim. Said victim advocate Barker:

> Those are the kinds of things that traumatize people who had chosen not to see what their daughters had been reduced to. The Oregon body find, to me, was an invasion of privacy. You have to remember that in homicides the family takes on the role of the victim, because they are the ones left to deal with the horror and the trauma of the victimization.[12]

In 1990, *Post-Intelligencer* reporters Michael Barber and John Hessburg speculated in an article that the serial killer may be involved in necrophilia.[13] As a result of that article, Tom and Carol Estes suffered renewed depression. They wondered if their daughter, Debra, had been dismembered. Worse, the speculative details caused great tension and became another psychological wedge in their troubled marriage.

In *The Search for the Green River Killer,* the authors revealed that the killer had inserted rocks in the vaginas of several victims. That graphic description caused more consternation among the victims' families and appears to have been the impetus for author Roderick Thorp to include similar information in his 1995 fiction book, *River: A Novel of the Green River Killings.* Thorp wrote this fictionalized scene of a victim: "Hot Lily's legs were spread and lifted as she would have done herself in life for sexual intercourse. Nestled in her pubic hair was . . . Looks like a bullet."[14]

For over twenty years, those images underscored such headlines, sound bites, and teasers as "slain woman dumped into the river," "nude and decomposed," "bones rattle local citizens," "Bones 12, Bones 13, Bones 14, Bones 15," and "strangled with her own clothing."

Victim families found it impossible to keep from becoming fixated on the images created by the mass media. Once exposed to the morbid information, their imaginations ran wild. Barker said:

> One mom talked about the horrific nightmares. She talked about animal
> activity and her daughter's remains. And she had daymares. She'd be driv-
> ing down the road and she'd have daymares. The trauma would go on for a
> very long time . . . she tried to commit suicide. . . . A lot of this is brought
> on by the media.[15]

The media were not the only ones to thrust morbid images of the victims at families. At one point in the investigation, investigators decided to
make themselves the caretaker of the mass images, and they faired as
poorly as many news media outlets at being discrete with private matters.
The end result was that law enforcement bombarded the public with some
of the most unforgettably disturbing images of the investigation. On December 7, 1988, the Green River Task Force in conjunction with Seattle-
King Crime Stoppers aired a two-hour national television docudrama on
the case. For years the task force had been unable to capture the killer. In
an attempt to shock an associate of the killer into calling police, investigators financed the docudrama and revealed that one of the victims, Mary B.
Meehan, was nine months pregnant when she died. Investigators hoped the
killer's wife or "significant other" would be stunned by knowing the killer
had murdered a pregnant woman. To emphasize the point, the task force
allowed the use of a videotape showing detectives excavating Meehan's remains in the woods. Nationally, viewers watched as investigators with trow-
els slowing unearthed a pregnant skeleton. "Those were actual police tapes
(of Meehan's skeletal remains)," said Lou Gorfain, one of the New York
producers hired to create the docudrama. "I've got to tell you, we were real
afraid of that footage . . . I mean, that was pretty grisly stuff."[16]

In the 1970s, former King County Police Detective Robert D. Keppel
was the lead investigator on the Ted Bundy serial case in Seattle. And in
the 1980s, Keppel became a consultant to the Green River Task Force. It
was while assisting the task force that Keppel began a dialogue with
Bundy, who had offered to help investigators catch the Green River Killer.
At the time, Bundy was incarcerated in Florida, on death row. As a result
of his interviews with Bundy before he was put to death, Keppel wrote a
serial killer book in 1995. Although the book was about Bundy and the
"Ted Murders," the publication was titled *The Riverman: Ted Bundy and I
Hunt for the Green River Killer.* The title and Keppel's relationship to the
Green River investigation signaled to Green River families and observers
that fresh revelations about the case could be revealed in the book. At the
time, the Green River Murders were unsolved, and many potential victims
remained missing. Instead, many of the scenes in Keppel's book graphically
described how Bundy killed. In one scene Keppel wrote, "He raised the
crowbar over his head and knocked her out again. The babbling
stopped."[17] In another passage Keppel described a search in the Bundy investigation: "1115 hours: Found fecal material with small hand bone."[18]

Green River victims relatives were left wondering if investigators possessed the same type of graphic physical evidence from the murder sites.

The Green River Murders case spanned so many years that it was inevitable that the Internet would play a major role in the spreading of murder-related details normally known only by the victims' relatives or investigators. Some murder details of how an individual is killed surface during a trial and are made public by news organizations, but most of the time graphic facts remain private, locked in investigative or court files. They are painful, guarded secrets enmeshed with the grieving process. In the Green River case, every detail of the slayings surfaced on the Internet soon after Ridgway was arrested. The images that traveled around the world in moments greatly traumatized the victims' relatives. The details of how each of the victims was choked, stripped nude, and hidden in the woods for future sexual gratification were released to the media and general public by the King County Prosecutor's Office in a document labeled the "Prosecutor's Summary of the Evidence." The 133-page document was so morbid the prosecutor's office attached a face sheet that said:

> *WARNING:* THE FOLLOWING SUMMARY CONTAINS GRAPHIC
> AND DISTURBING DESCRIPTIONS OF VIOLENT CRIMINAL
> ACTS AND MAY NOT BE SUITABLE FOR ALL READERS. IN
> PARTICULAR, FAMILY MEMBERS AND FRIENDS OF VICTIMS
> ARE CAUTIONED THAT THIS DOCUMENT DESCRIBES
> HIGHLY DISTURBING ELEMENTS OF THE CRIMES IN GRAPHIC
> DETAILS.[19]

News organizations created links from news sites and made the entire document available in digital form. The victims' relatives and friends could not keep themselves from reading the summary, and once they did they could not erase the vivid images from their mind. Fond, private memories of happy daughters, mothers, and wives were replaced by nightmarish murder scenes.

CHARACTER INTRUSION

The news media's characterization of the victims turned out to be one of the most painful aspects of the Green River case for the victims' relatives. Although the families were aware some of their daughters had turned to prostitution, they felt the media's character descriptions shed a negative light on the victims' entire lives. Repeatedly, the media painted a one-dimensional picture through the use of police mug shots and short descriptions like "drop-out," "prostitute," "tattooed body," and "troubled past." Crime magazines went beyond using an insensitive appellation once or twice in a story. In one issue a police magazine carried a story with the headline: "The River of Strangled Whores." In the narrative the author used the phrases: "pimps and whores have no warm feeling for cops" and "tossing whores in the river."[20] Many of the young women had exhibited distinct talents, and all of them had positive traits. In the end no one cared that victims like Opal Mills had extensive knowledge of the Bible and the women in it. And no one seemed to care about the children the killer made orphans. In mischaracterizing the victims' private lives, the media seem to distort and degrade their characters.

The media's portrayal of the victims had a direct effect on survivors. One teenage brother of a victim still missing was told by another boy at school: "Your sister deserved to die, because she was a hooker."[21]

The family of Kimi-Kai Pitsor, too, felt maligned. In a letter read in open court during Ridgway's sentencing, Kimi-Kai's brother wrote:

> Members of the media, I cannot forgive your actions. Since the beginning of the investigation into these murders, you have chosen to sensationalize and forever damage the names and families of Mr. Ridgway's victims. Why I ask? The answer has always been to make money.[22]

Those written comments were especially daunting and incriminating since he forgave Ridgway for murdering his sister. The brother's disdain for the news media's behavior had to be overpowering for it to overshadow the brutal acts of the killer.

In homicide cases—as in life—the lives of the victims and their surviving relatives are intertwined, inseparable. Parents of the victims felt tainted by what the media said about their daughters. Tom Estes believed negative reporting branded him a bad parent for letting his daughter "go astray." Said Estes: "We tried. Debbie was just headstrong."[23] Hence, one of the primary consequences of mischaracterization was that surviving relatives lost control of how people saw them in their private lives and lost control of their reputation. Many of the victims' relatives were outstanding citizens. Some worked at Boeing Co. Some lived in exclusive neighborhoods in Bellevue, Washington.

WANTON INTRUSION

During the Green River investigation, many relatives believed journalists used news gathering practices conceived to intrude into private matters.

That was the case in 1984 when the remains of victim Sandra K. Gabbert were found. "The media knew about it almost as soon as I did," her mother, Nancy Gabbert, said. "I started getting phone calls. . . . I'd give them anything they wanted—pictures, interviews, stories—just stay away from my house."[24] While Gabbert left her house momentarily, though, a television crew arrived at her home. Gabbert described what she saw, "We drove up . . . there was a man on the porch of my house . . . knocking at the door. And then we noticed that there were a couple of people in the yard across the street from my house. They had a camera set up pointed at my door."[25]

Over the years survivors of Green River victims moved to a new home or apartment, but they could not hide from the media when new developments occurred in the investigation. Reporters used city directories, real estate records, department of motor vehicle lists, voting records, and funeral home notices to locate people. If that failed, they went to the last address and talked to neighbors. Rebecca Marrero moved from her West Seattle apartment after her daughter, Becky Marrero, disappeared in December 1982. Several years later neighbors led a reporter to her new apartment. When Ridgway was arrested in 2001 and the media sought reaction and quotes, journalists used digital databases to locate many of the victims' parents and the children of several of the victims. When databases failed to point journalists in the right direction to locate Rebecca Marrero's daughter—who was an adult when Ridgway was arrested—they used traffic citations to obtain her latest address. In short, the victims' parents and children could run, but they could not hide, not even two decades after the killings began.

Reporters at *The Seattle Times* systematically sought ways to obtain information to ascertain if investigators were minimizing the number of potential victims. At times the information they sought involved private facts. In the state of Washington, the *legal* files of juveniles are public. Those files state the reason for an arrest and the final disposition of the criminal act. A juvenile's *social* file containing a history of the individual, relatives, and the extended family is not public. In the late 1980s, though, *The Seattle Times* discovered a state law that allowed access to social files if the information was used for "research" purposes. Using that law reporters were able to read some of the social files belonging to Green River victims. Many of the victims had juvenile histories of petty crime, delinquency, and dependency. The files included family histories, criminal histories, counseling assessments, information about physical and mental health, drug use, and parental sexual abuse. In the end, the reporters not only read the files of Green River victims, but also they examined files of teenagers who were potential victims: missing, but not yet added to the list of suspected victims; associates of those who had been put on the list; and other teenagers who had been cited or booked on sex-related offenses. The social files primarily were useful in studying the victimology of the case and evaluating the investigation, but at times they helped locate a relative or associates of a victim. And although under the law the journalists were barred from publishing information in the social files, they could use it when confirmed by relatives.

INTRUSION OF THE WRONGLY ACCUSED

By far the relatives and friends of the murder victims received the thrust of the news media's constant attention. During the investigation, however, journalists learned of a major suspect and made his entire life a part of the public domain. Investigators scrutinized over 20,000 suspects, but only went after a handful with search warrants and a concentrated effort of the entire Green River Task Force. The use of a search warrant by investigators became the media's measuring stick of an individual's possible connection to the killings. To police, a search warrant was a law enforcement tool to evaluate an individual when other methods—interviews, work schedules, or polygraph tests—failed to eliminate him. To the media, a search warrant meant the object of the search warrant *could* be the killer or *was* the killer. The use of a search warrant to the media, then, became synonymous with: The Long Hunt Is Over! As a result of the use of search warrants by investigators, major news organizations wrote extensively about a handful of men. The media's primary privacy transgression was publishing the men's names and photographs when no charges had been filed. In the end, the men had been wrongly accused, and no charges were ever filed in connection with the Green River serial case. To say the men's lives were deeply affected by the adverse news coverage would be an understatement. Some of the men felt their lives were ruined. At least one sued several news organizations and won. While the men once were the subject of intense media coverage, their privacy, for the most part, was restored as the investigation moved in other directions.

PRIVACY IN LIMBO

In this country the political system is based on a free flow of information. Under the U.S. Constitution, journalists are entrusted with the job of keeping the citizenry informed. News consists of events, people, and their activities. Journalists on the Green River case cited several reasons for approaching the victims' relatives: the public is interested in knowing how the family is reacting; there is a need for biographical information and a photograph of the victim; the family must be given a chance to make a statement; and the family may be able to shed light on the death. Relatives of the victims understood the public's interest in the deaths, but they felt journalists did their job with little compassion and made privacy concerns the least important aspect of the news process.

Many of the victims' relatives wondered if journalists were oblivious to privacy violations because sudden death had touched so few of them personally. The effect of media attention may be abstract to journalists, in spite of the fact that some cover sudden death often. Journalists might be more compassionate—and less intrusive—if they knew how profoundly the killings and journalistic practices hurt those it touched. There is some evidence to indicate journalists better comprehend the plight of crime survivors after they have experienced what crime victims go through. Phil Sturholm, former executive editor of KIRO TV News in Seattle, made that point in a letter to *The Seattle Times*. On July 31, 1989, his brother, a journalist, was stabbed to death. Wrote Sturholm:

> As our family read, listened, and watched this story unfold in the press, all of us were painfully aware of what was coming at us from the media. Common sense says the Sturholm family is as well prepared as any family in dealing with the media about a tragedy. But after having gone through such an ordeal, my thoughts now are . . . what about the families who are not prepared? If I felt threatened . . . what about families that never deal with the press until something such as this happens.[26]

In the Green River case, the victims' relatives and friends were thrust into the public eye by a killer and circumstances beyond their control. Surviving relatives maintain those circumstances and media news practices will always control their private life. In a fairly routine homicide—a single death where the victim is not well known outside his or her circle of friends—the newspapers run a short story, and the television stations carry a thirty-second news report. More sensational murders attract several days of coverage, but the media blitz on survivors and their privacy is short compared with serial murder cases. Media coverage in the Green River case is in its twenty-third year, leaving survivors of the victims wondering when the media will stop calling.

The "Intrusion during Grief," "Psychological Intrusion," "Character Intrusion," and "Wanton Intrusion" may never cease. The Green River families have been deprived of their right to be left alone. Even though Ridgway has been arrested and sentenced, more skeletal remains related to the Green River case may be found in the future, prompting renewed news media interest. The media, too, will seek out victim relatives if Ridgway is assaulted or killed while in prison. Sustained media coverage has led to isolating those who survived the victims. Decades of media attention and intrusion create a phenomenon that can be characterized as privacy in limbo. It is very unlikely they will ever get their private lives back.

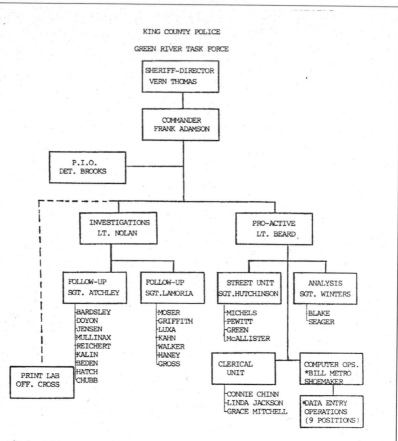

KING COUNTY POLICE

GREEN RIVER TASK FORCE

SHERIFF-DIRECTOR
VERN THOMAS

COMMANDER
FRANK ADAMSON

P.I.O.
DET. BROOKS

INVESTIGATIONS
LT. NOLAN

PRO-ACTIVE
LT. BEARD

FOLLOW-UP
SGT. ATCHLEY

FOLLOW-UP
SGT. LAMORIA

STREET UNIT
SGT. HUTCHINSON

ANALYSIS
SGT. WINTERS

- BARDSLEY
- DOYON
- JENSEN
- MULLINAX
- REICHERT
- KALIN
- BEDEN
- HATCH
- CHUBB

- MOSER
- GRIFFITH
- LUXA
- KAHN
- WALKER
- HANEY
- GROSS

- MICHELS
- PEWITT
- GREEN
- McALLISTER

- BLAKE
- SEAGER

PRINT LAB
OFF. CROSS

CLERICAL
UNIT

COMPUTER OPS.
*BILL METRO
SHOEMAKER

- CONNIE CHINN
- LINDA JACKSON
- GRACE MITCHELL

*DATA ENTRY
OPERATIONS
(9 POSITIONS)

*Federal Grant personnel

1. Organizational chart does not indicate two (2) positions eliminated in 198·.
2. Six outside police department personnel are also assigned to the GRTF (one ·
   which is part time and one which has been returned to his agency).
3. This does not include periodic staffing of FBI personnel.

CHAPTER

The Investigation . . . I

I thought it would be over in three months and we'd be looking for something else to do.

Green River Task Force
Commander Bob Evans[1]

Murders are some of the easiest crimes to solve. The clearance rates across the United States—in small and large departments, on the East and West Coasts—are quite high. In many cases the killer knows the victim and detectives simply work through the process of eliminating relatives, friends, coworkers, and acquaintances. At the conclusion of the meticulous investigation, one individual stands out as having the motive and opportunity to be the killer. Success in the solving of murders throughout history, then, figured prominently in the minds of King County Police administrators and investigators when the first victims of the Green River Killer were discovered in the Green River in the summer of 1982. Confidence was extremely high, and the prevalent thinking called for the case to be solved in a matter of weeks to a few short months. That would not be the case. It would be almost 20 years before residents of Seattle, the Pacific Northwest, and the United States would find out who killed over 60 young women in what became known as the Green River Murders case. Why did it take so long to identify the killer? And why did it take so long to gather the evidence to solve the murders? An analysis of the lengthy and complex investigation reveals an overall valiant effort by King County Police, the law enforcement agency responsible for overseeing the case since the slayings occurred outside the jurisdiction of the city of Seattle. At the height of the investigation in the mid-1980s, the King County Police were efficiently operating a multi-agency task force consisting of over 50 investigators and costing over $2 million a year. Investigators appeared to be doing all the right things to end the killings and catch the perpetrator. However, since the beginning of the investigation countless forces worked at undermining a successful outcome and especially a quick resolution. There were the politics, egos, inept vice officers, countless deviants, jurisdictional jealousies, dwindling resources, and aggressive journalists. Then there were the numerous investigative missteps and missed opportunities. And finally there was the killer. He, too, creatively influenced the direction of the investigation to his advantage. In the end the public was overjoyed at the arrest of Gary Leon Ridgway in 2001, but lamented over the lives that could have been saved if only he had been found out years sooner.

SUMMER 1982 TO 1984

The investigation into the first two victims found in the Green River resembled the handling of a routine homicide. Although both victims were discovered in the Green River, one was in a section of the river that fell under the jurisdiction of a suburb called Kent, and the other was in an area under the jurisdiction of King County Police. The idea that the death of Wendy L. Coffield in early July 1982 and the death of Debra L. Bonner in late July 1982 were connected crossed the minds of the investigators working each case separately, but they felt generally there was no link. Kent Detective R. D. Kellams was assigned to the Coffield case, while King County Police Detective David Reichert was charged with handling the Bonner case. Two dead, nude, Caucasian women in the Green River in close proximity seemed more coincidental than anything to the detectives working the cases. It was not until August 15, 1982, that the lack of a link came into question. On that day three dead, nude, black women were found in or on the bank of the Green River in the same area. The three new victims happened to be on the side of the river handled by King County Police. Since King County was investigating most cases, it took the lead in the investigation, and King County Police Major Richard Kraske convened a meeting of Seattle-Tacoma–area law enforcement agencies to compare notes on unsolved homicides. Interestingly, this was Kraske's second encounter with a major serial killer case. In the 1970s Kraske played a major role in the investigation of the "Ted Murders," in which Ted Bundy methodically murdered college coeds in Washington before moving on to Colorado and Florida to kill more young women. Kraske, King County Police Detective Bob Keppel, and the "Ted Squad" had failed to capture Bundy, but now Kraske hoped he would have better luck stopping the Green River Killer, despite the lack of experience of the detectives in the homicide-robbery unit. One of those detectives was Reichert, made the lead investigator on the Green River case since he responded to the Bonner discovery. The law enforcement agencies present at the meeting were King County Police,

Seattle Police Department, Kent Police Department, and Tacoma Police Department. Also invited was Keppel, who had left King County Police, but was working as an investigator for the Washington State Attorney General's Office. Although the intent of the meeting called for promoting cooperation, the varying investigative opinions made that difficult. Was there a pattern to the five deaths at the Green River? Some investigators felt there was, and some did not. Were the five deaths the work of a serial killer? Many of the detectives were hesitant to say they were. Keppel had no doubt there was a serial killer at work. His opinion, though, received minimal weight since many of the investigators did not like him. They thought he was a self-promoter, an egomaniac, who saw serial killers in every multiple murder case. Some investigators probably thought he was delusional. Unfortunately, the meeting was reduced to bickering over jurisdiction and personalities. The petty arguments detracted from the need to communicate and develop a strategy to catch the Green River Killer. So it was that in the first month of one of the biggest and longest investigations in history the meeting was permeated by a Machiavellian attitude. It was clear too many of the investigators were acting in bad faith.

To his credit Kraske ignored much of the interpersonal disagreements and decided to form a 25-member King County Police task force to investigate the river deaths. It was the biggest task force at King County Police since the "Ted Murders." Two of the detectives assigned to the task force were King County Police detectives Larry Gross of the "Warrants Unit" and Fae Brooks of the "Sex Crimes Unit." About the same time that Kraske publicly announced the creation of the task force, he quietly asked the FBI for a psychological profile of the killer. FBI Agent John Douglas provided a twelve-page profile. In brief, Douglas wrote that the killer was:

- Probably a white male who had a dysfunctional relationship with women.
- Organized since he tried to hide the bodies and appeared to spend some time at the river.
- Cunning in using rocks to weigh the victims down in the water to conceal them.
- Very mobile with a vehicle.
- Going to kill again.
- Like other serial killers, he would be prone to contacting police wanting to help in the investigation.[2]

The profile's final two points resonated the most with Kraske. King County Police immediately stopped the vice squad's "john patrols," in which female police officers dress as prostitutes to arrest the customers instead of the prostitutes. Police feared a police decoy would end up dead. The task force, too, decided to go after an ornery, Seattle cab driver named

Melvin Foster after he repeatedly called police to offer his perspective on the murders. He would turn out to be one of the investigation's first high-profile suspects.

Foster initially contacted King County Police on August 13, 1982, a day after Bonner's body was found in the Green River. He asked the 911 operator if police had considered that the killer might be a cab driver. The second time he called, Foster was patched through to investigators. Based on the profile and Foster's contact, the task force locked onto Foster. Investigators were certain he was the killer and believed it was only a matter of time before they came up with the evidence. In one interview Reichert butted heads with Foster, and an acrimony developed that seemed to taint Reichert's judgment on Foster's viability as a suspect for years. Both men possessed big egos. Foster liked taunting Reichert and the other investigators, and they responded with surveillance and search warrants. It would be years before investigators decided Foster probably was not the Green River Killer. By then, the damage had been done. Valuable time and resources were wasted while the killings continued. Foster's on-again, off-again battle with King County Police railroaded the investigation at its most critical time. And when investigators were unable to develop a case against Foster after several months—leaving police with no viable suspects—the task force was disbanded. Officials argued, in part, that the resources were needed to fight crime throughout the county.

Only Reichert and a handful of other detectives were assigned to work the unsolved murders even though it was obvious they could not keep up with the workload. Hundreds of tips were coming in. When the investigation finally would come to an end two decades later, the tips would fill 26,000 pages. Each day the tips and follow-up work created more mounds of paper. Somewhere in the department Kraske found a microcomputer, but there really wasn't any support staff to help input the information for case management. The small investigative team gave it a valiant effort, but detectives simply could not keep up.

By January 1983, the investigation had gone into such a lull—especially since no more bodies had been found—that the public had the impression the killings had stopped. Uniformed police officers on the street gave the prostitutes that impression, too. Everything on the strip seemed so normal again that the King County Police vice squad resumed "john patrols" with decoy officers. The relaxed atmosphere worked in the killer's favor as he picked up victims with impunity.

Although there were no obvious clues the serial killer remained active, King County Police needed reassurance the investigation was making some progress, and in March 1983, Keppel was asked to evaluate the county's effort. Keppel did not endear himself to the investigative team when he announced that he would only commence the evaluation when all the files were reorganized to fit his needs. In short, he told the team, the files were too chaotic to examine.[3] Reichert would later write, "As much as

I respected Bob, he possessed a strong ego and it was possible that his analysis would be affected by a desire to demonstrate superiority."[4] When Keppel completed his review a few months later, the team abhorred him even more. Throughout the 33-page report, Keppel criticized the investigation with lists of tasks undone by investigators. Primarily, Keppel pointed out that some witnesses had never been contacted and some tips had fallen through the cracks. Clearly, professional jealousy and animosity tended to detract from the investigation. In Reichert's mind, Keppel unfairly interpreted all of the investigative work in a negative way.[5] Keppel's confidential report quickly made its way to Kraske and Vernon Thomas, a former Seattle Police Department officer who was appointed the new sheriff of King County Police toward the spring of 1983, just in time to help rethink the investigative approach to the Green River Killer case.

While King County Police commanders contemplated their next move over the next several months, the killer kept plying his trade. And the King County Police vice squad—the undercover officers who worked the strip day-in and day-out and were the most likely to come across the killer— went about their job as if there had never been a serial killer abducting women on their strip. During the years the killer murdered most of his victims the vice squad did little to look for the killer. Instead, they confined their activities to arresting prostitutes and trying to build illegal gambling cases. That was their job, but they hardly bothered to ask the prostitutes they arrested about a killer, a more serious public safety threat. There existed a communication problem that hindered advocating a prudent, department-wide policing approach within King County Police. An analysis of King County Police vice squad expenditures reveals that during the killer's most prolific years—1982, 1983, and 1984—vice officers spent over $44,000 investigating prostitution and gambling. That amount included $25,000 on gambling investigations, over $3,000 on alcoholic drinks, about $1,800 on soft drinks, and $1,019 for 253 table dances at topless establishments. The money was spent at restaurants, hotels, and gambling houses on the strip. Sometimes the unit spent money renting three rooms at a nice hotel to arrest high-class prostitutes. Other times it would purchase cases of beer and assorted chips for props to nab prostitutes masquerading as "escorts."[6] Ironically the vice squad officers frequented businesses that the killer patronized. Vice squad reports illustrate what officers did at Trudy's. On January 27, 1983, a vice officer spent $7.50 on beer and pool games while investigating gambling activities.[7] On the same day the same officer spent $40 gambling at Trudy's. He "played in the card room in attempting to get info. from two other players in the game."[8] During his confession Ridgway told investigators he often went to Trudy's.[9] Vice officers also stopped by the White Shutters often on gambling investigations. One officer spent $38 at the business on April 6, 1983, to "re-contact gambling contacts." Thirty-three dollars was lost gambling and $2 went for "drinks."[10] Ridgway revealed in his confession that he dated prostitutes and possibly killed some in the parking lot of the White Shutters.[11] While confessing, Ridgway was asked: "Did you ever frequent the White Shutters?" He responded, "Yeah, every Thursday night . . . Parents Without Partners (meetings). . . . And I saw hookers in there too . . . and tell the people I'm going and then I'd meet her out in the parking lot and talk to her and have a date."[12] The abduction of Carol Christensen on May 3, 1983, on the strip illustrated how vice squad officers were so preoccupied with regular duties that they seemed oblivious to the killer. On that day one vice officer went into a Denny's lounge in the heart of the prostitution strip and had two beers.[13] On the same day the same officer crossed the street, walked into a hotel lounge, and bought a "soft drink" for himself and a "drink for suspect."[14] That same officer on the same day then went into a different lounge at the same hotel and bought an alcoholic drink for himself.[15] Meanwhile, a second vice officer spent $35 on a prostitution investigation at a massage parlor.[16] That same day the same officer visited an adult book store and viewed "porno films."[17] Christensen's body was found five days later in a wooded area about half an hour southeast of where she disappeared from on the strip. A supermarket paper bag from a large market on the strip covered her head.

While the vice squad spent time and money freely, King County Police commanders agonized over how to beef up their tiny Green River investigative team. Toward the end of 1983, King County Police had no choice but to reinvigorate its efforts. During that year eight young women had been found dead in rural, wooded areas of King County. Several of the victims were left near back roads of the prostitution strip. Police had played coy with the public, claiming there was no way to determine if the five women found in or near the Green River in 1982 were linked to the deaths in 1983. Perhaps there were two killers, one responsible for the river murders and one leaving his victims on land? In their own minds, however, commanders were almost certain the cases were related, and the killings had been ongoing all along. Adding to their discomfort were several missing person reports provided by the Seattle Police Department. The missing women fit the victim profile, which meant more potential victims. How many women were dead? No one knew.

In late 1983, King County Police Sheriff Vernon Thomas decided it was time to ask King County Executive Randy Revelle for authorization to create a large investigative team to identify and catch a serial killer who had plagued the county for two years. As soon as he received permission, Thomas selected Captain Frank Adamson to run the new effort: the Green River Task Force. Adamson, who possessed the administrative experience and patience to direct such a task force, was given free reign to select his team. Obviously he went after the best officers within King County Police and that created hard feelings that divided the department. Commanders complained that Adamson was raiding their units. Those officers chosen for the task force were ecstatic. Those who were not felt left out and resented the investigative effort. Soon the task force members were said to be a part of the "Green River Golf and Country Club." The rift became even greater when task force investigators were outfitted with stylish nylon green windbreakers identifying them as task force members. The politics of policing couldn't have been more bitter. As the lead investigator on the initial investigation, Reichert was selected for the task force.

1984 TO 1990

The Green River Task Force was an investigative work of art. It seemed to possess everything a major investigative team should need: money, a new computer for information management, talented investigators, and the authority to do whatever it felt necessary to solve what was becoming the biggest serial killer case in the country. The man leading the manhunt also had a reputation for building teamwork. Captain Frank Adamson was to report to only one individual at King County Police, and that was the sheriff. How could any serial killer—no matter how brilliant—be a match for such a massive, organized undertaking?

The task force consisted of over 50 investigators, most of whom were King County Police officers. Other major agencies involved with the task force were the Seattle Police Department, the FBI, the Washington State Patrol, the Pierce County Sheriff's Office, and the Port of Seattle Police, whose officers patrolled airport property adjacent to the prostitution strip. The cost for operating the task force that first year totaled $2,816,000: $2,420,000 for King County Police, the King County Medical Examiner's Office, and the King County Prosecutor's Office; $220,000 for the State of Washington crime lab and computer system; and $176,000 for outside agencies.[18] Organizationally, two lieutenants were directly under Adamson. One directed an "investigations" unit with the help of two sergeants, each directing several detectives. The second lieutenant headed the "proactive" unit with the help of two sergeants. One of the sergeants ran a "street unit," while the other ran an "analysis" section. Within that organizational structure operated a "victims team," charged with learning everything it could about the victims and their activities on the street, and a "suspects team," charged with developing and investigating the potential serial killer." Members of the proactive team specifically were to frequent the streets to gather intelligence and learn the habits of the women and men who made the streets their home. Also reporting to Adamson were two other individuals: Detective Fae Brooks, who drew the dubious distinction of dealing with the news media as the task force's public information officer, and Bob Keppel, who was to act as a consultant to the investigation.[19]

In early 1984, the Green River Task Force moved into its headquarters, the basement of the King County District Court. The location of the headquarters offered two major advantages: (1) investigators only needed to walk upstairs to the courthouse to locate prostitution arrest records and other material that might assist them in locating missing potential victims, and (2) the strip was only blocks away, allowing investigators to easily check out investigative tips and suspects. While the task force members were all smiles on moving day, a number of King County Police uniformed officers were not since the basement served as their south county precinct. They did not like being kicked out. The vice squad also found itself out on its ear. As the task force began to infiltrate the strip, the vice officers were instructed to move out. Why? The task force's strategy called for investigators to make friends with the prostitutes to get them to provide valuable intelligence and tips on who might be responsible for killing so many women. Investigators did not intend to allow the formation of a free-wheeling "red light district," but they preferred to befriend the victims of the killer, instead of antagonizing them.

From the beginning, it was clear the task force was in search of a needle in a haystack. So many of the murders had occurred so long ago, the task force first found that it had to re-create the haystack before looking for the needle. To that end investigators set out to find out who were the prostitutes on the strip and who were the men buying their services during the killing years. To identify potential witnesses and potential victims, a "missing persons" team sifted through thousands of missing person reports, hundreds of prostitution arrests, and dozens of Failure to Appear warrants. The investigators then spent weeks contacting relatives, friends, and acquaintances of missing women. Slowly they made the link between missing person reports and the women falling prey to the Green River Killer. And it was clear, after months of compiling lists of the many women who walked the street for quick money, that the total number of victims would be staggering. To expedite the identification process when victims' skeletons were discovered in the woods, the detectives set out to collect dental charts of the potential victims.

To help create lists of potential killers, the proactive team visited the jail to talk with women who had been arrested for prostitution. Primarily, they sought to identify "bad tricks" on the strip since it was evident the killer appeared to still be killing. As the men were scrutinized, they were categorized as "A" suspects, "B" suspects, or "C" suspects. The "A" list was reserved for those individuals most likely to kill and who had a strong connection to the strip and prostitutes. The cab driver named Melvin Foster remained a strong suspect in the case. Suspects and their vehicles surfaced, too, as detectives interviewed those who filed missing person reports on the women whose bodies had already been found. Several "boyfriend-pimps" of victims described an older-model pickup truck as being the vehicle the victim was last seen in. The pickup particularly was linked to the strip intersection of South 216th Street and Pacific Highway South. Composite drawings were done of the pickup and suspects. The more investigators looked for suspects, though, the more they realized that there were literally hundreds of men on the strip who fit the "A" category, hundreds of men out looking for kinky sex and with an urge to hurt women. There were a lot of sick people out there. Some of the men even dressed in woman's undergarments. The bottom line: there were too many good suspects.

While task force investigators made excellent progress reconstructing the haystack, hikers and mushroom hunters began stumbling across the bodies of more dead women. During the task force's first year, fourteen women were discovered dead in rural areas, including five in the month of April 1984. It seemed every weekend the Green River Task Force windbreakers dominated television news broadcasts as investigators recovered skeletal remains. Detectives became experts at processing outdoor crime scenes. When arriving at the "bone find," investigators determined the killer's likely path, then avoided it to preserve evidence. Instead, they developed a different route into the remains as they videotaped every move. The layers of leaves and twigs on the victim revealed the number of seasons that had passed. Once at the remains, investigators sifted the dirt for evidence: hairs, teeth, small bones, fibers. Often only the skull and a few bones remained at the scene. To locate more of the remains, the task force turned to experts such as Bill Haglund, the King County Medical Examiner's Office chief investigator who specialized in physical anthropology. To better assist the investigation, he studied the disarticulation of remains and the animals that were prone to carry away skeletal human bones. Haglund, too, helped in the efforts to identify the victims. He could determine race by the shape of the eye sockets and mandible. And he could ascertain gender by examining the ridges of bone over the eyes. Age could partly be determined by examination of the sutures on top of the skull. Since dental work was the most reliable method of identifying a victim, the skull and lose teeth were turned over to odontologists Dr. Bruce Rothwell and Dr. Thomas Morton, who compared the found teeth to dental x-rays collected from the families of missing and potential victims.

The removal of a set of remains from the woods did not end the task force's work at the scene. Next, explorer scout volunteers were called in to use machetes to cut down brush and blackberry bushes to allow investigators to search for more possible victims. It had become clear early in the investigation that the killer liked to deposit victims in clusters. It was not unusual for the scouts to clear land for weeks.

Haglund, the forensic dentists, and the scouts were only some of the experts employed by the task force. As the need arose, the task force also sought the help of a clinical psychologist to review suspect case files to determine if a suspect could be the killer; a forensic psychiatrist to analyze tapes and letters to identify psychopathic behavior dysfunctions; a tracker to examine tracks at some dump sites; and a forensic entomologist. On two occasions the task force asked Pierce Brooks to visit Seattle to offer investigative advice. Brooks was a respected California homicide investigator who was instrumental in getting the U.S. Congress to create a national computerized data bank to help investigate unsolved serial killer cases.

The task force even accepted an offer from Ted Bundy, who at the time was on death row in Florida. After receiving a letter from the infamous serial killer, task force members Keppel and Reichert flew to Florida to listen. Bundy offered several insights—such as that the killer would return to the dump sites to relive the kills—but the FBI already knew of those serial killer propensities.

The task force was well aware it was imperative that the victims be found. How else could investigators piece together the women's final hours alive and link them to their abductor and killer. However, as 1984 turned into 1985, detectives found themselves spending more time with archeology digs for remains than doing investigative work that could yield the identify of the killer. By then, other investigative concerns began to weigh heavy on the investigation. Those concerns were spelled out to King County Executive Randy Revelle by his staff assistant, Shelley Sutton. Wrote Sutton in a March 22, 1985, memo stamped "CONFIDENTIAL":

> There are a number of problems related to processing physical evidence and fingerprints that impede the progress of the investigation. First, the volume of physical evidence continues to overwhelm the Washington State Crime Laboratory. As of this writing, the Task Force has collected and catalogued 3,995 pieces of evidence, and each piece of evidence may contain hundreds of fibers, hairs, or other evidence that needs to be processed, analyzed for commonalities, and then compared. As of this writing, the backlog of lab requests stands at 123—80 with the State Crime Lab and 43 with the FBI Crime Lab.[20]

The memo further stated:

> Second, although the State Crime Lab has tried to be cooperative and supportive, particulary [sic] since new State Patrol Chief George Tellevik took over, the Lab's philosophy regarding its role exacerbates our evidence problems. The lab does not consider its role to be an investigative one—rather, the Lab believes its role is to confirm a suspect when an agency has already positively identified a suspect in a particular crime.[21]

Amid the ever growing lab troubles, in early 1985 the FBI momentarily stepped up its effort to assist by sending three FBI crime lab agents to Seattle to help search a vehicle belonging to cab driver Melvin Foster. Since King County Police still were uncertain if Foster was or was not involved in the slayings, it had authorized an undercover officer to purchase the vehicle. Eventually, the task force sent back to the FBI crime lab 34 pieces of Foster's vehicle, including the padded dash and moldings for a search of fingerprints through laser analysis. The car showed no evidence linking Foster to the murders, but, somehow, he kept managing to convince detectives he could be the Green River Killer.

The task force had to contend with other menaces: politics at multiple levels:

- When it appeared the killings stopped in Washington in 1984, the task force explored the possibility that the Green River Killer moved to Portland, Oregon. Since 1984, the city had been plagued with several unsolved cases resembling the work of a serial killer. When task force investigators contacted Portland police for information that would assist the task force, Portland refused to help. Portland feared being tainted by the infamous Green River case. Sheriff Vern Thomas had to make a special trip to Portland to speak to the chief of police to get cooperation.

- Toward the summer of 1985, skeletal remains belonging to several suspected Green River victims were found off rural roads just south of Portland. Some of the remains belonged to Denise D. Bush, who disappeared in King County in 1982 when she went to a convenience store to buy cigarettes. Upon learning that a murder victim had been taken across a state line, the FBI decided it had jurisdiction and entered the case. King County Police resented the feds suddenly encroaching directly on the investigation.

- At the end of 1985, the Green River Task Force lost its staunchest supporter, King County Executive Randy Revelle, the man who hired Thomas and authorized the funds and resources for the massive hunt for the killer. He lost the election to a fiscal conservative named Tim Hill. Hill and Thomas did not get along, and eventually Hill introduced regular reviews of the task force, which resulted in officers being reassigned. King County Police especially had trouble arguing against reductions when commanders had publicly stated, on numerous occasions, that the killings appeared to have stopped in March 1984 with the slaying of Cindy Smith. Eventually Thomas would grow tired of the political battles with Hill and resign.

No matter how often the ax fell on the task force, Captain Adamson did his job by being the eternal optimist. During the excavation of skeletal remains at a cluster site known as "Star Lake," Adamson told journalists: "I'm sure we're going to catch him. We're like a fisherman, throwing our net out again and again."[22]

In January 1986, Adamson made a bolder statement as his investigators finished recovering skeletal remains from a steep hillside near Mount View Cemetery about three miles south of Star Lake. Adamson told a *Seattle Times* reporter: "By this time next year I'm fairly optimistic we will have him in jail. I'm being optimistic about 1986. I feel good about this year."[23] The story ran the next day on front page: "Serial Killer Hunter Predicts Capture in 1986." Adamson's public comments angered Hill since the county executive's office was caught off guard. The news media also was caught by surprise, but quickly realized the task force probably already had identified the suspect. Virtually every news organization familiar with the case created teams of journalists to be on the ready the moment the suspect was arrested.

On the afternoon of February 6, 1986, Adamson's prediction appeared to be coming true. And as the task force converged on the home of Ernest W. "Bill" McLean just off the strip in south King County, so did dozens of journalists. The arrest turned into a media circus when a nearby store owner began selling popcorn and soft drinks. According to Reichert, neither he nor other task force investigators were privy to how McLean came to become the prime suspect. It was the FBI that concluded McLean appeared to be the Green River Killer. The FBI partly targeted the construction worker based on its own profile. Upon picking up McLean, agents and detectives took him into a room decorated with his photograph in the woods and filing cabinets with his name. Rocks resembling those used on the Green River victims also served as stressors. The arrest revolved around a psychological ploy to get McLean to confess. In fact, McLean calmly explained to King County Police Detective Jim Doyon and an FBI agent that he was not the killer. To prove it, he took a lie detector test and passed it.

That night marked the beginning of the end of the Green River Task Force. The task force had gone after the wrong man, and the news media crucified him and ruined his life. The investigative fiasco gave King County Executive Tim Hill the ammunition to begin dismantling the group, which had become an obvious political liability. From then on, it was mostly downhill for the task force:

- In spring 1986, the task force was moved out of its substation head-quarters and into an old, vacant junior high school. Sheriff Thomas cut three positions from the task force to finance the move. Shortly after that, an evaluation of the task force's manpower was conducted, and it resulted in deep cuts. And when a new precinct chief was needed, Thomas offered it to Adamson and he took it, along with a promotion to major.

- King County Police Captain James Pompey became the task force's new commander. During his tenure King County Police Detective Matt Haney decided to examine more closely a suspect who had been placed in the inactive list. The suspect, Gary Leon Ridgway, had been arrested in 1982 for soliciting a decoy police prostitute, and in May 1984, he had offered information to police. He claimed to have seen one of the victims. Ridgway was a former U.S. Navy man who had lived in King County most of his life. After a brief investigation, Ridgway voluntarily agreed to take a polygraph, which he passed, according to the examiner. Now in late 1986, something troubled Haney about Ridgway, and he resurrected the suspect's viability after doing additional digging. Haney discovered (1) Port of Seattle Police records in which a prostitute accused Ridgway of choking her in 1980. According to Ridgway, he assaulted the woman after she bit him. Police ended up letting Ridgway go. (2) A Port of Seattle Police report in which a Washington state patrol officer encountered Ridgway in a parked truck near a Little League field near the strip in 1982. A woman with Ridgway identified herself as Jennifer Kaufmann, which was an alias for Keli K. McGinnes, 18, who would turn out to be a Green River victim. In March 1984, the remains of Green River victim Cheryl L. Wims, 18, would be found in that same area, along with another set of skeletal remains that were never identified. (3) A Des Moines Police Department report that said Ridgway was a suspect in the disappearance of Marie M. Malvar, a suspected Green River victim whose remains had not been found. Ridgway's home was near the strip, and Ridgway had been placed under surveillance briefly in October 1986. When Haney showed the polygraph test to the FBI, they said it was flawed. Based on all that research, the task force obtained search warrants for his home on Military Road and vehicles and arrested Ridgway in April 1987. Again, the Green River windbreakers were seen carting off box after box of evidence. But again, investigators could find nothing proving Ridgway was the Green River Killer. The crime lab, too, claimed it could come up with no strong evidentiary link between items in Ridgway's home and vehicles and hairs and fibers found where the victims were deposited in the woods. Before releasing Rigdway, though, detectives routinely had him provide a saliva sample by sucking on a swab.

- Not long after Ridgway's arrest as a major suspect, Pompey died in a scuba diving accident; he surfaced too quickly and suffered an embolism. Pompey, then, was replaced by King County Police Captain Greg Boyle, who left most of the decision making to his lieutenants. His tenure was uneventful. About the same time, Sheriff Thomas grew tired of the politics and resigned. That ushered in a new task force commander, King County Police Captain Bob Evans, and a new sheriff, James V. Montgomery from Idaho. Montgomery took over the reigns of the department in the summer of 1988.

Under Evans the task force was forced to move, once again, from the school to the 12th floor of the King County Courthouse, where an old jail used to be in downtown Seattle. As part of the move, more investigators were cut from the task force. And by now, the FBI, Seattle Police Department, and the Port of Seattle Police had withdrawn their detectives from the multi-agency investigative team.

Convinced the Green River Killer may have moved—perhaps to Portland, Oregon, or San Diego, California, where unsolved murders of prostitutes plagued the cities—Captain Evans and Lieutenant Dan Nolan partnered up with Seattle-King County Crime Stoppers in hopes of finding the needle in the haystack. The task force and Crime Stoppers planned to create their own media show to appeal to the public for investigative tips. As the representative of Crime Stoppers, Myrle Carner convinced PEMCO insurance company to donate $150,000 for the production, which would include re-enactments, interviews with victims' families, and flying in detectives from all over the country to man phones to accept the tips. The program was dubbed "Manhunt Live: A Chance to End the Nightmare," and the phones lit up moments after the "docudrama" began that November 1988. Most of the callers could not get through, though. It was estimated that 100,000 people attempted to call in, but only about 10,000 were successful, meaning the tip to solve the case could have gotten lost.

Several of the calls, however, caught the eye of the task force. They pertained to a man named William J. Stevens, a resident of Spokane, Washington, a convicted burglar who enjoyed possessing police paraphernalia. Stevens became the next high-profile suspect and news media target when the task force served search warrants at his home in July 1989. But he was not the Green River Killer either. Another public embarrassment for the task force.

That was the Green River Task Force's last hurrah. By the end of 1989, the task force was no more. For all practical purposes, one man was left in charge of babysitting the case and answering the phone: Detective Tom Jensen.

The task force members dispersed reluctantly, demoralized. The killer appeared to have won. And King County Police was seen as throwing in the towel. The long investigation took a heavy toll on the investigators. In arguing against heavy task force manpower cuts after the Bill McLean fiasco, an investigator wrote to commanders of King County Police:

> It is well known that investigators assigned to major on-going serial homicide investigations frequently suffer premature burn-out, and other stress-related problems because of the inherent difficulties in this kind of case. We have seen some of these problems rear their head within the Task Force over the past 2½ years. For these officers to be told now that they are expendable, or that the investigation is winding down because it is not solvable, would be a blow very, very difficult for Task Force management to deal with. I do not believe the issue of morale can be over-stated in this particular case.[24]

The daily grind of the investigation probably affected investigators most dramatically. It could be argued that when the Green River case began in 1982, Major Richard Kraske had already been traumatized by the failed Ted Bundy investigation of the 1970s. While directing the Bundy investigation, he feared for his daughter's safety, and that was the focus of arguments with his wife.[25] When the Green River Killer surfaced, the case brought back anxiety and apprehension. Could he have been suffering from an untreated bout of posttraumatic stress disorder?

Green River Task Force Commander Frank Adamson initially refused to discuss the investigation with his wife, Jo. Eventually, his wife convinced him to open up and freely talk about the painful task of recovering the decomposed bodies of so many young girls.[26]

Detective Fae Brooks served as the task force's spokesperson for years. She battled daily with journalists, trying to keep too much information from leaking out and interfering with the investigation. She suffered nightmares of being overwhelmed by pushy reporters armed with pencils and microphones.

Task force crime analyst Detective John Blake became fixated on a criminal lawyer from Kent who represented prostitutes. The attorney had been arrested for soliciting a police decoy about a week before the first found Green River victim surfaced in the Green River. When other task force members refused to support his weak suspicions, Blake became angry and bitter and took a temporary disability leave for reasons of psychological stress. The leave became a permanent retirement.

Task force Lieutenant Dan Nolan retired shortly after the task force was closed down. He did not live to enjoy his retirement. An illness caused his death a short time later.

King County Police made a valiant effort to solve the Green River case with the formation of the Green River Task Force. The county's commitment to catching the killer was huge. By the time the task force was created, though, the trail was cold. Much of the evidence was gone. The wind had taken away fibers and Seattle's constant rain had washed the victims' bodies even as it contributed to their rapid decomposition. Before the task force began its exhaustive investigation, Ridgway had already killed most of his victims. Hence, when the task force began operating, it was already well on its way to being buried under a staggering number of victims and investigative leads related to their circle of relatives, friends, acquaintances, and abusive tricks.

1990 TO 2000

Almost overnight the frenzy of one of the biggest criminal investigations in history died down to the slow shuffle of one man: Detective Tom Jensen. He could call on other detectives for assistance, but for an indefinite time he would be the investigation. It was left up to him to answer the phones, which he despised doing since most callers now were either crazies or women trying to get back at a boyfriend or husband by giving the task force their name. It was left up to Jensen to prioritize any investigative activity that could be mustered by one man.

Jensen dabbled in many areas of the case, but for the better part of a decade, he focused on trying to find missing women who were new potential victims and identifying the skeletal remains of victims on the official Green River list. To locate women who disappeared in the 1980s, Jensen spent endless months tracking down their friends and relatives nationwide. It was not uncommon for him to contact law enforcement agencies in other states for help in checking out a lead. To give a name to the skeletal remains—all of which had been found between 1984 and 1986, including one just south of Portland, Oregon—Jensen turned to DNA. He methodically directed the laborious process of obtaining DNA from the skeletal remains to compare with DNA obtained from relatives of women reported missing and who fit the Green River victim profile.

Especially in the early 1990s, his efforts were interrupted by the disappearance of a number of women who fit the Green River victimology. One such woman was Marta Reeves, 36, who vanished in March 1990 while in Seattle. As the caretaker of the Green River investigation, it was his job to help ascertain if the disappearance of Reeves and other women were linked to the Green River case, which meant, if they were, that the Green River Killer was still active. There were so many similarities between the disappearances during the Green River era and the late 1980s and early 1990s that *The Seattle Times* published an exposé on November 21, 1991. The article suggested that the Green River Killer was back.[27] The article essentially made the argument that the most recent rash of disappearances and deaths were the work of the Green River Killer or a serial killer who operated in a very similar manner. The exposé strongly suggested that the Green River Killer had never stopped killing. King County Police had argued for years that the killings stopped in 1984. *The Seattle Times* story specifically pointed out that some of the women who had been found dead recently were discovered in rural, wooded areas near old Green River dump sites. That was the case with Reeves. Her remains were found September 20, 1990, off Highway 410, a few miles outside the town of Enumclaw in King County. Three Green River victims had been found off Highway 410 near Enumclaw in 1984. King County Police secretly assembled a small group of detectives to evaluate the possibility of an ongoing serial murder case. When the public learned of the existence of the mini-task force, King County Police commanders concluded there was no evidence to suggest a link between the most current disappearances and deaths and the infamous Green River Killer. Asked his thoughts on whether the Green River Killer was active in the 1990s, Keppel emphatically stated that he doubted the killer would return and risk detection.[28]

2001 TO 2004

As Jensen labored alone for years, many of the former Green River Task Force members moved up the ranks, gaining one promotion after another. Detective David Reichert was no exception. He had attained the rank of major in 1997 when Sheriff James Montgomery resigned to become the police chief of a Seattle-area community. Surprisingly, King County Executive Ron Sims appointed Reichert to replace Montgomery. And when the next election came around, Reichert ran for sheriff and won.

The events leading to the eventual serendipitous arrest of Ridgway began to unfold in the early part of 2001 when Sheriff Reichert called together 25 detectives who once were involved in the investigation. He asked for ideas to solve the case. For some time Jensen had been trying to use DNA regularly in the case, and there had been previous suggestions that investigators try getting DNA from victim vaginal washes and the saliva sample taken from Ridgway during the 1987 arrest. However, detectives had but a small amount of saliva and feared the DNA test would fail on such a tiny sample. By the time the meeting convened, technology had improved, and STR (Short Tandem Repeats), a faster and more accurate test, could be run on small amounts of DNA. To everyone's amazement, the DNA in the saliva sample matched DNA found in vaginal washes-swabbing of several Green River victims, including Carol A. Christensen. As yet another Green River Task Force took shape, detectives followed Ridgway on several days during October 2001. Finally, on November 30, 2001, King County Police Detective Jim Doyon and Detective Randy Mullinax arrested Ridgway on a four-page "Statement of Probable Cause" signed by Jensen.

Ridgway officially was charged with four counts of aggravated murder in the death of Marcia Chapman, 31; Cynthia Hinds, 17; and Opal Mills, 16; who were found in or near the Green River in 1982, and Christensen, 21, found in Maple Valley. If convicted of one or more counts, Ridgway faced a sentence of either death or life in prison without the possibility of release. In March 2003, Ridgway was charged with three additional counts of aggravated murder in the death of Wendy Lee Coffield, 16, and Debra L. Bonner, 23, whose bodies were discovered in the Green River in 1982, and Debra L. Estes, 15, found buried in Federal Way. But all those charges seemed to matter little a few months later when the King County Prosecutor's Office agreed to spare the life of the Green River Killer if he confessed and led detectives to other victim dump sites. The agreement sparked instant criticism. One question surfaced among all others: How can a man who kills over 60 women be given life imprisonment, while a man who kills one individual can be put to death?

During the summer of 2003, Ridgway started talking, and when he was done six months later, investigators were astonished at how he managed to elude the investigation for so long. He had been right there, on the strip, for all to see. Yet he had made himself invisible. More disturbing was the revelation that he had killed as late as 1998 and possibly into 2001.

REPORT OF MISSING PERSON

DATE: 05-03-83   TIME: 1030   CASE #: 83-00688

MISSING PERSON: MALUAR MARIE M   DOB: 4-1-65   SEX: F   RACE: Philipino

ADDRESS: 22856 30 AVE S #119   PHONE #: N/F 722-4149

HEIGHT: 5'02" WEIGHT: 105 HAIR: BLK   EYES: BLK   COMP.: DARK BUILD: SLIGHT
                                                          Philipino

CLOTHING: Blue Jeans, Purple Shirt, Black Coat

VEHICLE DESCRIPTION: YEAR: — MAKE: — MODEL: — LICENSE #: — COLOR: —

PHYSICAL/MENTAL CONDITION: NO Problems

LAST SEEN: DATE: 04-30-83 TIME: 2100 to 2200 LOCATION: At the Above residence

PROBABLE DESTINATION: To A Phone booth At SR 516 & SR 99 IN
the TRADEWELL parking lot Are

COMPLAINANT: WOODS, Robert L   HOME PHONE: N/P   BUSINESS: N/P

ADDRESS: 22856 30 Ave S #119   RELATIONSHIP: Roommate/Boyfriend

ADDITIONAL: Last seen on 04-30-83
     By APT on 05-02-83 At Apptox 1500 HR At
The Columbia Center on Hudson & Rainier
          Scar on Rt. Arm
     Morris, Monique   /   SS# 536-73-7410
     Garcia, Mario   /   4-1-63 ✓

POLICE DISPOSITION

ENTERED WACIC: Yes   REPORT GIVEN OUT TO (AGENCY):

LOCATED: DATE: TIME: AT:

ADDITIONAL:

CANCELLATION: DATE: TIME: BY WHOM:

INVESTIGATING OFFICER: _____   BADGE #: 23

6/79

Follow-up — MCSO

CHAPTER

. . . The Investigation II

5

Ah, in some ways I duped the police. I don't know how . . . I did it, but I did.

Gary Leon Ridgway
Green River Killer[1]

Even Gary Leon Ridgway was incredulous. For almost two decades, he eluded one of the biggest criminal investigations in history. The 55-year-old Utah native was as amazed as investigators, serial killer pundits, forensic psychologists, and the public because his life always has been one of simplicity. His mental faculties, especially, have been those of a child. The simper on his face says it all. His lifelong struggle to function—verbally and socially—can best be conveyed with a few snippets of his life in the Seattle area.

Since his childhood Ridgway got lost, often, not knowing where he was. And when he had to converse with anyone to get his bearing, he had problems articulating his predicament. That was the reason his parents assigned his older brother, Greg, to be his almost constant companion. The relationship between the brothers seemed reminiscent of John Steinbeck's *Of Mice and Men*. In school Ridgway received *C*s and *D*s and was considered a slow learner who couldn't remember what the teacher told the class. For several years Ridgway was enrolled in special programs to help him learn. Even during the summer, his parents drove him to classes designed to help him learn to read. "I felt sad because I couldn't learn," Ridgway said during his interrogation after his arrest for the Green River Murders.[2] His parents even had Ridgway hypnotized to get at the root of his learning problems and why he frequently responded to questions with: "I don't know. I don't know."[3] But that didn't work.

RIDGWAY: They wanted to put me . . . they did want to put me in a special
   program called Woods . . . Woodside?
DR. ROBERT WHEELER: You're crying as you remember that. Why are you
   crying?
RIDGWAY: Because I didn't want to go. . . . That was a school everybody
   made fun of . . . when the buses come by a kid I knew in the fourth
   grade, he was put in that bus and every time it came by everybody else I
   was with made fun of it and the people in there.
WHEELER: The retards?
RIDGWAY: The retarded people . . .[4] And I didn't want go. Greg wouldn't
   and my friends wouldn't be there. And when . . . whenever we saw the
   Woodside bus everybody would give 'em the fingers and yell at the bus. . . .
   I didn't wanna be treated like that.[5]

When Ridgway was asked questions outside of school, his brother
Greg answered for him. Clyde, the family dog, seemed to be the only living
being that Ridgway felt comfortable talking to about his problems reading
and learning. In high school, Ridgway tried coming out of his shell and
went out for sports:

> I started, ah, football later on. I started, ah, wrestling later on but I
> dropped out because my excuse was I got a job but . . . I couldn't, ah, re-
> member what I was doing in football, couldn't remember what I was
> doing in bas . . . And I didn't have that much initiative. I just couldn't, um,
> couldn't remember what they're talkin' about . . . wouldn't sink in.[6]

Despite his apparent learning disability, Ridgway was able to enter the
U.S. Navy. Asked how he handled boot camp, he responded, "I handled it
pretty good, but I had problems with uh, uh I was right up in the front and I
always made mistakes in marching. If they'd say left fl-flank, and I'd go the
wrong direction."[7] When Ridgway left the Navy, he obtained a job painting
trucks at Kenworth Trucks, south of Seattle in King County and adjacent to
the prostitution strip. At the truck company, the workers enjoyed creating
nicknames for each other. Ridgway was known as "Wrongway," because he
tended to misidentify the paints, resulting in trucks being painted the
wrong color.

Ridgway still was painting trucks and misreading paint codes at Kenworth in the early 1980s when his rage against women overcame him, and
he took to the streets to squelch it. Within hours of Ridgway's arrest at
Kenworth in 2001, the haunting questions arose: Why did it take nearly two
decades to apprehend Ridgway? How could he elude such a large manhunt? Luck played a big role. Ridgway seemed to get all the breaks year
after year. Innumerable police missteps, though, contributed heavily to the
lack of a quick resolution and an increase in the number of abductions and

murders. Perhaps the most important factors that made Ridgway so difficult to catch were his street smarts and familiarity with the prostitution
strip. Ridgway grew up near the strip, and every day he meandered through
the businesses and residential neighborhoods, learning the sounds and
memorizing the smells. During his confession, he seemed to know every
trash can and dead-end dirt road, like a mangy, skinny, stray dog who wan-
ders the streets at night after people go to bed. By the time Ridgway
agreed to divulge his secrets in exchange for his life in 2003, Reichert, the
first investigator on the Green River case in 1982, was the King County
Sheriff.

"You have good instincts," Reichert stated during one interrogation
session. "Do you know what I mean by that?"

RIDGWAY: I have uh, survival instincts . . . I think.
REICHERT: No, you have street instincts.
RIDGWAY: Yeah, street, too.
REICHERT: Yeah. That's why I think, part 'a the reason that you were so
    good out there. You kinda feel whether or not there was a cop around.
RIDGWAY: Um-hm. (yes) Feel whether there was a cop or a, a pimp, you
    know.[8]

THE GREEN RIVER

The good fortune that enveloped Ridgway in his serial killings was evident
from the beginning in 1982. Between July 15, 1982, and August 15, 1982,
Ridgway killed five women. Two of the victims had been fished out of the
Green River by August 12, 1982. The three others had not been discovered.
Two of the unfound had been weighted down in the river with rocks, and
the third had been left on the bank. On the afternoon of August 15, 1982,
Ridgway returned to the Green River to have postmortem sex with the
victim on the bank, then he planned to place her in the river with all the
others. When he reached the bank, however, a man named Robert
Ainsworth was floating down the river in a small raft. After the two men
exchanged pleasantries, Ridgway left quickly. Moments later, Ainsworth
discovered the two women in the water, and the river was overrun with police officers. Fortunately for Ridgway, Ainsworth was unable to provide
enough details to identify him, and no one happened to see his truck and
take down his license plate.

The Green River serial murders could have ended with only five victims had police had a little luck. And if Ridgway would have confessed in
the summer of 1982, investigators would possess plenty of physical evidence. It so happened that Ridgway had taken photographs of some of his
river victims with an Instamatic camera. Knowing police would search his

home if he was suspected of being involved, Ridgway hid the photographs in a crawlspace at the base of the Sea-Tac Red Lion, located off the prostitution strip near the Seattle-Tacoma International Airport. Once a week for several weeks Ridgway pulled them out to look at them. After about a month, he tore them up since they had fingerprints. Then, he threw them in the river. He ran over the camera with his truck to destroy it.

LIVING VICTIMS

Throughout the years there were many women who could have testified to Ridgway trying to kill them, but only two appear to have contacted police. Ridgway started choking—but released—about four women before the summer of 1982 when the initial Green River victims were found in the river.

- One potential victim escaped when Ridgway assaulted her near a Little League Field just north of the airport. Ridgway told investigators:

  > I paid her for the twenty dollars and tried to choke her and . . . she was just too big for me . . . I couldn't, ah, control her. And, ah, she's probably use to men beating her up or somethin' . . . we walked back to the truck and I apologize and apologize to her and . . . took her where I needed to drop her off and dropped her off . . . she didn't turn me in . . . I don't think.[9] I just begged and begged and begged the woman . . . the woman wouldn't tell anybody, pimp or you guys . . . but it wasn't really that violent . . . we just rollin' around and I just gave up on tryin' to . . . she was just too much for me.[10]

- A second woman survived an attack at Ridgway's home. When Ridgway tried to choke her from behind, somehow he put a finger in her mouth. She bit the finger until he removed his arm from around her neck.

  > We rolled a little bit and she just . . . just kept . . . had . . . had my finger in her mouth. If I coulda got it out and went further I would have tried but at that point my finger hurt more than . . . than killing her at the time. . . . And she, ah, got pissed off and asked me why I did that and all that stuff here, and . . . and, ah, I just told her I was sorry and everything and paid . . . paid for the sex I had and we walked out.[11] I just kept on bein' apologetic all the way through, "I'm sorry I did it. I've never done it before" . . . she didn't take down my license number, just walked off back to the strip or back to her boyfriend or whatever.[12]

Ridgway was uncertain when this incident occurred. And although Ridgway stated that the woman reported the attack to police, it was unclear what they did, if anything.

- In November 1984 a woman contacted the Green River Task Force to report that she was violently attacked while she worked as a prostitute in November 1982. A subsequent investigation revealed that Ridgway was the perpetrator. "During the sexual act that ensued, Ridgway placed the female prostitute in a police-like chokehold, forcing her to the ground face down."[13] When Ridgway momentarily released the chokehold, the woman managed to break free and escape. She ran to a nearby mobile home trailer park and never saw her assailant again. When contacted in February 1985, Ridgway admitted choking the woman, but claimed he did so after she bit him. No charges were filed.

Asked why so many woman failed to report him to police or delayed in doing so, Ridgway explained:

> I just tell the woman I'm sorry, frustration or whatever, make up a lie to 'em and . . . and, ah, she's already got the money and . . . and, ah, told 'em don't, ah, don't tell anybody this has never happened before. You know, almost bend down kiss their feet, you know, all that stuff here.[14]

POLYGRAPH

Although not many assault survivors contacted police about Ridgway, there seemed to be enough troubling information for authorities to seriously consider Ridgway a suspect. He had been arrested in a prostitution sting in 1982, and he had contacted the Green River Task Force in 1984 to say he might have seen one of the victims in 1983. Ridgway's overture reminded investigators of the FBI profile, which warned that serial killers tend to interject themselves into a case by offering innocuous information. Prudently, detectives focused on Ridgway then turned to one of law enforcement's most venerable investigative tools to ascertain truth. In 1984, Ridgway was asked to take a polygraph. He happily did so and he passed it. Upon close examination years later, the test was declared flawed. The questions given to Ridgway seemed to lack specificity. And, tragically, the test results misdirected the investigation. It was generally understood, however, that the polygraph examiners probably were not entirely to blame for the false reading. Somehow Ridgway was able to take advantage of the situation, although he was being deceitful. How did he beat the polygraph? When asked, Ridgway responded:

> I . . . (yawn) excuse me . . . I just was gonna take it and, and uh, I thought for sure pass it.[15] I just was, (yawned) excuse me, I just uh, relaxed and took the polygraph. I mean there's no uh, I didn't practice anything . . . just relaxed and answered the questions and . . . whatever came out. Uh, maybe I was too relaxed.[16]

MARIE M. MALVAR AND CAROL CHRISTENSEN

When law enforcement agencies in King County seemed to have the opportunity to catch Ridgway early in the serial killings, miscommunication or no communication turned the opportunity into a missed opportunity. That is what happened with the abduction and murders of Marie M. Malvar and Carol Christensen. The Green River Murders case could have been solved in April 1983—less then a year after it began and after 22 women were dead—had police been more alert and communicated with other law enforcement jurisdictions.

It was the night of April 30, 1983, that Malvar climbed into Ridgway's pickup truck on the prostitution strip. Malvar's boyfriend was nearby and tried following the truck in his own vehicle, but lost the pickup truck as it turned onto South 216th Street. While the boyfriend searched the neighborhood streets frantically, Rigway took Malvar to his house a short distance from 216th Street. Malvar turned out to be Ridgway's most difficult kill. She fought and struggled, and before she died she scratched his arm with her long nails, leaving deep scars. A short time later, Ridgway was pulling Malvar's body down a steep, wooded hill a few miles southeast of his house and the prostitution strip.

After a couple of days of searching, Malvar's boyfriend discovered a truck similar to the one used to abduct Malvar. It was parked in front of Ridgway's home on Military Road. The boyfriend summoned the Des Moines Police Department, which patrolled that area of the county. Sergeant Greg Fox and a second officer responded. Ironically, Fox and Ridgway had worked together at a bazaar about 20 years earlier. Ridgway was too embarrassed to remind the officer of their past relationship. It was unclear if Fox remembered. Recalled Ridgway:

> Greg Fox came a couple days later and he had an officer and he asked me about Malvar and he asked if it's okay for him to check the house and so an officer. . . . I'm quite sure it was another officer, walked in and walked out. Didn't see anybody . . . I was working right by the front gate. I talked to him over the fence and leaned up and talked to him.[17] I had to hide my arm because it was scratched and he would have seen it and asked, "how did you get scratched?" So I hid it.[18]

The officers' approach seemed lackadaisical, at best. They did a poor job of looking in the house; they asked Ridgway few questions; and they failed to notice his scarred arm. A tremendous opportunity was missed. More aggressive police work—in light of widespread news media reports of a serial killer operating only a few months before—could have led to a thorough search of Ridgway's home. The search could have led to the evidence to charge him since he had been killing women in his bedroom. On separate occasions Ridgway had found a ring and a watch in his bedroom belonging to victims. In the house, too, investigators could have found a hiding space behind a drawer under the kitchen sink. It was there that Ridgway hid jewelry taken from his victims. Occasionally, he took the jewelry out to hide it under rocks and utility posts adjacent to roads in south King County. He did so to avoid having incriminating evidence in his house in case police ever suspected him. Investigators also might have found in his truck a rug or wool blanket Ridgway used to wrap victims in. By the time the Green River Task Force searched Ridgway's house in 1987, the rug and blanket had been tossed out. Most important, the officers who went to Ridgway's house after the Malvar murder could have caught Ridgway in a lie if they had pressed him with a few questions. Ridgway told Fox he was out of work. In fact, Ridgway had a job. After the officers left, Ridgway chastised himself for telling a lie that could prompt the officers to question him. If the officers had found grounds for taking Ridgway in for questioning, they could have found Malvar's identification in his pants pocket. For several weeks he kept the identification in his pocket and likely had it when he abducted Carol Christensen May 3, 1983, from the prostitution strip, then left her in a rural area known as Maple Valley.

The visit by Des Moines police spooked Ridgway into staging Christensen's body so it would not be associated with all the other Green River victims. After having sex with Christensen at his home, Ridgway redressed her, put her in the woods, placed two fish on her upper torso, sprinkled meat about the body, and placed an empty bottle of wine at her crotch. Ridgway, then, placed a Larry's Market grocery bag over her head. The staging worked. For years investigators debated whether Christensen was or was not part of the Green River serial case.

While putting Christensen in the woods, Ridgway escaped another close call.

> As I was leaving there, I got to the . . . out the driveway, right next to me, a officer in a white State Patrol, was going out of the next dirt road so I drove up to the . . . took a right, stopped at the stop sign and I . . . trying to figure out which way I went.[19] Holy, holy crap, you know, (laughs) . . . officer didn't, didn't realize that he . . . was, uh . . . that close to catching me. Uh, that was, a, a, a, a big one.[20]

In case his vehicle left tire tracks at the Christensen site, Ridgway bought new tires for his truck and threw the old ones in a river.

In the week following the murders of Christensen and Malvar, Ridgway became even more creative to throw police off. He took hotel matches, car rental leaflets, and travel material and spread them around the hillside where he dumped Malvar's body. The planted evidence was intended to make investigators believe the killer was a person who had flown into the Seattle area on a sojourn. Ridgway also sprinkled cigarette butts about to make detectives think the killer smoked. He would leave cigarette butts and gum wrappers at other sites as well in the future.

Next, toward the end of May 1983, Ridgway took Malvar's identification and dropped it on the floor of B Concourse at the Seattle-Tacoma Airport. Again, he wanted to create the impression the killer had flown in and out of the city. On May 27, 1983, a custodian cleaning the carpet discovered Malvar's driver's license at Gate B4. The custodian turned the license in to the lost-and-found department of the Port of Seattle Police, who contacted the Des Moines Police Department since it was that agency that was investigating Malvar's disappearance. Des Moines police never bothered to pick up the license, and in October 1983, it was destroyed routinely, along with any fingerprints Ridgway may have left on it. There is no evidence, either, that Des Moines ever contacted King County Police about its encounter with Ridgway. Another missed opportunity.

Ridgway talked in detail about an apparent transformation of his killing series to avoid being caught:

RIDGWAY: Just gettin' rid of the evidence. Um, not be seen and always have some kind of excuse in case you . . . somebody comes up and talks to you, you know.

DET. JON MATTSEN: I mean, that was early! That was the beginning of your reign . . .

RIDGWAY: Yeah.

MATTSEN: You know, the . . . the top dog of . . .

RIDGWAY: Um hmm.

MATTSEN: . . . of serial killers.

DET. RANDY MULLINAX: So this was a learning process for you?

RIDGWAY: This was a learning process, yes. . . . It was learning and getting it better. Better. Foolin' you guys.

MATTSEN: Was that your whole goal?

RIDGWAY: Yeah.

MULLINAX: You like foolin' us, didn't you?

RIDGWAY: Yeah.[21]

KELLY M. WARE

In mid-July 1983, Kelly M. Ware, 22, got into Ridgway's truck near downtown Seattle, and she was never seen again, until her remains were discovered four months later in a shallow grave near the Tyee Golf Course adjacent to the Seattle-Tacoma International Airport. Her case affirmed the notion that officers of the various law enforcement jurisdictions that patrolled south King County and the airport area were not alert and were not suspicious enough.

A few days after killing Ware and leaving her body in a wooded area near a golf course, Ridgway had custody of his son, Mathew, for the weekend. And after attending a birthday party, they headed home in Ridgway's truck. When Mathew fell asleep, Ridgway decided to have post-mortem sex with Ware. Suddenly a Port of Seattle police officer appeared. During his confession, Ridgway explained what happened:

> It was dark, you couldn't see my truck and the only way I got up off of her havin' sex with her is because I saw the lights of the . . . the officer comin' in.[22] I came as a cop was coming outta the car, the . . . the airport security, and I had to hurry through to get to the front of the truck so that I could talk to the officers so they wouldn't . . . go back and look. And then I talked to 'em and I told 'em my son was in the car, told 'em that I was, ah, needed to take a pee. . . . And, ah, he bought it as soon as . . . and he pulled out, and I just followed him so that he was satisfied that nothin' . . . nothin' funny goin' on in there.[23]

A day or so later, Ridgway returned to the area, had post-mortem sex with the victim again then buried her. Ware's body lay only about 20 feet away from where Ridgway spoke with the officer.

CONSTANCE E. NAON

The golf course was the site of another bizarre incident in 1983. That summer Ridgway abducted Constance E. Naon from the prostitution strip, killed her, and laid her body on the ground near the golf course. He planned to return the next day to bury her, but in the meantime he picked up another prostitute.

> I brought a woman to a site where a dead body was . . . I found a prostitute I was gonna take her to that same site and I forgot that she (Naon) was laying out right around where, ah, the, ah, walked up to the trail to take the woman to have sex and kill her . . . I forgot that I left a body there . . . all of a sudden there's a woman laying there naked.[24]

Asked what the prostitute did when she saw the body, Ridgway said, "She ran to the truck and I didn't have that killing frenzy in me to . . . to kill her otherwise I woulda killed her in the front of the truck. I think she said, 'Let's get outta here.'"[25] Sometime later, Ridgway went back to where he put Naon and leisurely dug a hole to bury her. Although he dug for over an hour, no one reported seeing him.

KIM L. NELSON

The disappearance of Kim L. Nelson—known as "Star" on the street—revealed some of the more subtle mistakes Ridgway made.

In the early morning hours of November 1, 1983, Nelson and a prostitute named Paige Champion decided to work together near a bus stop on the prostitution strip near South 144th Street. Champion got a "date" first. When she returned 15 minutes later, Nelson was gone and did not return that day or night. A couple of days later, Champion was at a 7-11 convenience store on the prostitution strip at 2 A.M. when a man came up and asked about the tall, blond woman who had been with Champion at South 144th Street. The man then flashed a big wad of money to encourage Champion to date him. Champion refused, fearing the man had something to do with Nelson disappearing since only once had Champion and Nelson paired up to solicit customers on the strip. Champion was unaware Nelson was dead until her remains were found in the summer of 1986, and the Green River Task Force contacted Champion. The man who approached Champion that morning at the 7-11 turned out to be Ridgway.[26]

EVASIVE MOVES

Even though Ridgway sometimes acted careless and forgetful in his killings—like the time he killed a woman and left her in the back of his pickup at work all day—he premeditatedly tried to evade detection in many ways. Some of his ideas came from the mass media, specifically detective magazines, true crime books, and television programs. "So I knew . . . what evidence was and . . . knew what you're lookin' for or what," Ridgway told investigators.[27] Other ideas he thought of while he observed police decoys and prostitutes on the strip as he relaxed sipping coffee inside a Kentucky Fried Chicken on the strip. Once he even waved at a prostitute from the business, and she came inside to meet him. After he finished his coffee, he took the woman for a date and killed her. Ridgway employed a variety of techniques and schemes to beat his pursuers:

- On occasion, he used plastic gloves to avoid leaving fingerprints.
- If a victim scratched Ridgway during the slaying, he clipped their nails while they were in his bedroom and flushed the nails down the toilet. He was aware skin under the fingernails could provide evidence.
- He stripped almost every victim of their clothing to make identification difficult and get rid of any fiber evidence that might link him with the victim. Routinely, he tossed their clothes and identification cards out the window as he drove on rural highways. A few times he left a victim's clothing in boxes at a Goodwill drop-off station.

- He hid condoms under a rock near the produce delivery area at the rear of Fred Meyer.
- If Ridgway picked up a prostitute and thought someone was following him, he'd drop the woman off and would not date.
- Ridgway made it a point to avoid passing by an area where police were processing a scene after a body was discovered.

> I stayed away from those areas . . . 'cause I've heard sometimes they film people that come in. And film everybody, like they did with the uh, uh, these sites. 'Cause guys like to come back to see where they killed people, and then they're in the audience. I've heard that.[28]

- Ridgway enjoyed taking his victims' jewelry, but he went through great pains to physically disassociate himself from it, unlike other known serial killers. After murdering a woman, he'd keep the jewelry in a plastic bag for a few days. He then would hide it in several locations in south King County: by a tree, a highway guardrail, or a lamp post in a Safeway parking lot.

> I've heard about them . . . savin' the jewelry and saving mementos and, you know, body parts. Ah, which is all . . . which is all evidence. If it's away from me, it's in a plastic bag, there's no fingerprints on it, no. . . . Ah, the body parts I didn't . . . you know, didn't care for the body parts. No, that wasn't even in the picture. But the jewelry I knew that a lot of times that's where they get caught is they . . . most the guys leave . . . keep the jewelry or mementos close.[29]

Sometimes, Ridgway took jewelry to work and tossed it into the women's bathroom for female employees to find.

> And it's my way of maybe sometimes maybe getting back at the people at Kenworth, some of the women. 'Cause hey . . . (unintel) . . . you see 'em walkin' around with, ah, somebody's stolen. . . . I just could hear 'em in the bathroom say they found a watch or . . . and I'd see how many. . . . in one way I wanna see who's gonna be honest and who's gonna be not honest.[30]

On occasion, Ridgway expressed his pleasure at his success:

> Well I was in a way a little bit proud of not being caught . . . like removing the clothes. Not leaving anything . . . any fingerprints on it, using gloves. Changing tires on my vehicle one time after I. . . . I think after I dropped Christensen off. Not bragging about it. Not talking about it.[31]

Ridgway felt so at ease he considered posing victims with a hand "giving the finger" to King County Police investigators.[32]

RELOCATING SKELETAL REMAINS

The scheme that created the most serious investigative problems involved the relocating of skeletal remains of several victims. Ridgway came up with that creative idea to throw off investigators and have them believe the Green River Killer had moved south to Oregon. His trick worked.

After the Green River Task Force was formed, Ridgway decided to scrounge around several Green River victim dump sites in King County for bones to move to Oregon. When he was done collecting various bones, he had skeletal remains from Denise D. Bush and Shirley M. Sherrill, who disappeared and were killed in 1982, and Tammie C. Liles, who was killed in the summer of 1983. Ridgway visited the Mountview Cemetery area and found the skull belonging to Kimi-Kai Pitsor, but he dropped it and couldn't find it in the dark. Ridgway threw the bones in two separate plastic bags and placed them in the trunk of a sedan he was driving.

About the time Ridgway decided to execute his plan, he realized he had visitation rights with his son, Matthew. That did not stop Ridgway. He simply put his son's bicycle in the trunk with the bags of bones and headed for Oregon. While Matthew slept, Ridgway threw the bones out into two semirural areas. He then quickly returned to Washington with his son. As he drove away from Portland, he threw the plastic bags out the car window.

In late April 1985, two sets of skeletal remains were found just south of Portland near a community named Tualatin. One of the remains was identified as belonging to Liles. The other was never identified because the Portland-area medical examiner's office somehow lost the remains. In mid-June 1985, the skeletal remains belonging to Bush and Sherrill were also found just south of Portland on Bull Mountain in a community known as Tigard.

Ridgway wanted the bones to be found.

DET. TOM JENSEN: Did you know that by depositing those bones in Oregon you were gonna involve the FBI in this case?
RIDGWAY: Y . . . uh, yes.
JENSEN: And you knew that that would screw us up really big time, didn't ya.
RIDGWAY: Yeah, yes, I would because a body's bein', goin' across the border, yeah.[33]

As soon as the Seattle office of the FBI learned some of the Green River victims were taken across state lines, it entered the case, and forced the Green River Task Force to let it take the lead in some aspects of the investigation. Eventually the FBI lacked the resources to keep a sustained presence in the hunt. The jurisdictional bickering did little to advance the investigation. At the time, neither King County Police nor the FBI were aware they had been had by the killer, who knew more about their institutional behavior than they knew about his personal propensities. They were being toyed with.

To the investigators and psychologists who interviewed Ridgway after his capture, his cognitive skills seemed a paradox. On the one hand, his intellectual capacity appeared to be almost nonexistent, yet he possessed refined critical thinking skills. He knew what to say and do when police came close to catching him. And, no doubt, he was cunning. FBI Agent Mary Ellen O'Toole of the National Center for the Analysis of Violent Crime was impressed and visited Seattle several times to try to fully grasp Ridgway's deviant thinking: "Just from listening to you, you're always thinking and you're on your toes and you're thinking ahead.[34] You're having to think under pressure, and you're having to make some choices because you know what your intentions are, but you also know you've been stopped several times, or at least seen . . . that's pretty impressive . . . you're still able to think on your feet."[35] Ridgway responded:

> I'm always thinking I don't want any attention. Don't want to be outside drinking a beer so if anybody could see when I went back to the truck or anything. I got in and looked around and just drove out normal. Not spinning the tires or nothing to throw any attention to me.[36]

King County Sheriff David Reichert's resentment of the FBI's encroachment in the case through the years was evident during Ridgway's interrogation in the summer of 2003:

REICHERT: They do like to hog the show.
RIDGWAY: Yeah, the, uh, FBI lady comes in here and they stop everything when she comes in.
REICHERT: They did, they stopped everything for her?
RIDGWAY: Uh-ha. They stopped everything and had me meeting with her last week.
REICHERT: Well, yeah, the FBI, I mean, that's heavy duty stuff.
RIDGWAY: Uh-huh.
REICHERT: I'm just the Sheriff.
RIDGWAY: You're just a, a County Sheriff, not a . . .
REICHERT: I'm not FBI.
RIDGWAY: You're not, uh, they kind of walk all over you.
REICHERT: (laughs).
RIDGWAY: (Unintelligible) try to take things away from you.
REICHERT: Uh, they got a few nice . . . people.
RIDGWAY: You know how the movies are, they always bring up, uh, the FBI wants to take over this case.[37]

When in control, Ridgway could be lucid, insightful. And if given an opportunity, he could turn the tables around. For a moment, Ridgway seemed to be interviewing Reichert.

RETIRING FROM KILLING

Even when Ridgway agreed to confess, he was hesitant to give up many details. That frustrated Detective Tom Jensen:

JENSEN: If you wanna laugh in our faces for not catchin' you . . . go nuts.
RIDGWAY: Um-hm. (yes)
JENSEN: You won . . . the first twenty years . . . or the first nineteen. We won now, okay.
RIDGWAY: Um-hm. (yes)[38]
JENSEN: But if you wanna laugh about the first nineteen years, you go ahead. You can throw it in my face all you want.
RIDGWAY: Um-hum. (yes)
JENSEN: I don't care what you do. Just tell me. You, you, right now, are the best serial killer that, that this country has ever known. . . . You are the man. We wanna know how you did it, that's all.[39]

When Ridgway finally opened up, he dropped a bombshell on everyone: he had not stopped killing in 1984 as everyone thought he had. In fact, he believed he killed into 2001, the year he was arrested. Ridgway claimed to have trouble remembering some of his most recent slayings, but he provided investigators enough information to confirm he murdered:

- Patricia Barczak. She was killed in October 1986, but her remains were not found until February 1993 near Green River Community College in an area where a Green River victim was dumped in the mid-1980s.
- Roberta Hays. She was last seen in February 1987, but she was not found until September 1991. Her remains were off Highway 410 in the general area where Green River victims were left in the mid-1980s.
- Marta Reeves. She disappeared in March 1990. Her remains were found in September 1990 off Highway 410, just three miles from Hays.
- Patricia Ann Yellowrobe. She was found in King County August 6, 1998, shortly after she had been killed.

It was evident to investigators that Ridgway most probably murdered many more women than those four since 1984, but Ridgway insisted he could not recall specifics of other kills, preventing officials from charging him with more slayings in the late 1980s and throughout the 1990s.

Only Ridgway knows, still, if he intended to minimize his murderous activities to support his contention that he was doing what other serial killers throughout history had been unable to do: stop killing. Ridgway called it retiring.

Ridgway's assertion angered Detective Randy Mullinax:

> Why the fuck should we believe that suddenly Gary Ridgway has got, ah, the will and the where with all to say "I'm done, that's it, not gonna kill anymore prostitutes. Sixty-three's my limit, that's it, can't kill anymore."[40] . . . You liked killin' . . . you just told me you liked killin' people. . . . That must be a pretty strong addiction, it ain't somethin' you put a fuckin' patch on your arm and just get over. I mean that just doesn't go away one day, "oh, that's it, I'm not gonna kill anymore."[41]

Even after investigators and psychologists pointed out to Ridgway that research had shown a serial killer's drive to kill and use prostitutes is too overpowering to override, Ridgway insisted he was on his way to retiring. At times during the interrogation, he was convincing:

> I was beatin' the system. I knew that nobody . . . very many people never stopped killing, and it was me to get back at you guys and have you guys waste your time tryin' to pin me on other murders. Yeah, that would be. . . . that's one of the motives, too, but not the underlyin' motive of stoppin', 'cause I know you guys would keep on lookin' and keep on lookin'. . . . It is a very strong addiction. But it's true, I knew I could . . . the major thing was for Judith (Ridgway's wife) . . .[42] . . . losing every thing and, ah, going . . . going to jail, going to prison, um, and, ah, the cats outta the bag and every . . . everybody, ah, ah . . . would know and, ah, it would be a real hard one to, ah, look Judith in the eye . . .[43] . . . but also . . . to get you guys keep on goin' on a steady track . . . you're looking into San Diego, mirror image . . . the paper says "Mirror Image of Seattle," looking into maybe Portland, Hawaii. They're just throwin' that money around to . . . to go after, and I'm just sitting back there, watchin' TV, doin' . . . doin' things, and here is you guys are goin' on wild goose. . . .[44]

Gary Leon Ridgway, in fact, hoped to reduce his killing to greatly lessen the chances of getting caught. Then he planned to move away from the Seattle area, leaving investigators to look for the needle in the haystack for years to come. Said Ridgway: "My general opi . . . opinion, uh, yes, I didn't think I'd ever get caught."[45]

U.S. Department of Justice

Federal Bureau of Investigation

In Reply, Please Refer to
File No.

FBI Academy
Quantico, Virginia 22135

August 24, 1984

Detective Bruce Kalin
Department of Public Safety
King County
W-150 King County Courthouse
Seattle, Washington 98104

Re: Letter and three tapes sent to Supervisor John E. Douglas,
     Criminal Profiling Program, Behavioral Science Unit (BSU).

Dear Detective Kalin:

        The purpose of this letter is to respond to referenced
material that was sent to me by Tonya Yzaguirre, Latent Print
Examiner, King County Department of Public Safety, for my review
and analysis.

        It is my opinion that the author of the written
communique has no connection with the Green River Homicides.
The communique reflects a subject who is average in intelligence
and one who is making a feeble and amateurish attempt to gain
some personal importance by manipulating the investigation. If
this subject has made statements relative to the investigation
which was not already released to the press, he would have to
have <u>access</u> to this information (Task Force).

        The verbal communiques were reviewed and it is my
opinion that they are unrelated to the written communique.

        I am not familiar with the areas that your subject
furnishes as being the location of other bodies. I would assume
that when you in fact located another victim it was in the
general vicinity.

        Your caller is not specific enough to establish himself
as the "Green River Murderer". However, he does have the capacity
to imitate and be a "copy cat" killer.

nvℓ

CHAPTER

Communiqué

6

It is my opinion that the author of the written communiqué has no connection with the Green River Homicides.

John E. Douglas
FBI Profiler[1]

Journalist Mike Barber was working at the *Seattle Post-Intelligencer* when a copy aide dropped a letter on his desk. The letter had already been opened and paper-clipped to the envelope, which bore the words "very important." It had been postmarked in Seattle on February 20, 1984. The first line of the letter made it clear that it was no ordinary letter from a disgruntled reader. It read: "whatyou eedtonoaboutthegreenriverman . . . dontthrowaway."[2] Barber and *Post-Intelligencer* (*P-I*) reporter George Foster were assigned to keep track of the Green River Murders, which had taken on added importance the month before with the announcement of the formation of the Green River Task Force. Barber had covered the police beat often enough to know the value of evidence. He copied the letter and put the original in a clear plastic lunch bag. During that process, he went to work drawing lines between the typed words because the writer put no spaces between his words.[3] As journalists at the *P-I* studied the copy of the tantalizing letter, the news organization did its civic duty and gave the original to the Green River Task Force. Green River Killer Gary Leon Ridgway wrote and sent the letter, but investigators would not know that until he confessed in 2003. For nearly 20 years, the communiqué sat in a file collecting dust.

The handling of the communiqué by the Green River Task Force and the FBI reveals the need for law enforcement and social scientists to rethink their treatment of communiqués in serial killer cases. This was not the first time investigators hunting for a serial killer in the United States mishandled a communiqué and ignored its potential investigative value. It is apparent a more systematic investigative approach to better evaluate and utilize communiqués in serial killer investigations would better serve law enforcement and the public.

The two-page letter that arrived at the *P-I* that winter day in 1984 was Ridgway's most sophisticated and boldest attempt to lead the investigation astray. He obviously did not care which Seattle newspaper received the communiqué and passed it on to police. He wrote on the envelope "Seattle postintelligencer," but he addressed it to the other major daily newspaper in town, *The Seattle Times,* at "fairview n john . . . PO Box 70."[4] While Ridgway seemed careless with that aspect of his plan, he thought out the misinformation he sought to plant in the minds of investigators. Many of the behaviors Ridgway attributed to the killer in his letter pertained to the "evidence" he had been planting all along at several dump sites. He had littered some areas with gum wrappers, cigarette butts, and motel and travel material. The letter said:

I first onebokenordislocaarmwhy
2oneblackinriverhadastoneinthevaginawhy
3whysomeinriversomeabovegroundsomeunderground
4insurancewhogotit
5whostogainbytheredeaths
6truckisoutofstatefatherhadpaintedorinriver
7somehadfingernalscutoff
8hehadsexaftertheydeadhesmokes
9hechewsgum
i0chancefirstoneblackmailedhim
iiyouworkmeornobody
i2thinkchangedhismo
bussnesmanorsellman

i3carandmotelreservation
i4manseenbiglugageoutofmotelwasheavyneededhlp
keysidcardatroadi8whos
i5wheresclosesomeringsandmisc
i6outofstatecop
i7dontkillinourarealookinoutside
i8onehadoldscarse
i9momaplehadredwinelombroscsomefishanddumpedthere

20anydurgsprselling
2iheadfoundwhofounditwhereisrest
22whendidtheydieddayornight
23whatburntheremouthsorisitatrick
24whytakesomeclothsandleavereast
25thekillerwheresatleastonering
26realestmanisoneman

27longhaultruckdriverlastseenwithone
28somehadropemarkesonneckandhands
29onebla einriverhadbraononly
30alstrangledbutwithdefermetheds
3ioneblackinriverhadworedformetro
32mosthadpimpsbettingthem
33escortmodelingforcedthemofffearofdeth

34maybepimphatergetbackatthem
34whofindstheboneswhataretheytherefor
35manwhithgunorknife
36someonepaidtokilloneothersarethideit
37killwhotheyareorisitwhattheyare
38anydeaddiferthenrestt
39itcouldamanportlandsomeworkedthere
40ehatkindofmanisthis

therewasabookliftatdenneysigotthisotof
   itbilongsto cop

callmefred[5]

Interestingly, the number of lines in the communiqué—counting the two introductory lines and the three lines at the end after he stopped using numbers—was almost identical to the number of women Ridgway had murdered up to that point, although investigators had only linked about half of the victims to the serial case. The intent of the letter was to mislead the Green River Task Force, but to do so it needed to convince investigators it, in fact, came from the Green River Killer. To establish his credibility, Ridgway included many details of the murders that only he or those close to the investigation would know:

- The broken or dislocated arm mentioned in the first line referred to Wendy L. Coffield, who had suffered serious trauma to one arm when she was killed.
- Line two revealed a "stoneinthevagina" of one of the river victims. That was correct, and that idiosyncrasy was a guarded secret within the investigation.
- Line three was an effort to link for police the death of the many women found dead throughout King County. Some had been in the river, some on the ground easily visible, and some had been buried.
- Line seven stated that some of the victims' fingernails were cut off. This was true, but investigators were unaware the killer had been cutting off some of the fingernails to destroy evidence.
- Line eight talked about necrophilia. Investigators suspected this from the sexual propensities of previous serial killers and the way some of the Green River victims were found in the woods.

- Line fifteen alludes to the victims' missing clothes and jewelry.
- The information in line nineteen reveals very guarded information related to the murder of Carol Christensen in the summer of 1983. The letter writer knew of the fish and wine bottle left with the body. The writer even knew the brand of the wine.

The communiqué contained so many investigative details that it was difficult to believe it did not come from the Green River Killer or someone privy to his murderous misdeeds. Who else would possess so much "secret" information? One or two details could have been leaked or may have been inadvertently revealed to someone, but the letter writer seemed to know quite a bit about information that often is used as polygraph keys. It was possible the writer was an investigator or someone close to the investigation. If that was the case, however, the Green River Task Force was obligated to unmask that individual before irreparable harm was caused to the investigation. And what motive might have driven such an individual to railroad the investigation? The simplest explanation seemed to be that this particular letter came from the killer, and investigators should set in motion a strategy to evaluate the communiqué and how it could be used to identify the murderer.

The *Post-Intelligencer* could only guess at the authenticity of the communiqué, but it tried to communicate with the letter writer. It placed an ad in the Personals: "callmefred. got your message. interested in talking with you. mike. Write."[6] No one responded.

King County Police records reveal that the Green River Task Force initially did little or nothing with the communiqué. There appeared no urgency. The letter ended up with the King County Police Lab, and the first entry in the Latent Lab Work Sheet is dated July 18, 1984, five months after the letter was sent. The handwritten entry stated: "While talking with Det. Kalin and Durin I showed them the letter from Fred. They ask me to send it to the FBI for some tests and the Behavioral Science Unit."[7] The letter was sent the following day to the FBI via overnight service. Tonya Yzaguirre, latent print examiner for King County Department of Public Safety, wrote, "Some of the information contained in the letter has not been made public which leads us to believe the person writing it may somehow be involved. The pen marks were put on the letter after it arrived at the newspaper office."[8] Two weeks later the FBI Laboratory sent a letter to King County Police stating that it had examined the envelope (Q15) and letter (Q16) and found:

Q15 and Q16 were searched through the appropriate sections of the Anonymous Letter File without effecting an identification. Representative copies will be added to that file for future reference purposes.

The typewriting impressions on Q15 and Q16 correspond with the laboratory standards for an Olympia style of type having a horizontal spacing of 2.60mm per character. Characteristics were noted in those typewriting impressions which indicate that the typewriter used to prepare those impressions is equipped with a fabric ribbon. These typewriting impressions are suitable for comparison with known typewriters. If a future typewriting comparison is desired, Q15 and Q16 should be resubmitted at that time.[9]

The FBI's Latent Fingerprint Section examined the envelope and letter for fingerprints and discovered "one latent fingerprint of value" on the letter.[10] Those results were put in a letter to King County Police on August 17, 1984.

Eventually, the letter made its way to the desk of John E. Douglas of the FBI's Criminal Profiling Program, and he put his observations in an August 24, 1984, letter to King County Police:

It is my opinion that the author of the written communiqué has no connection with the Green River Homicides. The communiqué reflects a subject who is average in intelligence and one who is making a feeble and amateurish attempt to gain some personal importance by manipulating the investigation. If this subject has made statements relative to the investigation which was not already released to the press, he would have to have <u>access</u> to this information (Task Force).[11]

Not only was Douglas stating there was no connection between the communiqué and the Green River Killer, but also he strongly insinuated that the letter writer, culprit, was amid investigators. Perhaps the most unsettling aspect of Douglas' analysis was his conclusion that the letter writer was "making a feeble and amateurish attempt to gain some personal importance by manipulating the investigation." How had Douglas arrived at that conclusion? What theoretical basis—in criminology, psychology, sociology—supported that statement? Douglas did not explain his synthesis in the letter, but admitted he was wrong in 2003 after it was learned Ridgway was the author of the communiqué.

With the FBI's conclusion that the 1984 letter had not been written by the Green River Killer, the Green River Task Force reasoned the letter writer was being truthful in saying the communiqué represented notes from a detective's notebook left at a Denny's. The letter writer put it this way: "therewasabookliftatdenneysigotthisofitbilongsto cop."[12]

In July 2002, eight months after Ridgway's arrest, King County Police pulled the 1984 letter out of its files and sent the flap of the envelope and stamp from the envelope to a private laboratory in Maryland. It apparently took the lab a long time to determine that it could find no DNA. It conveyed its results to King County Police in a July 2003 letter, a year after the lab received the request. By then, Ridgway was confessing.[13]

LETTER EXPLICATION

Ironically, by the time investigators sat down with Ridgway to chronicle his murders, they had long forgotten about the letter sent to the news media. So had Ridgway. The two sides zeroed in on the communiqué only after Ridgway referred to a letter almost as an afterthought in the first days of his confession. Crime laboratory scientists had failed to find DNA on the envelope flap and stamp, because Ridgway did not lick the envelope or stamp. He intentionally used water. Also, he wore gloves while handling the letter. According to Ridgway, he recalled writing two letters, but he only mailed one of them. He intended for the communiqué go to *The Seattle Times,* but, instead, the postal service delivered it to the *Seattle Post-Intelligencer.* And what happened to the typewriter used to write the letters? Gary said he sold it at a swap meet or garage sale.

During the confession, Detective Tom Jensen particularly was interested in extracting details of some of the statements made in the communiqué. He asked about the letter's first line, the reference to one broken or dislocated arm:

RIDGWAY: The first, first lady, Coffield, was in the river. Uh, for some reason I was still mad at her. I uh, broke her, or dislocated her . . .
JENSEN: Why?
RIDGWAY: Why? 'Cause I was mad at, still mad at her, I think.
JENSEN: For what?
RIDGWAY: I don't have a answer for it.[14]

Regarding line 23 in the communiqué—whatburntheremouths—Ridgway responded:

> That's some'n to throw 'em off thinkin', 'cause I, I've heard somewhere along the line that some woman back east, or somebody, was killed and they, they put stuff in their, the woman's mouth or the, the person's mouth. So that was some'n to throw you, throw you guys off. . . . No truth at, at all, no. It's just another way of screwin' with ya.[15]

Jensen also was curious about a book with investigative notes being left at Denny's. Rambled Ridgway:

> That's to throw off the Task Force thinkin' that somebody had a . . . left their. . . . a guy would have a ledger, or for a woman would be a diary, at Denny's . . . think this is not the Green River Killer, it is somebody that got this stuff and he's . . . he's giving it out, um, um, 'cause he has the Green River Killer's ledger. I think that's what I was tryin' to accomplish. . . . Get ya to think you're . . . you're goin' down one way, and here it is somebody found this ledger, and most people would turn it in but here this guy here's a . . . he wants somethin' out of it. He wants . . . he wants the

newspaper to pay money. Maybe that's what the deal was, maybe that's why I put that there. . . . I don't remember, but I thought it was more about the . . . the whole, ah, tryin' to throw it off.[16]

After repeatedly having Ridgway explain and expound on various aspects of the communiqué, Jensen stated,

I gotta tell you somethin' . . . when we read . . . went over your letter the other day, people out there were just amazed at how . . . basically how brilliant it was. I mean it was . . . it fooled John Douglas and it was just a great letter. I mean it was . . . it accomplished its purpose . . . it wasn't written by some stupid idiot, you know. You tried to . . . you can sit here and make yourself out to be a, a blithering idiot sometimes, but you're not . . . that's not what you are. You don't have to play that role anymore because you gave it up when you wrote that letter. Okay? It proved just how smart you were. Even though it looks goofy, it proved just how cunning and smart you are on this.[17]

Since Ridgway communicated with the Green River Task Force with a letter, investigators wondered if he had tried contacting any of the key figures involved in the investigation via telephone. Ridgway claimed he never attempted to contact Green River Task Force Commander Frank Adamson or King County Sheriff David Reichert.

JENSEN: (Bob) Keppel? Keppel was the expert on everything.
RIDGWAY: Keppel? No, I didn't, I was more out getting prostitutes.
JENSEN: Ann Rule?
RIDGWAY: Ann Rule?
JENSEN: She's an expert on everything.
RIDGWAY: Ann Rule is a . . . no.[18]

Uppermost in the minds of investigators was whether Ridgway would have mailed more communiqués:

RIDGWAY: I would have, ah, probably, um, wrote somethin' else . . .
JENSEN: If we'd have acknowledged that we got the letter . . .
RIDGWAY: Un-huh (yes).
JENSEN: . . . then you might have . . . may have made further communication.
RIDGWAY: Un-huh (yes).
JENSEN: That makes sense. . . . Did you watch for our response?
RIDGWAY: Ah, yes I did watch for a response but there was nothin' come up. Figured the letter got. . . . I figured the letter got lost.[19]

Ridgway indicated he would have written again even though investigators could attempt to detect patterns and clues in the communiqués. Somehow, Ridgway felt he could outsmart police.

In one confession session, Dr. Judith Becker asked, "You might have then written something else?" Ridgway responded,

> I mighta wrote somethin' to make a, ah, I might even ask for help or some-thin'. Ah, ah, you know, because killing so many it was ... it was bothering me, and I mighta asked what would a guy do that's a serial killer do to get help if he wants to stop? I think I probably woulda put that in there. Um, and let maybe that mushroom out because I needed to have. ... this is the letter they think from the Green River Killer or somebody that's playin' with 'em, and maybe it isn't the Green River Killer, maybe it's a killer or somethin', maybe he's killed somebody before but not these women. His way of seeking help, and then there might be a psychologist from some-body will suggest things. I ... I ... maybe I mighta put somethin' in there, ah, ah, "catch me ... ," you know, I wasn't gonna ... "catch me if you can" or anything but I woulda put somethin' in there to ... it would have ... whatever mood I was in, and that mood might ... might change.[20]

Green River Task Force investigators—like the average police officer or private citizen—doubted Ridgway's sincerity in seeking help. No one would blame them. However, in fact, several serial killers who have sent communiqués in unrelated cases in the past have shown a propensity for asking for help in their communiqués. A part of the killer seemed to want to stop killing, but they do not know how and they could not get them-selves to turn themselves in.

King County Sheriff David Reichert decided to be the last person to ask Ridgway questions during the confession:

REICHERT: So the day you got arrested, you felt like you had a knot in your chest?

RIDGWAY: I had a knot in my chest because I, I, I put it all off ... well, be-cause I got caught, but also because of uh, it's my time ... thinkin' about it, it's my time to give these bodies up (Reveal where he hid the remains of several missing women) and I was, I was fighting myself inside—should I give 'em up or should I ... or should I, I not. And I was waiting ...

REICHERT: You would've never turned yourself in, though ...

RIDGWAY: No, I would not have. ... No. But uh, like I said, in those uh, let-ters that I mailed in ... I would have communicated that way through and give the bodies up—but without givin' myself up.

REICHERT: But you only wrote the one letter.

RIDGWAY: I only wrote the one letter.

REICHERT: And you didn't sign your name to it.

RIDGWAY: No, I didn't, and I wouldn't ...

REICHERT: So we didn't know who it was from.

RIDGWAY: No. And even the F.B.I. didn't think it was from that, but ...

REICHERT: Yeah.[21]

RIDGWAY: If I would'a had communication between you the same way as more letters through the mail, I would'a coughed 'em up earlier and you would'a had more . . .

REICHERT: But you didn't wanna do that because you didn't wanna get caught.

RIDGWAY: Yeah . . . but I could, I could do that where I wouldn't get caught.[22]

The sheriff seemed oblivious to the value of what Ridgway was revealing. No matter the risk of getting caught, he seemed open to the possibility of communicating with investigators if they had shown an interest in his communiqué. In admitting his mistake in an interview with journalist Mike Barber in 2003, Douglas also failed to understand the opportunities communiqués presented. Douglas stated that he did not feel there was anything else to do with the letter.[23] His comment goes to the heart of the need for a more sophisticated method of evaluating serial killer communiqués and how to use them as investigative tools. Law enforcement agencies should view a communiqué—letter, poem, or random telephone call—as an opportunity to begin a conversation with the killer. Serial killers are almost impossible to identify, and the communiqué provides investigators with a direct link to the killer. The longer investigators can keep the conversation going, the more likely the killer may provide a clue that could lead to a mistake, revealing his/her identity. Law enforcement must be proactive. Ridgway never contacted the news media again, because, partly, he was unsure if his letter ever arrived. King County Police could have made the letter public to use the media to let the killer know he had succeeded in connecting with investigators. Then, teams of psychologists, linguists, and criminologists could have attempted to convince Ridgway to keep the communiqués coming. They could have identified his need to reveal the dump sites and prodded him into making a mistake.

In many serial murder cases, there have been bogus communiqués, but past serial cases involving communiqués show that the actual killer had no problem providing details no one else knew, allowing police to separate the false confessors from the individual they needed to communicate with. In serial killer investigations, investigators must be willing to shed traditional investigative practices and culture—such as keeping communiqués secret to use as polygraph keys—to creatively and successfully use communiqués to solve a case. Law enforcement should also make it a point to reveal the content of communiqués soon after they are received to allow the public to assist more in the investigation. Private citizens who may suspect an individual or be familiar with the killer's handwriting or philosophy are apt to make a connection when the case is fresh in their minds during the slayings.

WASHINGTON COUNTY
PUBLIC SAFETY BUILDING — 146 N.E. LINCOLN
HILLSBORO, OREGON 97124

DEPT. OF PUBLIC SAFETY
BILL PROBSTFIELD, Sheriff
(503) 648-8894

NEWS RELEASE

ON JUNE 12, 1985 A BULLDOZER OPERATOR DISCOVERED A SKULL WHILE CLEARING ACREAGE NEAR S. W. 133RD AND BULL MOUNTAIN ROAD NEAR TIGARD. ON JUNE 14, 1985 THE REMAINS WERE IDENTIFIED AS BELONGING TO DENISE DARCEL BUSH, WHO WAS ON THE GREEN RIVER TASK FORCE MISSING LIST.

A SUBSEQUENT SEARCH OF THE AREA RESULTED IN THE DISCOVERY OF OTHER HUMAN REMAINS.

THE SECOND SET OF REMAINS FOUND AT THE BULL MOUNTAIN SITE HAS BEEN IDENTI-FIED AS SHIRLEY MARIE SHERRILL, A 19 YEAR OLD WHITE FEMALE.

IDENTIFICATION WAS MADE BY JOINT EFFORTS OF THE KING COUNTY MEDICAL EXAMI-NER'S OFFICE, THE MULTNOMAH COUNTY AND OREGON STATE MEDICAL EXAMINER'S OFFICE AND THE OREGON STATE HEALTH SCIENCES UNIVERSITY.

DRS. LUNDY, FRED SORENSON, DOUG BARNETT AND ROBERT SHERIDAN COMPRISED THE TEAM OF 1 ANTHROPOLOGIST, 2 RADIOLOGISTS AND 1 ORAL DIAGNOSTIC SPECIALIST THAT MADE THE IDENTIFICATION.

MS. SHERRILL WAS REPORTED MISSING TO SEATTLE POLICE DEPARTMENT BY HER MOTHER ON NOVEMBER 25, 1983.

HER LAST DOCUMENTED CONTACT WAS IN PORTLAND ON OCTOBER 18, 1982, HOWEVER SHE WAS REPORTEDLY SEEN IN SEATTLE SINCE THAT TIME.

MS. SHERRILL WAS KNOWN TO FREQUENT THE SEATTLE AIRPORT STRIP.

MS. SHERRILL WAS ADDED TO THE GREEN RIVER MISSING LIST ON DECEMBER 29, 1983, AS TASK FORCE DETECTIVES FELT THAT SHE HAD RETURNED TO SEATTLE PRIOR TO HER DIS-APPEARANCE.

TASK FORCE OFFICIALS ARE CONSIDERING THE POSSIBILITY OF ADDING BUSH AND

CHAPTER

Investigation and Media Conflicts

7

I would be as fair and as open to everybody I could until one of them (journalists) fucked me and then I just wouldn't deal with that person.

Green River Task Force Commander Bob Evans[1]

The relationship between law enforcement and the news media historically has been antagonistic. For journalists, covering the crime beat without friction is impossible. What a journalist seeks, police officers often tend to want to keep confidential. It is an inherent friction born out of the very nature of the two institutions: one is based on publishing daily events as they happen, whereas the other seeks to gather information methodically and confidentially until it can be presented in a structured setting before a judge and jury. More often than not, the traditional friction between members of the media and law enforcement is relatively minor, because the daily confrontations are over routine burglaries, assaults, and traffic accidents. More serious incidents, such as homicides, raise the level of friction. In those cases journalists become more aggressive and seek more details. Similarly, investigators make more of an effort to hold back details. The more sensational the murder, the more journalists assigned to cover the investigation. The more sensational the homicide, the more investigators assigned to the case. The clash between these two institutions, then, is almost in direct proportion to the size of the news event. But in even the average sensational homicide, more often then not, the tug of war dissipates in a few days or weeks as police activity dwindles and the media deem the event old news.

The relationship between law enforcement and the news media in the Green River murders case did not deviate from the historical acrimony. This serial murder case propelled the traditional police-media friction to monumental proportions. The clash in the Green River murders fostered a crisis response where the media pulled all stops in attempting to discover investigative details, while police took extraordinary measures to conceal them. The battle over information and what should be made public in the Green River Murders case flared up from the beginning. When the murders began in 1982, the case attracted heavy coverage from newspapers and television stations throughout Washington and Oregon. *The Seattle Times,* the *Seattle Post-Intelligencer,* and KIRO TV News assigned the greatest recourses to the case. When it became clear in the mid-1980s that the body count neared 50, the case received national prominence. *Life, People,* and the *London Observer* carried lengthy articles on the case. *NBC Nightly News* gave the case several minutes, and *20/20* did a 20-minute segment on it. The *Times-Union* of Rochester, NY, had a lengthy article in December 1989. *The New York Times* published front-page stories on the killings and *Time* magazine devoted a page to one of the prime suspects in the late 1980s. *USA Today* also followed the case several times. Even *Oprah* and the *Sally Jessy Raphael* show featured aspects of the case. Scores of national news organizations—print, broadcast, cyber—covered the story when Gary Leon Ridgway was arrested in 2001. *Time* magazine, alone, devoted five pages to chronicling the murders and arrest. To some degree, the extensive coverage, especially in the early years of the case, proved positive since it maintained political pressure on politicians and police administrators to continue the investigation.

Coverage spanned 20 years, and throughout those years the friction between investigators and journalists over information was intense. The instances and decisions that spawned the greatest conflict between investigators and journalists during the lengthy Green River Murders case can be divided into two categories: (1) media behavior that influenced law enforcement investigative decisions and how investigators dealt with journalists; and (2) law enforcement investigative decisions aimed at manipulating the media to harness it and control what information the public received.

MEDIA BEHAVIOR THAT INFLUENCED LAW ENFORCEMENT DECISIONS

THE GREEN RIVER

Two events in the first few weeks of the Green River serial investigation set the tone for the relationship between investigators and journalists: one involved King County Police Major Richard Kraske and the other KIRO TV News, the CBS affiliate in Seattle.

On August 15, 1982, the bodies of three young black women were found in or on the bank of the Green River. The discovery was significant because two other young women had been found in the river in July and early

August. The finding of three more women clearly indicated a serial killer, yet no media appeared at the scene. The King County Sheriff's Office intentionally did not notify the media, which was routinely done with a message on a police code-a-phone. Kraske did not want reporters interfering with the processing of the scene and pressing him for answers as he contemplated the ramifications of the case. He did not want a repeat of the problems he experienced while he headed the investigation into the Ted Bundy serial killings of the 1970s. During the Bundy investigation, Kraske recalled that at one crime scene reporters "outflanked" investigators and walked onto the area where a victim was found. In the Green River case, Kraske waited to notify the media until after the scene was processed. He did not put a message on the code-a-phone until 10:30 P.M. that Sunday as he prepared to call it a day. In fact, the department's public information officer, Pat Ferguson, was not told of the new development. When reporter Dave Birkland of *The Seattle Times* telephoned Ferguson at home at 2 A.M. Monday to obtain information about the slayings, he hit a dry well. Ferguson told Birkland he knew nothing of the three victims and went back to bed.

The lack of notification infuriated reporters and created deep distrust. Kraske's decision also stripped the department's media spokesman of credibility.

It was the investigators who were furious a few days after the three black women were discovered at the river. Attempting to set a trap in case the killer returned with more victims to the river, investigators staked out the Green River. According to police, a KIRO TV News helicopter flew overhead and revealed the stakeout. KIRO TV News officials repeatedly denied the police allegations on the stakeout. Real or imagined, for the remainder of the investigation investigators often claimed KIRO's action denied them a chance to catch the killer in 1982. The media countered that surveillance should have been started after the second victim was found. Then police would have caught the killer in the act of depositing the three black women in mid-August.

The two incidents polarized members of both institutions and set the stage for the deterioration of their relationship in this case.

After his arrest, Ridgway was asked about the helicopter incident and if it deterred him from returning during the stakeout:

RIDGWAY: Green River I think they news people . . . news cameras gave you away.
SHERIFF REICHERT: Yes they did. Fortunately for you.
RIDGWAY: No, they didn't give it to me, no.
REICHERT: No, I mean, fortunately for you.
RIDGWAY: The boater caught me.
REICHERT: Yeah. But you would have come back even after that?
RIDGWAY: Not after the bodies were found.

REICHERT: Right.
RIDGWAY: I think I heard about it that night on Sunday night.
REICHERT: But you would have come back just to screw us . . . screw with us.
RIDGWAY: No.[2]

WITNESSES

As soon as investigators announced in the summer of 1982 that a serial killer appeared to be at work, the local news organizations took the traditional big-story approach and assigned numerous reporters to the story. Journalists inundated the prostitute strip in Seattle and Tacoma. Some journalists interviewed prostitutes, while others tried to trace the victims' last few hours alive. Yet other journalists attempted to find relatives and friends of the victims. There were so many journalists that some of them were contacting acquaintances of the victims before investigators. Police cried foul, charging that individuals untrained in interviewing were contaminating information that might help identify the killer.

The news organizations covering the Green River case seemed oblivious to damaging the investigation and continued to search for interviews aggressively. Some news organizations argued that journalists were getting to witnesses first because King County Police was understaffing the investigation.

MELVYN FOSTER

More often than not, the news media was unaware of the identity of suspects in the Green River case. That was not the case with a former cab driver named Melvyn Foster. He chose to make journalists aware of his precarious position in the eyes of investigators. He attracted detectives because he had met several of the initial victims on the street, and he approached detectives to help in the investigation. If Foster was not the killer, he found himself compelled to make his case public to clear himself. King County Major Kraske said investigators were looking at no one else. One day Foster became so frustrated at being followed by investigators that he contacted KIRO Eyewitness News reporter Hilda Bryant to complain he was innocent, but investigators would not leave him alone. In fact, he informed Bryant he was being followed that moment. Bryant agreed to rendezvous with Foster, but asked him to give her enough time to get a cameraman. As Foster arrived for the rendezvous, Bryant and the cameraman approached the detective following Foster. Bryant made the investigator look foolish and incompetent, since he was caught appearing to be unable to conduct surveillance discreetly.

It takes years for investigators to forget such media behavior. The ambush interview only added to the feeling that journalists covering the

Green River investigation always were out to humiliate police, even if it meant collaborating with questionable characters astute at manipulating the media.

EDITORIAL CARTOON

When the Green River Task Force went after suspect Ernest W. "Bill" McLean in 1986, it angered Sheriff Thomas that an out-of-control news media convicted McLean in print and broadcast reports. McLean turned out to be the wrong man and the high-profile mistake eroded Thomas' support for continued operation of the task force. Thomas became even more infuriated at *The Seattle Times* when it ran an editorial cartoon poking fun at the task force for going after McLean because he fit the FBI's profile of the potential killer. The cartoon by Brian Basset depicted a boy in a tree house that did not allow girls. Several officers associated with the "Task-Farce" pointed rifles at the boy.[3] After that, Thomas angrily brought up the cartoon every time he bumped into a *Times* reporter.

THE SEATTLE TIMES SPECIAL REPORT

Most news coverage of the investigation was reactionary. The majority of the time stories focused on the latest body find, another search by police, or the identification of another victim. *The Seattle Times,* however, assigned two reporters full time to the case early in the investigation. Over the years the reporters were able to reconstruct much of the investigation by compiling computer printouts of every arrest and prostitution citation on the prostitution strip from 1982 to 1984; gathering every missing person report and arrest report on all the victims; and obtaining documents listing every arrest and expenditure by King County Police's vice unit, the detectives whom on a day-by-day basis worked the closest to the victim population. *The Times* obtained the vice records by filing public record disclosure requests.

In 1987, *The Times* published a report titled "Green River: What Went Wrong." It chronicled the investigation and listed a series of investigative errors, including the decision in 1982 to de-emphasize the investigation after assuming the killer had left the area. He had not. The report's primary conclusion: investigators missed their chance to catch the killer in the summer of 1982 since they knew the type of victim being killed and from where the killer was abducting his victims.

The special report further polarized both sides, but by now neither side seemed to care since investigators appeared to be getting nowhere and journalists found there were fewer reasons to contact investigators since there were few new developments.

"THE SEARCH FOR THE GREEN RIVER KILLER"

When King County Police disbanded the Green River Task Force in 1989, essentially ending the active investigation, the two *Seattle Times* reporters who had been following the case since 1982 wrote a book. Since the beginning of the case, investigators had shared little information about the investigation with the public or other law enforcement agencies. The reporters' intent was to reveal details that had never been made public. They hoped those details would convince a citizen to realize they possessed valuable information about the case and come forward with the clue that might solve the case. The book publisher offered a $50,000 reward for information that would solve the case.

To the dismay of investigators, the book published detail after detail about the case, including how many of the women were killed and how their bodies were left at the crime scenes. Investigators felt angry at losing valuable polygraph keys.

SEATTLE WEEKLY

From the moment Gary L. Ridgway was arrested on November 30, 2001, police, the news media, and the public wondered if he, in fact, was the Green River Killer. Investigators claimed DNA tests linked Ridgway to several victims, but they were reluctant to say that he was responsible for all 49 victims. In November 2002, Carlton Smith, one of the former *Seattle Times* reporters who co-authored the book on the Green River case, freelanced a story to the *Seattle Weekly*. The story's headline read, "Truth or Death." Smith focused on whether prosecutors should make a plea agreement with Ridgway to learn the truth about the rest of the victims. Smith wrote a persuasive argument, but he seemed to go out of his way to castigate police. Smith repeatedly attacked the investigation, pointing out what he thought were deficiencies. For the article, Smith appeared to have helped the defense team identify the various body dump sites, making it seem he was in the defense camp, helping the defense team find holes in the prosecution.[4]

LAW ENFORCEMENT DECISIONS AIMED AT MANIPULATING INFORMATION

GREEN RIVER TASK FORCE

The Green River Task Force was created in 1984. In planning its investigative strategy, investigators carefully thought out the role of the media and the need to systematically control—manage—information about the case. Whereas in 1982 and 1983 King County Police tried to keep information from leaking out, it was done haphazardly and more by individual investigators. Investigators now intentionally sought to control every piece of information. To that end, the task force designated one person, Detective Fae Brooks, to be the spokesperson. Task Force Commander Captain Frank Adamson was the only other person authorized to discuss the case with the media. There would be no access to individual detectives. In fact, King County Police refused to divulge who was on the task force. Among the journalists, Brooks was notorious for giving out little information at crime scenes or about new women added to the list of potential victims.

KIRO's John Lippman sent a complaint letter to King County Executive Randy Revelle: "As you know, taxpayers are paying money for a separate public information officer for the Green River Task Force. It seems illogical to us that she only answers media questions during 'business hours.'"[5] Lippman sent a letter to the sheriff when Brooks failed to notify the media of a body find: "I'm disappointed to hear that the news media was again shut out by the Green River Task Force this weekend. It was not until Monday morning that we were told of the weekend operation near North Bend by the Task Force. . . . What kind of public information is that?"[6]

Jack Hamann of KING TV5 epitomized the feelings of reporters assigned to cover the case:

> The media relations just deteriorated terribly. I think she (Brooks) is a very able and intelligent woman and good officer . . . but she was the wrong person . . . because she had a way of giving us some sort of feeling that we did not have the right to ask the question that we were asking. It's a real tough skill to be a public relations officer for law enforcement and she wasn't one of the best.[7]

An internal memo by Revelle staff assistant Sam Sperry revealed the level of media dissatisfaction:

> Generally, reporters complain of "lack of access" to GRTF detective and of a "lack of cooperation" in helping them get information. . . . They want greater and more frequent access to the people doing the work, the detectives. Reporters blame a negative attitude in general, on the part of the department, toward the press.[8]

Sperry suggested regular weekly briefings and that Brooks be available around the clock. The sheriff's office and the task force ignored the suggestions and nothing changed.

The task force was so successful at keeping journalists at bay it was featured in the magazine *Law and Order*. In the article Brooks revealed she had a recurring dream of hordes of journalists mobbing her for answers. The same article congratulated Brooks and Adamson for developing a system to keep journalists away from task force investigators.[9]

KOMO RADIO REQUEST VS. KIRO TV REQUEST

The Green River Task Force received two major overtures from news organizations the year it was formed in 1984.

In June, Ken Kohl of KOMO Radio wrote to King County Executive Revelle:

> Our primary purpose is to establish a line of regular communication between KOMO Radio and the Green River Task Force for the purpose of telling the inside story of the men and women of the Green River Task Force. . . . I feel KOMO Radio's team of award-winning broadcast journalists can do the best job handling the story because of our sensitivity to the area and its people, and because of our empathy with the job the Task Force faces.[10]

KOMO promised to embargo any story the task force felt would jeopardize the investigation. Revelle declined the request, arguing that it would be unfair to the rest of the media and KOMO's access could "interfere with their (task force) important duties and conceivably cause a breech of security."[11] The denial easily was defensible, but, ironically, the KOMO request was the type of relationship investigators often said they wanted with news organizations.

While the Green River Task Force and the county rebuffed KOMO's request, they jumped at a request by KIRO TV News. The station offered to put up a $100,000 reward for information leading to the arrest and conviction of the Green River Killer. By late 1984, KIRO and task force officials were having news conferences announcing the reward. As part of the offer, KIRO produced a series of news reports on the investigation. KIRO, too, created a campaign to inform the public of the reward and promote its program. KIRO ran commercials with the theme: "Someone Knows Something." The rest of the news media in the Seattle area cried foul, accusing KIRO of buying its way into information from the task force.

SAN DIEGO

In 1987 King County Police Captain Bob Evans became the new commander of the Green River Task Force. He was easygoing and promised to make himself available to journalists. His philosophy: "I would be as fair and as open to everybody I could until one of them fucked me and then I just wouldn't deal with that person."[12] Evans' willingness to sit down and talk with individual reporters informally about the case came in handy to the task force. When the task force could get little cooperation from San Diego on information pertaining to the slaying of over two dozen prostitutes in Southern California, the task force set up an informal meeting with *The Seattle Times* reporters covering the case. At the assignation in a restaurant, a task force officer offered that the San Diego deaths were worth a deeper look because they might be related to the Green River case. The reporters already had been keeping track of the San Diego deaths, but that meeting gave them a final push to convince editors to fly them to San Diego. The reporters spent a week in San Diego, visiting all the sites where the victims had been found. The subsequent article speculated on whether the Green River Killer was responsible for some of 32 deaths in San Diego.[13] The story prompted a storm that attracted the television networks and the California media. Less then a month later, several San Diego County and San Diego City homicide and vice officers flew to Seattle to learn how to form a task force. In early August, a group of task force detectives traveled to San Diego to better study the California deaths. The task force was pleased in how it used the media to force San Diego to cooperate. Green River Killer Gary Leon Ridgway is not believed to have murdered in San Diego.

NATIONAL DOCUDRAMA

In 1988, the Green River Task Force desired to use the media to psychologically manipulate someone who might know something about the case or the killer. The task force felt someone knew the killer and might be protecting him. Task force officials thought they could use psychology to flush that witness out. There was one major hurdle to the task force's plan: It did not control the means of communication, and the news media would never agree to cooperate and publish information intended to trick or manipulate readers or viewers. The task force solved its problem by partnering up with Seattle-King County Crime Stoppers, which took the lead in obtaining funds from a private company to finance the production of a two-hour, reality-based docudrama for airing on national television. The program included re-enactments, news footage of body recoveries, and interviews with key investigators. The program was titled "Manhunt Live: A Chance to End the Nightmare." As part of the program, the task force flew in investigators from all over the country to man dozens of phones. The task force even convinced actor Patrick Duffy to moderate the program. Although the task force had succeeded in creating its own program, it needed the news media to get the word out that the docudrama was to air December 7, 1988. To get publicity, the task force called a news conference December 6, 1988.

At the news conference Evans revealed that one of the Green River victims was nine-months pregnant and was buried. The information was being released, he said, in hopes that someone who knew of the killings would be repulsed that a pregnant woman was killed, in addition to prostitutes, and would contact the task force.

The local media felt the task force was setting a dangerous precedent by financing its own forum to present the case to the public. All the years of friction came to a head during a question-and-answer session at the conference:

REPORTER: When crime stoppers was invited in, at that news conference we were in fact told there would be no information made available to these people that will not be made available to the local press, and now, suddenly, we're hearing that we decided to release the information about how these people were or were not buried. To release the fact that one of them was eight-months pregnant . . .

SHERIFF JIM MONTGOMERY: We are advising you, the local press, before it is aired nationally. . . . I'm not here to necessarily be given the third degree . . .

REPORTER: Please, just explain to those who don't know . . . this docudrama is . . . it is not a documentary, it is a docudrama . . . and you in fact have control of the facts that are aired. And it is considered a manipulative effort to catch a killer.

MONTGOMERY: I certainly wouldn't call it a manipulative effort . . .

Later, KIRO reporter Brian Wood asked, "If this works, is this a good message. . . . I mean is it a message you'd like to . . . have other law enforcement agencies . . . bypass the local media especially on these national issues."

LT. DAN NOLAN: We're not bypassing you jack. This is obviously an effort not to bypass you. And you guys are all bent out of shape cause you've got a local interest in it. That's great. We all understand that. This has become your forum . . . to take a shot at the police department. And we knew that you were going to do that. And that's great, if that's where you want to go. I hope to God it solves a lot of cases because we'll stick it right up your . . . O.K.

MONTGOMERY: I feel we're being badgered at this particular point.[14]

The docudrama aired the next day and brought in thousands of tips, some of which helped solve cases across the country. None of the tips, though, led investigators to Ridgway.

NOT-A-TASK-FORCE

King County Police always maintained that the Green River Killer operated between 1982 and early 1984. Even when the Green River Task Force was disbanded in 1989, officials remained adamant the killings stopped in March 1984. During the mid-to-late 1980s and the early 1990s, however, many women were abducted from the street, killed, and deposited in wooded areas. The deaths of those women resembled the Green River case so much that *The Seattle Times* published a lengthy story speculating that the Green River Killer or someone with a very similar modus operandi was killing in the area. King County investigators were wondering the same thing, but did not want to make that publicly known. Quietly, they gathered a small group of detectives to try to ascertain if the Green River Murders were related to slayings in the late 1980s and early 1990s. Anticipating the news media would inquire if a task force had been formed for the renewed investigation, investigators decided to dub the new investigative group "Not-a-Task-Force." By using such an appellation when journalists called, detectives felt they could say there was no task force in operation.

SHERIFF DAVID G. REICHERT

Historically, information released to the public primarily came from the captain running the investigation or a public information officer working closely with the task force. All that changed on November 30, 2001, when Ridgway was arrested in connection with the case. As soon as an arrest was made, King County Sheriff David G. Reichert took the lead as the spokesperson on the case and made it his mission to counter any negative statements made about the investigation. In the past two decades, the sheriff and investigators had made themselves virtually unavailable to discuss the case. Reichert, particularly, yelled angrily at journalists at the dump sites. Now, he courted them. Reichert agreed to almost every interview request, whether for print, radio, television, or cyber. The day after Ridgway's arrest, Reichert appeared on virtually every newspaper front page in the Seattle area. For weeks it was nearly impossible to read or hear news reports about the case without Reichert being quoted. In the coming months, it became clearer why Reichert took the lead in the dissemination of information: He announced his candidacy for a U.S. Congress seat being vacated by a fellow Republican. In seeking the lion's share of media attention on the Green River investigation, Reichert became the only investigator or politician to ever use the Green River case for political gain. To further link his role in the Green River killings and his political campaign, Reichert worked with a ghost writer to pen a book about the case. The book was titled "Sheriff David Reichert . . . My Twenty-Year Quest to Capture the Green River Killer . . . Chasing the Devil." In the book Reichert gave little credit to anyone for helping solve the Green River Murders case, although scores of investigators and agencies worked day and night for 20 years to gather the bits and pieces they hoped would eventually lead to an arrest and conviction. According to the book, Reichert made all the major strategic decisions all along the way. *Chasing the Devil* came out just before the election, which Reichert won easily. And as of 2005, his new title was U.S. Congressman David G. Reichert.

OUTCOME

The primary duty and mission of law enforcement in the Green River Murders case should have been to provide the resources and strategy to investigate the death of young women in an effort to apprehend the person or persons responsible for the deaths. The primary duty and mission of the news media should have been to provide the resources to keep track of the investigation to inform the public on the progress of the case. Overall, both institutions fulfilled their primary obligation over the course of the investigation. It is clear, though, that in doing their job investigators and journalists did so in a manner that often was irresponsible and contrary to the public's interest. The irresponsible behavior and decisions revolved around the gathering, releasing, withholding, or manipulating of investigative information. Investigators and journalists forever will be at odds, to some degree. As a result of the institutions' conflicting functions, some tension will always exist. In the Green River Murders case, investigators and journalists fed on creating tension, which turned into antagonistic behavior, which eventually spawned acrimony.

Major Richard Kraske made a critical mistake at the start of the investigation in deciding not to contact the news media when several women were found dead in the Green River. He should have opted for finding ways to keep the media at a distance at body finds instead of attempting to keep the discoveries secret. In not contacting the news media, Kraske ignored a law enforcement agency's responsibility to operate in an open, public manner when it can and to inform the public, via the news media, of a public safety issue. As commander of the Green River Task Force Captain Frank Adamson approved information-control procedures that systematized the withholding of information. The news media generally goes along with the withholding of information that might damage the investigation, but the task force's policies called for releasing virtually no information. The task force refused to release the names of detectives on the task force and often only released a name and an age when a victim was found dead, pushing journalists into an investigative mode to obtain the simplest of information for victim profiles and the manner of disappearance. The task force never provided an explanation for keeping secret the names of the investigators. Ultimately, investigators caused an irreparable rift when they financed the production of a docudrama and included investigative information previously denied the news media on the basis that it would harm the investigation. The sponsoring of a docudrama, in fact, translated into law enforcement refusing to recognize the legitimate function of the media in society. News organizations saw the move as an attempt to operate in secrecy and avoid scrutiny in a democratic system based on open government. In retrospect, the task force chose to put its energy into producing the docudrama about the same time it was de-emphasizing its probe of a suspect named Gary Leon Ridgway, who eventually was charged in the case in 2001, but not as a result of any information brought in by the television program.

The Seattle news media was also at fault at the beginning of the investigation by creating tension and distrust. They made many irresponsible blunders in covering the case and those mistakes seemed to bolster the task force's decision to eventually bypass the traditional news media with the docudrama. Airing the surveillance stakeout on television at the Green River was inexcusable. KIRO TV News reporter Hilda Bryant ambushing the detective following suspect Melvin Foster was uncalled for and so was the polygraph test the television station later gave Foster. These instances amounted to interfering in the investigation, as did journalistic interviews of friends and relatives of some of the victims before police could speak to them. Charges that journalists can interfere in investigations by contaminating witness information during interviews are not new. Law enforcement officers in many other major cases across the nation have made similar complaints. Although the Green River Task Force had been disbanded in 1990 by the time the book *The Search for the Green River Killer* came out, the true-crime narrative revealed sensitive investigative details investigators hoped to keep secret until a viable suspect was arrested. It could be argued that the authors and other journalists failed in their civic duty to respect the criminal investigation process. Instead of simply reporting on the progress and quality of the investigation, the media became a participant in the investigation when it published investigative clues in hopes of attracting the tip that could solve the case. In making such revelations, the journalists could have seriously damaged the investigation or efforts to eventually prosecute the perpetrator.

In analyzing the relationship between investigators and journalists over the span of the investigation—specially some of the events and decisions that caused the most friction—it is evident that neither investigators nor journalists tried very hard to establish a professional relationship that would lead to trust and credibility. In fact, members of both institutions seemed to relish antagonizing each other. Each lost sight of the other's vital role in society. The travesty continues since the relationship between the investigators and journalists involved in the Green River Murders case never improved. The investigators are now high-ranking officers who run King County Police. And many of the journalists involved with the coverage of the case remain reporters or editors at Seattle news organizations. Obviously, the scene is still set for future major confrontations since neither law enforcement nor the news media has taken the initiate to improve communication and create a professional relationship to alleviate potential conflicts.

RIDGWAY INTERVIEW TAPE LIST

Tape #	Date	Day #	Examiner(s)	Locations
1	6/13/2003	1	DPA Brian McDonald	
2	6/13/2003	1	Det. Randy Mullinax, #01486 Det. Tom Jensen, #05517 Det. Jon Mattsen, #00463 Det. Sue Peters, #05802	
3	6/13/2003	1	Det. Tom Jensen, #05517 Det. Sue Peters, #05802	
4	6/13/2003	1	Det. Jon Mattsen, #00463 Det. Sue Peters, #05802	
5	6/14/2003	2	Det. Randy Mullinax, #01486 DPA Ian Goodhew Atty Mark Prothero Atty Anthony Savage	
6F	6/14/2003	2		
7F	6/14/2003	2	Det. Randy Mullinax, #01486 Det. Tom Jensen, #05517	- Leisure Time Resort
8F	6/14/2003	2	Det. Randy Mullinax, #01486 Det. Tom Jensen, #05517	
9F	6/14/2003	2		
10F	6/14/2003	2		
11F	6/14/2003	2	Det. Randy Mullinax, #01486 Det. Tom Jensen, #05517	
12	6/14/2003	2	Det. Randy Mullinax, #01486 Det. Tom Jensen, #05517	
13	6/14/2003	2	Det. Jon Mattsen, #00463 Det. Sue Peters, #05802	
14F	6/15/2003	3		
15F	6/15/2003	3	Det. Sue Peters, #05802 Det. Tom Jensen, #05517	- King's Restaurant - Lewis & Clark Theater Dumpsite - Jewelry dumpsites - Grandview Park - Kent-Des Moines Road - Lake Fenwick
16F	6/15/2003	3		
17F	6/15/2003	3	Det. Sue Peters, #05802 Det. Tom Jensen, #05517	- Lake Fenwick - 292nd and West Valley Highway Dumpsite
18F	6/15/2003	3		
19F	6/15/2003	3	Det. Sue Peters, #05802 Det. Tom Jensen, #05517	- 292nd and West Valley Highway Dumpsite
20	6/15/2003	3	Det. Jon Mattsen, #00463 Det. Tom Jensen, #05517	
21	6/15/2003	3	Det. Randy Mullinax, #01486 Det. Jon Mattsen, #0463	
22	6/16/2003	4	Det. Randy Mullinax, #01486 Det. Sue Peters, #05802	
23	6/16/2003	4	Det. Randy Mullinax, #01486 Det. Sue Peters, #05802	
24	6/16/2003	4	Det. Jon Mattsen, #00463 Det. Tom Jensen, #00517	
25	6/16/2003	4	Det. Jon Mattsen, #00463 Det. Tom Jensen, #5517	
26	6/17/2003	5	Det. Jon Mattsen, #00463 Det. Tom Jensen, #05517	
27	6/17/2003	5	Det. Randy Mullinax, #01486 Det. Jon Mattsen, #00463	

CHAPTER

Confession or Deception? . . . I

8

Bullshit! I'm calling bullshit on that!

Detective Randy Mullinax
King County Police[1]

King County Corrections Officers had barely forced Gary Leon Ridgway into a white jail jumpsuit after his arrest in late 2001 when King County Prosecutor Norm Maleng insisted on telling everyone that he would refuse to spare Ridgway's life in exchange for a guilty plea. In a news conference just days after the arrest, Maleng stated that he would refuse to bargain with the death penalty. He would later explain his rationale this way:

> The question leaped out to me just as it does to you: How could you set aside the death penalty in a case like this? Here we have a man presumed to be a prolific serial killer, a man who preyed on vulnerable young women. I thought, as many of you might, if any case screams out for consideration of the death penalty, it is this one.[2]

Four months later, Maleng again emphatically stated publicly that he would seek the death penalty if Ridgway was convicted. As time went by, though, Maleng privately reconsidered his rationale and was open to discuss a possible plea when Ridgway's attorneys approached him with a proposition in the spring of 2003. They told Maleng that Ridgway did not want to die. Yes, he had murdered over 60 women, but he wished to live. And in exchange for his life, Ridgway offered to reveal all: his delinquency as a youth, his sexual propensities as an adult, and, most important, his secret burial grounds for the missing victims. After that meeting, Maleng reversed himself, but both sides agreed to keep the agreement secret. The public was not to be told. What changed Maleng's mind? He came to believe that justice could be served by society getting answers to two decades of questions. Ridgway could provide those answers and more if he confessed. And Maleng desired to bring "closure" for the families of the victims whose remains had not been found. Ridgway seemed the only individual who could lead investigators to the undiscovered bodies. If Ridgway confessed, too, everyone would be certain that he really was the individual who had been murdering all those women in King County.

Secretly, in early June 2003 King County Police detectives removed Ridgway from the King County Jail and transported him to a building in South Seattle. In that structure investigators created a small bedroom for Ridgway and a stark interview room equipped only with sophisticated video and audio equipment. As the confession began and investigators ventured out to over 20 rural, wooded areas to confirm dump site locations supplied by Ridgway, word started leaking out that Ridgway was talking. Officials repeatedly were asked, was Ridgway cooperating with prosecutors and investigators? Was he confessing? The public especially thought it had a right to know since the county had already spent millions of taxpayer dollars on attorneys, investigators, and clerks for both the prosecution and defense. And that was only for pretrial preparations. Several million dollars were to be allocated by the county for the lengthy, high-profile trial. In spite of that, everyone associated with the case lied to the public. The intent of the officials' silence and parrying was to deliberately mislead and deceive. No one has ever offered an explanation for the secrecy and deception. Prosecutor Maleng and Sheriff Reichert refused to answer the questions. Dan Donohoe, the spokesman for the prosecutor's office, told reporters the prosecutor's office was scheduled to go to trial in July 2004 and any comment on the case would be made in court. Lead Defense Attorney Anthony Savage stated that his client's plea was not guilty, and he was looking forward to going to trial. In fact, Savage had sat in on the first day of the confession, and when Savage made his comment, Ridgway had been confessing for over a month. It was obvious there would be no trial. Perhaps the individual who was the most blatant in misleading the public was King County Police Detective Kathleen Larson, the spokesperson for the renewed Green River investigation. Week after week during the summer of 2003, she was asked how investigators suddenly were identifying specific wooded locations to search and actually finding Green River victims. None had been found for nearly fifteen years. She would say that investigators had chosen the locations based on cumulative evidence gathered over the years. Larson especially hedged when the remains of Green River victim Pammy Avent, 16, were found on August 16, 2003, near the community of Enumclaw, Washington. How did investigators come to search the area? Larson wrote in a news release: "It was determined during our review of the cases that these areas were not searched in the 1980s."

The truth was that Ridgway led investigators to that specific site during confession field trips.[3]

While it became obvious to the public that prosecutors, investigators, and defense attorneys conspired to deceive the public, it was not so easy for investigators to initially realize Ridgway was being deceptive, too, despite the plea agreement that was intended to spare his life. Ridgway seemed cooperative, but as the confession progressed, investigators began noticing traditional signs of lying:

- He was overly polite, very much the obsequious suspect.
- He gave brief answers.
- He rephrased questions before answering them, which gave him time to think of his answers.
- He hesitated often with "ums" and "ahs."
- He claimed to have memory problems.
- He tended to minimize his emotions, actions, and the gravity of the murders.
- He was less than forthcoming.

The confession was expected to be a relatively quick and easy process since Ridgway was required to answer every question truthfully. The opposite turned out to be true. The light interview that was to assist Ridgway confess and chronicle his reign of horror evolved into a six-month, turbulent interrogation punctuated with tears, anger, threats, and, what appeared to be, inappropriate deals. Investigators were forced to employ every interrogation and persuasion technique imaginable to coerce the Green River Killer into divulging the raw details. Some interrogation strategies worked. Others did not, leaving investigators angry and unfulfilled.

BONDING WITH CIVILITY

The interrogation of Gary Leon Ridgway began on June 13, 2003, with investigators doing everything they could to please their suspect. Although investigators possessed evidence to charge and most likely convict Ridgway of seven slayings, they lacked the proof to show he truly was the Green River Killer, responsible for all the murders. Investigators believed that if they were altruistic, Ridgway would be even more prone to divulge the truth and demonstrate he was the prolific killer. In brief, they planned to treat Ridgway like a gentleman to entice him to return the favor by opening up. And they intended to borrow a page or two from the field of counseling and feign compassion. At the start of the day investigators greeted Ridgway cheerfully and used small talk to relax him and give him the impression his interrogators cared about him. During the first few days, the interrogation began this way:

DETECTIVE RANDY MULLINAX: Did you get breakfast this morning?
RIDGWAY: Yes, I did.
MULLINAX: And the usual Randy's breakfast?
RIDGWAY: Rand . . . the usual Randy's breakfast.
MULLINAX: Everything all right there?
RIDGWAY: Yeah.[4]
DETECTIVE JON MATTSEN: How did you sleep?
RIDGWAY: Slept about 2 o'clock and then woke up and went back to sleep about 3:00. Slept pretty good.
MATTSEN: What did you have for breakfast?
RIDGWAY: I had two pancakes, sausage and an egg, I think, one egg.
MATTSEN: Was it decent?
RIDGWAY: It was okay.[5]

At the beginning of the confession, especially, investigators addressed every complaint related to Ridgway's meager living quarters. They brought him his "night guard" and then allowed him to take a "sleep aid" (sleeping pills) to help him sleep on the nights the murders kept him awake. The conversation at the end of the first day reflected the interrogators' approach:

MATTSEN: Alright. Is there anything else?
DETECTIVE SUE PETERS: I think we're gonna take a break here and I'm not sure if we'll wrappin' up for tonight, but we'll check with the other people outside. . . .
RIDGWAY: Un-huh (yes).
PETERS: Appreciate your help Gary, thank you.
MATTSEN: Do you need a drink, or . . . ?
PETERS: A pop?[6]

Investigators yearned to know the answers to thousands of questions those first few days, but they made it a priority to take field trips in a van to give Ridgway an opportunity to point out locations where detectives could find the missing victims. To everyone, the ability to produce the skeletal remains of an unfound victim would be the ultimate evidence of involvement in the serial murders. The field trips—taken under heavy guard—provided investigators a more leisure atmosphere to connect with Ridgway and treat him like a "human being." While inspecting a rural area in King County, even those involved mused over such a large investigative search team.

DEFENSE ATTORNEY MARK PROTHERO: Does this look like a bunch of cops standing here?

RIDGWAY: Tourists. Tourists trying to figure out where Incredible Universe is.
PETERS: Real estate venture.
RIDGWAY: Yeah.
PETERS: That's what I told the guy yesterday.
RIDGWAY: Somebody came over and talked to ya?
PETERS: A guy drove by and I said, "We're looking at some real estate . . .
  That would be joint venture. Apartment complex."
RIDGWAY: Um marijuana fields.
PETERS: Yeah.
RIDGWAY: They were looking for marijuana fields.
PETERS: There you go, that's a good one.
RIDGWAY: That wouldn't be it.
PETERS: No, not 30 people.
RIDGWAY: Well if you guys look for marijuana fields I know how . . . . ordi-
  nary police do . . . . they probably take that many out cause they are usu-
  ally patrolled by the growers.[7]

During those first few field trips, Ridgway and the investigators talked
about almost everything: Seattle Mariner games, police officers' retirement
parties, and some of the better fast-food restaurants to get a juicy hamburger.
The more field trips, the more Ridgway became comfortable enough to joke
with his guards. Some of the bantering on both sides, though, seemed inappropriate. A field trip on June 15, 2003, prompted the following exchanges:

- RIDGWAY: Look at the box over there . . . over there on that crosswalk
  over there, straight ahead, over this way, see it?
  DETECTIVE TOM JENSEN: Probably a garage sale. Do you want to stop
  at some garage sales this morning. (Laughing)
  RIDGWAY: Yeah. You guys could pick up some clothes for me. Wait there's
  a free box, we'll grab a couple of pairs of pants there. (Laughing)[8]

- RIDGWAY: I used to always drive Peasley Cannon since we always lived
  out there. We used to go to Wal Mart and go to IHOP for their
  Wednesday special. . . . Wednesday or Tuesday they had two for
  one senior citizens and Judith got hers free. So that was kinda traditional. That was in late 90s when we lived up there. . . . Should I
  scream in his microphone.
  PETERS: No, don't do that.
  RIDGWAY: I'm just kidding.[9]

- PETERS: You don't think you would have pulled in here?
  RIDGWAY: No. I don't think I would, no. There was no . . . the . . . there
  wasn't as high a vegetation on this side if there was any.
  PETERS: See the no dumping sign.
  RIDGWAY: No dumping sign. That probably wasn't even there. You're
  not going to fine me, are you? (Laughing)[10]

After driving all over King County for two days, the conspicuous Green River search team grew weary of the small talk and no results. Ridgway led them to several wooded areas where he thought he dumped bodies, but no remains were evident. Several times during the field trips, he seemed unsure if he had guided the team to the correct location. As expected, the landscape had changed over the past 20 years. Areas with low brush now supported tall vine maples and alder trees. Still, investigators interpreted the wasted outings as a result of deception. Jensen was the first to reveal his impatience and frustration with Ridgway.

JENSEN: Well, hey, first of all, let me tell you, Gary, I'm getting a little frustrated here. Okay?

RIDGWAY: Uh . . .

JENSEN: Like we're 0 for 2, 0 for 2 yesterday . . .

RIDGWAY: I know, I am too.

JENSEN: . . . I gotta say we're close to over twelve now. And it's getting a little frustrating, you know.

RIDGWAY: Um-hm. (yes)

JENSEN: I just, just wanna let you know that . . . if you're blowin' smoke up my ass, eventually it's gonna come out my ears.

RIDGWAY: This is very depressing for me, too.[11]

The lack of quick progress prompted detectives to change strategy. They stopped the field trips and headed to the interrogation room to begin asking tough questions as a video-audio system recorded every word, every gesture. While teams of two detectives asked questions, defense attorneys sat nearby listening, ready to guide Ridgway. Outside the interrogation room scores of detectives observed and listened. Some fed questions to the interrogation team via a laptop computer. Others went out into the field to run down information that would confirm or negate statements made by Ridgway. Still others studied Ridgway's every gesture and inflection.

OLD GARY, NEW GARY

Next to the skeletal remains of missing victims, Green River investigators most wanted to recover jewelry and other sentimental personal items the victims wore when they disappeared. Detectives hoped to return the mementos to the victims' families. The quest for jewelry became the center of the investigators' next interrogation strategy. They did not abandon trying to cajole Ridgway into confessing, but they introduced an often-used law enforcement technique to get him to divulge the rawest details. The technique called for disassociating the suspect from the crimes, allowing him to talk essentially in the third person.

Detective Peters led the way in asking Ridgway what happened to the jewelry worn by Mary B. Meehan and what were the details of her death. The jewelry was unique, Peters said, and her family would like to have it back. Meehan had been the victim who was nine months pregnant when she disappeared from the prostitution strip. When Ridgway stumbled through vague responses, Peters pressed on, illustrating how prepared the interrogators were.

PETERS: That was in September, the 15th.

MULLINAX: It was a Wednesday. And you worked a dayshift that day, Gary. You worked . . . from uh, 4:45 in the morning till like 5:15, your regular get-off time.

RIDGWAY: Um hmm.[12]

PETERS: Why did you kill her? You should be very good at remembering that.

RIDGWAY: Uh, I can't remember. Maybe there's somethin' in . . . in my medical . . . somethin' happened that um . . . is that . . . it might've had . . .

MULLINAX: Well, I'll tell you that two days earlier you had cut your finger, your little finger. And they had put a band aid on it at work. And that's the only thing in the med . . . medical records.[13]

To help Ridgway stop resisting, Peters pointed to a photograph of Ridgway in the early 1980s.

PETERS: This Gary I believe knows why he took that jewelry. I really believe that.

RIDGWAY: I've got it . . . I've got it blocked in my mind. This . . . not at this time comin' out. It . . . I mean, I, I don't know how to access uh, the right words to say of um . . .

PETERS: Tell us what that Gary did.

RIDGWAY: And I undid the clasp or anything or pull it over the top of her head. Uh, I didn't have . . . my rage was over with from the . . . uh, I didn't uh . . . well, except for the one I, I bit. Um, I didn't um . . .[14]

PETERS: . . . this Gary, the bad Gary, I mean now 'cause you've killed someone, do you want to get the hell outa there? (crosstalk)

RIDGWAY: In that location . . . in that . . . in that v—, because it's right on the street, yes. I, I had to . . . I had to hurry to dig the hole, and I had to hurry to put it . . . and I had to hurry to leave. Other places were secluded and I could take my time.

PETERS: Okay. How many times did you go back and re-look?

RIDGWAY: N—, only never out of . . .

PETERS: Don't say "never" Gary . . . all week you've been telling us "never" and it's always . . . there's been a couple . . . (crosstalk)

RIDGWAY: To look . . . okay . . . okay . . . okay.

PETERS: Be honest. We're getting to understand this Gary now. We're taking steps. They're slow, but this Gary, how many times did he go back?[15]

For two days investigators used the good-Gary/bad-Gary techniques to get Ridgway to discuss revisiting the crime scenes.

DET. MATTSEN: . . . that Gary is much different than the Gary that we are talking to and have talked to the last five days. It's apparent to us and we've had extensive conversations, as I'm sure you see us huddled around. . . . That . . . you are a bright individual and that when you speak to us, although you may have your only little way of thinking about things, you're able to recall a lot of details in these scenes and a lot of details about your activities 20 years ago. . . . We want to get to that person that is different than the person we have before us now. The person that's talking to us. . . . On another kind of side note, we've talked and I got to tell you I'm not totally comfortable that you're providing all the information that you have about some of these individual scenes so I just want to make sure, and it's clear with you, that you can tell us anything about these individual scenes. That it's okay for you to tell us and that we're not going to be shocked about anything that you tell us, okay?[16]

Rigdway finally succumbed and revealed he had urges to revisit the victims to have sex.

Added Jensen: "It's okay if you did. All right. Nothing to be ashamed of. Thousands of people have done it before you. You're not the first one. And you're not the only one and you're not going to be the last one. So that's one of the things that we need to know. If you . . . it's going to come out."

Wisely, Jensen used the technique of downplaying to entice the suspect to feel more comfortable with his horrid revelations.

RIDGWAY: This is . . . the Gary I was before . . .[17]

JENSEN: I know it but this is the guy we want to talk about. If he went back, if he had an urge to have sex with their bodies after they were dead. That's him. That's not you. We need to know what this guy did.

RIDGWAY: Yes, I did lie about that. I went back one time before and . . . on some of them . . . that, like I said, got to give it out, I can't keep holding it in.

JENSEN: No. It's building up inside you like a bad cheeseburger and you've got to . . . you need to take a shit.

RIDGWAY: And that's why I had to bury them because . . . I couldn't . . . they were in locations where I . . . that's why went and took them out further out where I wouldn't be able to go. I buried them and from there on out I stopped doing that.[18]

MATTSEN: It is taken twenty years, ah, to actually get to this stage. And I can understand, ah, what just transpired in that for the first time in the last five days we feel we've gotten you to a point where you're being honest with us in . . . .

RIDGWAY: Un-huh (yes).

MATTSEN: And that's a big thing Mr. Ridgway. . . . It's a very big thing for us to be able to sit across from you and to feel that you are allowing the truth and the information to come through to us.

RIDGWAY: Thank you.

MATTSEN: I want you to be aware, just like my partner Detective Peters did yesterday. . . . We're not talkin' about the Gary that's sittin' across from us right, we're talkin' about this Gary. So if you have any doubt, if there's any flicker in your mind about whether or not you should disclose something, whether or not you should go that avenue, whether or not you should explore that a little bit longer. I want you to look down at this Gary, right here. I want you to be able to recognize that this is the person that we're after . . .[19]

RIDGWAY: The other Gary.

MATTSEN: The other Gary. . . . This is what you need Gary, this is what you need to become . . . to be able to get a good nights sleep.

RIDGWAY: Un-huh (yes).[20]

MATTSEN: I'll tell you what Gary, you've given us a lot of information this morning, stuff that we, in the group, Randy and I both, Tom, Sue, the rest of the detectives, we all knew. But this morning was the first time you were a man and you let it come out to us.[21]

Sometime during the night the good-Gary/bad-Gary routine went to Ridgway's head, literally. And on the morning of June 18, 2003, he entered the interrogation room with authority and purpose. After asking if the video-audio system was operating, Ridgway angrily launched into a halting proclamation:

Well last night I went to sleep after I got a . . . a . . . second time . . . or first time I got up and the other GARY came into my mind the . . . the rage, the power, the control. Um, he's . . . he's . . . he's really, really pissed off about the, ah, not listening to me, not, ah, you, um, you guys are, um, ah, not listening to me about the, ah, the photographs that I . . . I . . . I tore up couple days later. I never put a . . . I never put a body . . . left a body in the house. You guys are tryin' to control me and I'm not gonna let you do it. I never slept with a woman overnight with a . . . a dead woman. Sure I screwed 'em a few times. Um, ah, fighting with the other . . . the new GARY and the old GARY is both a . . . a . . . a . . . a . . . ah, give you as much as I can on the old GARY. But, um, not . . . I'm not mad enough to, ah,[22] No, the new GARY is a candy ass . . . he's . . . he's a wimp.

Investigators played along with the charade.

JENSEN: Who's . . . who's been talkin' to us all along?

RIDGWAY: It's been mostly him and candy coating it to . . . to not knowin' . . .

JENSEN: . . . the new GARY is not a wimp because the new GARY . . . a new man was born yesterday, and I think that was the new GARY. When he started lettin' this stuff go that was a new man.

RIDGWAY: Mean . . . meaning . . .

JENSEN: A real man.

RIDGWAY: . . . yesterday, that was . . . that was the . . . that was the other GARY. This . . . this is me back in '82 . . . '82, not what he is. He . . . he didn't have any guts to stand up for himself. He . . . he let women . . . (unintel) . . . he use 'em, he let woman take control and I want control, I don't to have to have him control. He's not anymore . . . he's just . . . he's just there for . . . I don't give a . . . he's the . . . the good side and I'm the bad side. He's . . . I'm the one that did it, he didn't do it, he's different then. An I, ah, I killed every one of them and . . . and I was . . . my satisfaction I did have sex with 'em, ah, I think every one except for one that I killed, um, the pregnant one. And I killed 'em on the spot and, or it was . . . and then some I moved, some of 'em I didn't. The jewelry I didn't give a shit about the jewelry. I did hid . . . it is true I hid them in the same place the old . . . the new GARY said in all places. And where I threw the . . . threw the clothes off the . . . off the bridge, that's true. And it true where the hundre . . . ah, 216th where I dumped the . . . the damn, ah, ah, the damn plastic bag with the, ah, cans in it because they probably had fingerprints, and some clothes are dumped there. I was scared because I was in Tacoma and drivin' outta Tacoma around . . . in the evening 'cause I heard a house was bein' searched, and so I dumped 'em, I panicked. I didn't . . . I never kept any women overnight. Ah, I'm different . . . I am different than any other. Just the hatred of the women and the . . . the jewelry I put like by the tree, by that IHOP, and I'm not lying, whatever. I did take someone to the airport I think one . . . ah, and I took it to the same . . . next day or the day after, and not a week or a month later. You know, you're putting things in my mouth and I'm not gonna take it. I'm in control here and . . . and I'm . . . and I'm . . . I'm in charge, that's the way I wanna be . . . I never been that way, and then when I was . . . I was in charge when all these women I killed.

JENSEN: This is the old Gary?

RIDGWAY: This is the . . . this is the old Gary, '82 Gary, not the new one. I . . . I hated 'em so much. I did take a pictures, three . . . three or four pictures of the women, put 'em in that location under the Sea-Tac Red Lion. I did tear 'em up. Don't tell me I . . . it's hard to tear things . . . those up because I did . . . or cut 'em, or . . . I did tear 'em up. I did write a letter, now that I remember I think I either . . . either wrote it to the, ah, police station or, um, *Seattle Times* magazine. I . . . I didn't hide any jewelry under the hou . . . under the house, in the house. So you're gonna be wastin' your damn time by goin' over there.[23]

Ridgway's outburst put investigators on the defensive. And their civility disappeared when they caught Ridgway lying, changing his story on specific murders, again. Initially, Ridgway claimed to have killed all his victims with an arm chokehold. Then he offered that sometimes he used a rope or cables. Regarding where he hid the victims' jewelry, the number and locations kept changing. It did not help Ridgway's position that detectives who went out to look for the jewelry under rocks and bushes could not locate any. Ridgway, too, concocted a story on how he came to have a scar on his arm. He told a wild story about pimps pouring battery acid on his arm. In truth, he finally admitted, that was the arm gouged by Marie M. Malvar in her unsuccessful struggle to live. Ridgway had provided detail after detail of how he killed, but he had failed to offer any information that would lead to physical evidence—skeletal remains, jewelry, a victim's clothing, an item with fingerprints—to back up his claim of being the Green River Killer. Even if detectives wanted to believe his every word, they could not since there was no corroborating evidence. Other obstacles hindered the process. At times Ridgway's answers to questions contained tidbits of information from the investigation conducted by King County Police and the King County Prosecutor's Office. How was he privy to such information? His attorneys had allowed him to read reams of records provided by police and prosecutors to the defense under "discovery," meaning Ridgway was aware of the evidence against him. That made it even more challenging for the interrogators to elicit information known only to the Green River Killer. In frustration, Mattsen asked, "W–what's the truth here? . . . Is the old Gary gonna tell us the truth? Is the new Gary gonna come off? Because . . . you're not livin' up to your agreement. Your agreement was to tell us everything you knew about. . . ."

RIDGWAY: My, my mind is not workin' the way that you, you want it to do. It's not workin' . . . it's, it's not workin'.

MATTSEN: I understand that, GARY, and that's why we gave it five or six days. We still don't have anything from you, do we? I mean I'm kind of at a loss. I, I . . . tell me, GARY, I'm willin' to work with you. I, am willing to show you all the respect that you deserve in this process here.

RIDGWAY: Um-hm. (yes)

MATTSEN: But I also expect to get a little bit 'a information. A little TINY bit of information that we can use to help us resolve some of these issues. Gary, have you done that?

RIDGWAY: I've given ya' a lot 'a information, I th . . .

MATTSEN: You have?

RIDGWAY: I thought I did.[24]

INCITING

While observing Ridgway's obvious attempt to promote the concept of a split personality with his "Old-Gary" routine, investigators noticed that he seemed to provide more revelations while angry. So they made it a point to goad him into getting upset. They tried name-calling. They called him "candy-ass" and "wimp."[25] They asked him to be a "man" and "step up to the plate."[26] Then, they mixed anger, insults, and sarcasm:

- Gary, you didn't give us any information on those three. . . . It's like watching paint dry this morning when you're trying to give us explanations of cases that you say you did and that you know about . . . you're acting like you're in here acting like you're asleep. . . . Bullshit! I'm calling bullshit on that! . . . Zippo Gary. You provided zippo information this morning. I could have provided more information.[27]

- We aren't going to have any more of this crap like we did this morning. That was a pathetic performance. . . . That is unacceptable. And we're not going to let you sit here and put on this little act for us and not confront you from now on. You are not controlling and dictating how this interview is going to take place.[28]

- That was [a] pathetic morning. Jon and I should have stayed at our desks and drank coffee. We would have learned more. Do not waste our time or your time with that kind of a session. . . . We have not dedicated our lives and our careers to this to let you come in here and blow as Tom Jensen would say, "smoke up our ass." And you've been doing that for the last couple of days and it's ending today. Do you understand me?[29]

As the interrogation sessions grew more heated and acrimonious, investigators used, more often, the most vulgar terms to describe how Ridgway sexually used and killed his victims. The interrogators sought to unsanitize the murders to apparently force Ridgway to confront every disgusting detail of his acts and be honest, but their repeated vulgarities regarding the victims seemed inappropriate. Ridgway used the terms "breasts" and "ladies." Investigators sometimes referred to specific victims' physical attributes and insisted on speaking about the victims' "tits" and how Ridgway liked "fucking 'em."[30]

To further agitate and unstablize Ridgway, investigators took to suddenly canceling field trips, something Ridgway looked forward to since they were an opportunity to get out in the city or woods. One morning Ridgway was ready to go when King County Police Detective Raphael Crenshaw stormed in and said, "You're not goin' anywhere. Take his ass back to his fucking cell and when you wanna start tellin' the truth you let us know."[31] On another occasion, Detective Tom Jensen explained the reward system to Ridgway this way: "Do you think we are going to take you for another ride? . . . You haven't earned a trip. Because you haven't given a shit. . . . So you're really just talking to hear yourself today. . . . All right. Well, I gotta go feed my dog."[32]

For weeks the investigators' scorn was evident in almost every discussion. Sometimes it surfaced in the smallest of ways:

MATTSEN: See, you've gotten comfortable, you've gotten comfortable saying I don't remember I don't remember killing anybody after the bum fuck . . . don't say that anymore.
JENSEN: You don't need to pinch yourself to keep yourself . . .
RIDGWAY: No, I'm not pinching myself.
JENSEN: You're . . . you're gonna hurt yourself.
RIDGWAY: Kneading kneading myself.
JENSEN: Don't pinch your hands anymore, I don't want to see you doing that again.[33]

The interrogators' efforts at exerting control of Ridgway and his environment—with various bullying strategies reminiscent of high school teenagers picking on an unpopular student or an abusive husband castigating his wife—seemed to have little success since Ridgway had a mental disability and probably did have trouble with memory. Bullying appeared to be the wrong psychological tool to pry loose years of details of his crimes. Ridgway confided one day:

> Every day I get up in the morning. I fold up my . . . my . . . my sleeping bag. I put the pillow on there. I put my towel and I'm ready to go back to prison . . . back to jail. Every day I come in here, I think I'm going to go back.[34] I figure today is going to be the last. I think you can put me back. That's okay.[35]

BARTER

Investigators were so desperate to locate and obtain any personal items belonging to the victims that they made a very unconventional offer to Ridgway a month after the beginning of the interrogation. In exchange for revealing the location of any jewelry belonging to the victims, Detective Randy Mullinax offered to support arguments for Ridgway to be allowed to keep some of it. Mullinax said, "We'll let you have that to do with what you want . . . you can keep that. It will be our gift to you . . . maybe we'll do some of the old swamp meet stuff with you right now."[36] Mullinax clearly was lying to Ridgway since King County Police had made it a mission to recover the jewelry for the families. They would never allow Ridgway to keep any of it, especially since he, more than likely, would use it to relive his murders. The victims' families, too, were the rightful owners of the jewelry.

PSYCHOLOGICAL SOFTBALLS

King County Police would have shifted to the traditional good-guy, bad-guy approach—also known as the hot-cold technique—but they would have had trouble finding an investigator who could play the good guy. All the investigators had already taken turns verbally beating up Ridgway. To him, his mind seemed black and blue, puffy. It fell on several psychologists collectively to play the good guy: Dr. Robert Wheeler, acting on behalf of prosecutors and police; Dr. Mary Ellen O'Toole, an FBI profiler helping the prosecution, but also there to gather information for the National Center for the Analysis of Violent Crime; Dr. Christian Harris, primarily working for the defense; and Dr. Judith V. Becker, also with the defense. They all were invited to pry into Ridgway's psych to help every one understand his motives and ascertain how many women he killed. The doctors sometimes asked sharp, challenging questions, but, for the most part, they were gentle with Ridgway as they walked him through his life and relationships with family, teachers, schoolmates, and women. By and large, they addressed the suspect as "Mr. Ridgway." Although all the doctors were charged with getting the truth—convincing Ridgway to comply with the confession agreement—each crafted his or her persuasive arguments around Ridgway's life and why they had been asked to speak with him.

Throughout the interrogation, Ridgway claimed he wanted to divulge much more information about the murders, but he had trouble extracting it from the deep corners of his mind. And when he did manage to identify valuable details, Ridgway claimed he found it difficult to articulate what he was thinking. Dr. Wheeler used that alleged desire to cooperate for the base of his interview of Ridgway. While Dr. Wheeler repeatedly told Ridgway he was there to help Ridgway verbalize information valuable to the investigation, the doctor did not provide Ridgway with any communication tools or techniques to articulate his thoughts. Hence, Ridgway regurgitated his standard reply to most of the questions: he did not remember. It was important for Dr. Wheeler to get Ridgway to identify his first murder victim. Investigators believed Ridgway had killed long before he murdered the first woman in the Green River serial case. When Dr. Wheeler asked Ridgway to identify his first murder victim, Ridgway insisted it was Wendy L. Coffield, the first found victim in the Green River case. That upset the doctor. Off-and-on during the four-day interview, Dr. Wheeler asked Ridgway: "Are you trying to insult me?[37] Mr. Ridgway, do I look like a complete moron?"[38]

Dr. Christian Harris was given one day with Ridgway and that interview produced the most perplexing exchange. It appeared the doctor simply was attempting to scare Ridgway into telling the truth.

DR. HARRIS: Yeah. And then you say you're not gonna lie anymore, and then they catch you again.

RIDGWAY: . . . have a, have a problem with lyin', yeah.

DR. HARRIS: Yeah. So a good way of getting executed would be to keep lyin', wouldn't it.

RIDGWAY: It would be, yes.

DR. HARRIS: And you, you do think morally that's what should happen to ya. Morally and by law.

RIDGWAY: And, and, and, and, and by law, yes.

DR. HARRIS: Why have you not committed suicide?

RIDGWAY: Well, it's . . . uh, I ha . . . I haven't planted a seed in there to, to try. Uh . . .

DR. HARRIS: Why not? I mean you've let everybody down, you cry when you talk about letting your family down. You, yourself, feel you should die because of what you've done. Why haven't you committed suicide?

RIDGWAY: I just don't, don't uh, I don't know . . . I don't know why. I n-never tried it.[39]

Dr. Becker came across as the opposite of Dr. Harris. Dr. Becker sympathized and empathized with Ridgway. She illustrated the most support for his memory problems, his inability to recall details of when and how he abducted many of his victims.

While Ridgway revealed some embarrassing personal details and sexual deviant behavior to Dr. Wheeler, Dr. Harris, and Dr. Becker, he primarily bonded with Dr. Mary Ellen O'Toole of the FBI. She served up the most persuasive statements, some of which appeared deceptive. Her offers to Ridgway resonated so well that he openly discussed his bedwetting and sexual attraction to his mother. Dr. O'Toole threw a lot of softballs to Ridgway—which actually produced significant insights to explain some of his motivation for killing—but she slipped in a curve ball now and then. Dr. O'Toole began her interview of Ridgway in mid-July 2003:

- On the first day Dr. O'Toole met with Ridgway she used flattery to entice him to begin talking. She explained that the FBI constantly was in search of special serial murder cases to do a "case study," and the Green River Murders case seemed very special. Of course, she stated, Ridgway would have to provide many details for the FBI to be able to ultimately decide to make it worthy of being a "case study." If the case were selected, she further explained, that would be very beneficial for Ridgway since it meant a long-term relationship with the FBI, which would break up the monotony of prison.

- Next Dr. O'Toole pointed out that Ridgway was in a unique position to provide information that would help teach profilers, detectives, and attorneys about serial killers. Dr. O'Toole said:

We really need to have certain kinds of information that make it worthwhile. We can't use a particular case study and just say, "well he was real iffy on this and so we're not sure what was going on." "He was real vague on this and people weren't really sure." Do you see what I'm saying? There's certain key parts to your development, the fire setting, the anger, the rage and all of that. What you said was good stuff but there's still a lot more and that's what I'll need to consult with ... to my folks about to whether not to ... that it's going to be to their interest and mine to continue with this.[40]

- The psychological expert especially caught Ridgway's attention when she said no one apparently helped Ridgway when he was a boy and now Ridgway's revelations could help with intervention in the future.

DR. O'TOOLE: Does that make sense?
RIDGWAY: I want to help some other kids from doing the same thing I did.
DR. O'TOOLE: You could have been helped probably early on, do you think so?
RIDGWAY: Only if I probably would have sought into it.
DR. O'TOOLE: Do you think you're in a position now to help somebody else?
RIDGWAY: Um huh.
DR. O'TOOLE: Do you think you're willing to take the risk to do that?
RIDGWAY: I think I am.
DR. O'TOOLE: And do you think you're willing to put yourself out there on a ... on kind of a difficult situation to do that?
RIDGWAY: Yes I am but it's scary.[41]

Dr. O'Toole was very successful at getting Ridgway to supply a detailed chronology of his deviant behavior. The doctor had success, in part, because she encouraged the use of clinical-academic terms. That sanitizing approach allowed Ridgway to discuss specific behavior and propensities without having to deal with the vulgar aspects of such deviancy, that is, dirty aspects abhorrent to the average individual. The use of more a sophisticated language, too, allowed him to feel educated and instructor-like, just as Dr. O'Toole wished him to feel.

After a week of interviewing Ridgway for hours at a time, Dr. O'Toole took a break, and Dr. Robert Wheeler stepped back in the interrogation room. Dr. Wheeler made it clear he was unhappy Ridgway provided much more information to Dr. O'Toole.

DR. WHEELER: I was unpleased that you made progress with Dr. O'Toole.[42] I'm disappointed because of the lies of omission to me. All the stuff that you could have told me that you had an opportunity to, and you still chose to lie about it.
RIDGWAY: She ... she ... she walked through it a lot better and, you know, broke my, ah, any kind of barriers down. ... Better than you did. She's ... she's professional on it. And I know you're ...

DR. WHEELER: Un-huh (yes).

RIDGWAY: . . . a professional too, but. . . .

DR. WHEELER: No offense . . . no offense taken.

RIDGWAY: No, but it's . . . you know, the, ah, she just knew how to, ah, draw it out because she . . . she . . . that's what she, ah, does everyday.[43]

Dr. Wheeler needed to hear more.

DR. WHEELER: Let's go back and talk about the things that Dr. O'Toole . . . that you felt were helpful. So she sat next to you, she understood how a prostitute thinks and feels. . . .

RIDGWAY: Un-huh (yes).

DR. WHEELER: . . . and was able to talk to you the way a prostitute would talk. Is that right?

RIDGWAY: Yes.

DR. WHEELER: Is that what you're saying? What else did she do that was helpful to you?

RIDGWAY: Well she, ah, you know, coaxed me into, ah, goin' through how I . . . how I killed 'em, and, ah, ah, puttin' what my . . . I think she talked to me a little about what my feelings were when I was killing 'em. Um. . . .

DR. WHEELER: So you respond to the coaxing, is that what your saying?

RIDGWAY: Yeah, I respond to the coaxing.[44]

DR. WHEELER: How did it make a difference with Dr. O'Toole sittin' next to ya?

RIDGWAY: . . . well with every time . . . every time when SUE comes in she sits there.

DR. WHEELER: Who sits there?

RIDGWAY: Sue . . . Susie . . . Susie Peters.

DR. WHEELER: So the women sit next to you. And why do you think that is?

RIDGWAY: To help me out. You know, use the woman's perspective on it.

DR. WHEELER: Woman's perspective. And what is it that you like about having the women sitting next to you?

RIDGWAY: Well, I get to look . . . as I'm talkin' to 'em get to look into their eyes, and so far here when I'm in the middle of talkin' to you or some-thin' I'm thinkin' I gotta look some place else when I'm thinkin', it kinda throws off the . . . yeah.

DR. WHEELER: I don't think you're bein' straight with me.[45] Did you like being touched?

RIDGWAY: Yeah, that's . . . she touched me a lot of times she . . . she'd, you know, put my hand on her arm and . . .

DR. WHEELER: Did that feel good?

RIDGWAY: It feeled, ah, you know, closeness in a way.

DR. WHEELER: Un-huh (yes).

RIDGWAY: Ah, she wanted to get, you know, right down and get personal
what I, ah, . . . so she'd touch me in the arm sometimes. . . .
DR. WHEELER: She was gentle. . . .[46]

A woman's touch obviously had made a difference. However, even Dr.
O'Toole failed to get satisfactory answers to two questions that were driving
the interrogation: (1) Who did Ridgway murder before starting to kill prostitutes as part of the Green River Murders case? (2) Where was Ridgway still
hiding jewelry taken from his victims? According to Dr. O'Toole, history
showed that serial killers killed long before their slayings were detected, and
serial killers tended to keep keepsakes to relive their kills. But Ridgway refused to budge. He insisted he did not kill prior to 1982, and he had no jewelry to give up. Dr. O'Toole concocted one more trick, a version of the offer
Detective Randy Mullinax had made earlier in the interrogation process.

DR. O'TOOLE: But have you thought about how you can maintain that
meaning that it had. That significance that it has for you without giving it
to the victim's family. I mean that's kind of a fine line there. . . . And if
you found a certain way with which that stuff could be handled . . . if you
found a circumstance under which that stuff could be recovered that
would still afford you the emotional value that you attach to it. Would
that be an option for you?
RIDGWAY: That would be an option but the jewelry is . . .
DR. O'TOOLE: Let me pose an option that has had happened in another
case. And as we talked yesterday, it seems to me that what is important
to you to get some control back or into your life . . . take back some control which is an important place for you. . . . Is to be able to tell people
your story.[47] Tell people what . . . how you'll educate people. How you
were so successful at what you did and how law enforcement made a lot
of mistakes, didn't they? . . . One of the areas that I'm just offering as a
possibility for you, considering your set of circumstances. . . . As a training tool to teach people, but not give them back to the victim's families
has been done in another case and it seems to have been pretty effective
is to allow, say for example, a unit like our unit, the profiling unit, to use
that . . . those items . . . that material in kind of a training environment
for new profilers to come in and see these are things that are associated
with, for example, the Green River killer. These are the kinds of things
that this person was able to maintain over a period of time kind of like a
museum. . . . How does something like that sound?
RIDGWAY: That's sounds okay but I've got . . . I've got my case . . . my case
is a little bit different than most. . . . I'm not like an ordinary murderer?[48]
DR. O'TOOLE: I'm offering a possibility to you that you may want to consider in terms of how you will remain extraordinary to you know forever
in terms of your work. . . . I think it is important that people understand

that you were very successful and that [you] remained successful for a long period of time and to have things remain hidden at this juncture. I would think would not be how . . . it does you no good. And this is about you and this about how people can learn from you. This is about you. This is not about the victims. It's about you, Mr. Ridgway.[49] . . . Possibility?

RIDGWAY: It is a possibility but the thing is why every other . . . every other serial killer always keeps their possession. I didn't keep 'em. I threw the clothes out. I didn't save the jewelry for very long and I gave it to Kenworth, some employees.[50]

Dr. O'Toole's offer was dubious, to say the very least. The victims' families probably would never allow the FBI to keep the jewelry and treat it like museum pieces.

RAW PHOTOGRAPHS

Eventually investigators decided to try to jar Ridgway's memory with the raw photographs of his victims. Intermittently, investigators showed Ridgway slides of decomposing women to take him back to his hunting days in order to pry loose details of each murder. With each set of victim slides, they asked, What do you see in the picture? Who do you think is the victim? Where did she die? When did you first meet that person? How did you make contact with her? Where? How did you kill her? Did you have any conversation with her? Did she ask you not to kill her? Did she talk about her kids? Did you take her to your house? Where in your truck did you kill her? Did you visit her after she was dead? Why does it look like you had sex with her after you killed her? How often? Did you use a condom? How did you pick where you dumped her? Did you drag her down the hill? Didn't anyone see you? What were you thinking when you were killing her? How did it feel? Did she fight? Scratch you? Why did you bury her? How long did it take you? Did she have any ID? What did you do with it? Her clothes? Did you take any jewelry? What did you do with the jewelry? Did any of the women ever ask if you were the Green River Killer?

The sessions turned out to be productive, at times, but Ridgway gave inconsistent statements, angering his interrogators and prompting them to ask, again, why he was lying. There were many and varied reasons why Ridgway lied or appeared to be lying during the six months of the interrogation:

- He was a pathological liar. He had lied so often for so many years that he could not keep himself from making up information. It took less effort to lie than to remember the truth.

- He did not want to be seen as a monster so he tried to sanitize how he treated and killed his victims. He especially did not want people to know he practiced necrophilia.
- After lying to his attorneys, Ridgway had to be consistent, hence he lied to his interrogators.
- He sometimes lied, he claimed, to please interrogators when they refused to accept his initial answers.
- He initially lied about killing in the late 1980s and 1990s because his wife Judith would be devastated to know he frequented prostitutes and killed during their marriage.
- Ridgway probably suffered from a short-term memory problem, but investigators only wanted to believe his lack of memory was the product of lying. Ridgway had trouble remembering the names of his interrogators—Detective Tom Jensen, Detective Randy Mullinax, Detective Jon Mattsen, and Detective Sue Peters—in spite of sitting across a small table from them for months. And even up to the time he was arrested in 2001, Ridgway could not remember his home address and phone number when making transactions at swap meets.

During one interrogation session a detective asked Ridgway what he had written down on a tablet. Ridgway said he jotted down a reminder: "I will not tell a lie. I will tell the truth. Think before opening my mouth. And don't . . . do not guess."[51]

Eventually, Ridgway's writing tablet was taken away as punishment for so many inconsistencies and outright lies.

BODY FINDS

Ridgway had told an enormous number of big and little lies and had, in many ways, misled interrogators. In retrospect, however, it does not appear that he was deceptive in leading investigators to undiscovered human remains. Detectives initially were unsuccessful in locating remains at the locations pointed out by Ridgway during field trips. It was backbreaking work digging through years of leaves, dried branches, mud, and standing water. To their credit, investigators kept searching the sites and finally started discovering a skull here, an entire skeleton there. King County Police had not found a missing victim for almost 15 years when the skull of Pammy A. Avent was located in mid-August 2003 just east of Enumclaw, Washington, along Highway 410. The 16-year-old disappeared in October 1983 from Seattle. In the coming weeks and months, investigators found the remains of April D. Buttram, 17, who disappeared from Seattle in August or September 1983, and Marie A. Malvar, 20, who disappeared in April 1983. She had fought the hardest to live. Human bones found in a ravine off the Kent-Des Moines Road leading to the Green River also were linked to Ridgway that summer as a result of his confession. With those emphatic, although tragic, results, Ridgway finally convinced his interrogators he, in fact, was the infamous Green River Killer.

Investigators entered the interrogation room in a jovial mood each time they were about to share the good news of a discovery with Ridgway. The Green River Killer did not jump up with joy or told his interrogators "I told you so!" He simply said: "That's good. That's real good."[52] The discovery of remains prompted investigators to employ an old adage in interrogations: *"Treat a duchess like a whore, and a whore like a duchess"*:

DET. JENSEN: What do you want for dinner tonight?

RIDGWAY: Dinner tonight, ah, I think I'm gonna have . . . I don't know what they're gonna have, lasagna or somethin' like that.

JENSEN: Oh, we . . . we figure we owe ya somethin' for a bone, okay. We got a bone so what do you want for dinner?

RIDGWAY: . . . how 'bout salmon or somethin'?

DET. SUE PETERS: Somebody's gonna have to go fishin'.

RIDGWAY: Somebody's gonna have to go fishin', yeah.

FIRST ATTORNEY IN THE ROOM: I'll volunteer for that duty.

SECOND ATTORNEY: Ah, steak and lobster, I know you guys just forgot to ask us.

JENSEN: Well, you give us a bone and we'll do that.[53]

With each body find, investigators became more civil, again. They asked if Ridgway was being treated okay, if he was getting his medication, if he was using the exercycle regularly. They even let Ridgway get a haircut. "No complaints," responded Ridgway.

MASSIVE CONFRONTATION

Just when Ridgway thought he had finally pleased his interrogators and the arduous interrogation was coming to an end, investigators introduced another interrogation technique intended to shake him up and convince him to honestly explain why he had taken several victims to Oregon. Detectives had waited for the right time to reveal previously undisclosed evidence and unleash their persuasive assault. In response to repeated questions over the summer, Ridgway contended he sought to mislead the Green River Task Force in gathering a few skeletal remains and dumping them in Oregon to make it seem the killer had moved away from Washington. The way Ridgway described his evasive scheme, he visited several dump sites and picked up a few bones here and a few bones there, put them in two plastic bags, tossed them in the trunk of his car, and drove about three hours to an area just south of Portland. Through the years authorities had discovered two sets of remains in a rural area known as Tigard and two sets of remains in a wooded area near Tualatin. Only a few miles separated Tigard and Tualatin. Investigators felt certain Ridgway was hiding the real motive behind depositing four victims in another state. Perhaps he had done something to those victims that made him out to be even more of a monster in the eyes of the public. In early October 2003, investigators walked into the interrogation room and confronted him. Detectives revealed that almost an entire skeleton had been discovered in Tigard, and that contradicted Ridgway's claim of only taking a few bones to Orgeon. The evidence indicated Ridgway had transported the victim, Shirley M. Sherrill, 17, to decompose in Oregon soon after death. Or perhaps he killed Sherrill in Oregon? That would open the door for Oregon authorities to prosecute Ridgway in their state. They would not be bound by Washington's confession agreement, hence it would not behoove Ridgway to say he killed Sherril or Denise D. Bush in Oregon and dumped them in Tigard. According to investigators, forensic anthropological examination indicated that animal activity on the skeletal remains was more consistent with the victim being left in Oregon soon after death. Ridgway appeared dumbfounded by the revelation, but was adamant that he could not recall why he would have taken Sherrill's entire body to Oregon. And he reiterated his earlier claim that he was not responsible for the death of the two women found near Tualatin, who were on the official Green River list. One of those victims was Tammie C. Liles, 16, who disappeared in June 1983 from downtown Seattle. The other victim has never been identified. Investigators were not pleased with Ridgway's response, to say the least, especially Detective Tom Jensen: "You don't have to like us . . . but at least respect us, okay. . . . And the same thing for your attorneys. Give them the respect they deserve, okay, and give us the respect we deserve."[54]

Investigators brought in Detective Rafael Crenshaw for the second phase of the massive confrontation. If anyone could threaten Ridgway into being more frank, Crenshaw could.

CRENSHAW: Well I see everyday, I'm out in the field bustin' my ass, I come back here, what do I see? Got your feet propped up on the table back there, drinkin' your water, havin' your lunch, readin' a magazine, doin' your little crossword puzzles, tryin' to do 'em. You can't even do those, you gotta cheat to . . . to finish a crossword puzzle. Isn't that true? . . . What you're tryin' to do is just prolong this thing. You want us to go out there and bust our ass, waste our time while you just sit here in the lap of luxury. That's what it is . . ."[55]

RIDGWAY: It's not . . . not what I feel is luxury, no. There's . . . what else . . . what else am I suppose to do in my room just sit back, ah. . . .

CRENSHAW: We give you assignments all the time. You got all goddamn day to think. And then I sit today, actually I listened to the interview, I wanted to smack your face. It was ridiculous the stuff at Jolly . . . Jolly, ah,

Rogers, ah, ah, spot over here off of 216th. I think it's the first time we'd heard that. Have you mentioned that to us before? And was it the first time you'd mentioned taking bones there? . . . A hundred and twenty-three days into this, and then the light bulb just came on?

RIDGWAY: Yeah, some of it just comes on, yes.

CRENSHAW: That's ridiculous, it is, it's absolutely unacceptable because when you tell the story you tell it with a little smirk on your face. You do, I sit back there after spending my whole summer, the past four months, every single weekend, every single day almost out there searching at these sites while you're sitting back here kinda takin' it easy, and all of a sudden you tell us a story like that with a smirk on your face.

RIDGWAY: There's no smirk on my face, no.

CRENSHAW: I watched the video. You laugh, you do. I been out to Lake Fenwick eight separate days, spending eight or nine hours at a time. It's just not me. I work with a whole list a guys that are ready to kick your ass we're so sick of it. It is, we've reached that point where we've basically just had it. I don't know what else to say to ya. You know, you know these things and you sit here and you try to play stupid, "I don't know." We've torn the whole . . . we deforested Lake Fenwick. We've deforested. There's nothin' left, nothin' left.

RIDGWAY: There's gotta be a body out there.[56]

CRENSHAW: Our problem here, at least from my point of view is that we've treated you way too nicely. We do . . . before you got here I busted my ass running around gettin' your shit, got you a sleepin' bag, got ya a . . . a mattress to sleep on. People are bringin' ya food, movies to watch, newspapers to read, magazines to read.[57]

The verbal barrage rankled Ridgway and he stuck to his previous positions:

- He killed no one prior to 1982 when the Green River series began and he only murdered "prostitutes."
- He had no jewelry in a secret hiding place belonging to the victims.
- Although he was killing four or five women a month from 1982 to 1984, he managed to control his killing urge and only murdered four women after 1984, the latest being in 1998.

On December 15, 2003, the day before the interrogation was to end, Detective Jon Mattsen summed up the interrogators' feelings toward the marathon interrogation:

Gary, we have thirty investigators sittin' here watchin' this everyday that includes senior prosecution staff, other homicide detectives, all the interviewers, all the, um, administration support staff. . . . I mean everybody's watchin' this, and not one of us believes your little version here.[58]

The Green River Killer's confession led investigators to this site near Enumclaw, Washington, where they found the remains of Pammy A. Avent on August 18, 2003. *(Photo by Natalie G. Guillén.)*

CHAPTER

... Confession or Deception? II

9

Like yesterday, we had pretty interesting talk about some ... pretty interesting subjects, don't you think? Yeah, like two guys just sittin' in a bar.

David G. Reichert
King County Sheriff[1]

On August 18, 2003, King County Sheriff David G. Reichert walked into the interrogation room. It was his turn to try to convince Gary Leon Ridgway to end the game, stop being deceitful. As part of his persuasion strategy, he donned his official green and brown police uniform and combed his hair neatly. His thick hair had been jet black in the summer of 1982 when he responded to the Green River to guide the discovery of the first victim of the Green River Killer. Now his hair was completely gray. Reichert smiled broadly as detectives ushered Ridgway in to see him. To make Ridgway feel at ease, Reichert ordered that the suspect's handcuffs be removed. Some officers might have been hesitant to be in a room with an uncuffed serial killer. Reichert was not. He was confident in his physical strength; after all he lifted weights all his life to stay fit.

Reichert had put a lot of thought into his approach. His grandfather had been a Lutheran minister, and Reichert was an Elder in his own church. Reichert knew, too, that Ridgway had come to believe in God in recent years and was attending church services regularly. That nexus gave Reichert the opening to appeal to Ridgway to use the Bible as a guide in his confession. Reichert pointed out that he and his uniform represented the government, and the Bible stated that people should give to Caesar what belongs to Caesar. In other words, Ridgway should give to Reichert and King County the bodies of the missing women and the victims' jewelry.

Ridgway agreed with the Bible passage about Caesar, but calmly explained that he had nothing else to give Caesar. In his stuttering-stammering style of talking, Ridgway said he had done his best to lead investigators to body sites, and he had already told everyone what he did with the jewelry.

Several times Reichert emphasized that prison was a dangerous place, and Ridgway needed God to go with him and God would only look after Ridgway in prison if Ridgway repented, confessed his sins, and told the truth. Ridgway claimed he understood that and that he had told the truth to the best of his ability. Reichert countered that Ridgway needed God or someone with power like Reichert to survive prison life. If Ridgway gave up the location of more remains and led detectives to jewelry, Reichert offered to allow Ridgway to contact the sheriff anytime for help. Reichert said, "I know a lot of people. You know we should probably keep in touch after you go off to prison because there could be some things that you need." Then he added: "There's nobody else that has the relationship that you and I have. It's just the two of us."[2]

During their conversation that first day, Reichert focused on God and creating a bond between the two men to win Ridgway's trust and confidence. Whenever possible, Reichert used the word "we" and "us."

REICHERT: So three days ago on August 15th, 21 years ago . . . you and I were standing on that river bank.
RIDGWAY: On a Sunday.
REICHERT: They're always going to tie us together. Our lives are tied together.
RIDGWAY: Um-hm.[3]

Methodically, Reichert then touched on the commonalities the men shared:

- Both were dyslexic and had trouble reading.
- Both received poor grades in school.
- Both grew up poor and their family shopped at low-budget stores.
- Both lived and worked in South King County.
- Both were in their 50/s.

To further entice Ridgway to talk, Reichert tried "self-disclosure." Perhaps if he revealed something personal about himself—life with a domineering mother—Ridgway would reciprocate.

REICHERT: You know, I read once, uh, that you saw your, your mother hit your father over the head, it was in one of these articles I was reading, with a plate or something.

RIDGWAY: (Unintelligible) plate, that's what Marcia said, I don't know what that means. I don't know remember that.

REICHERT: Oh, you don't? . . . I saw my mom hit my dad over the head with a frying pan.

RIDGWAY: That's a coincidence, yeah.

REICHERT: (Laughs)

RIDGWAY: (Unintelligible) wake, wake him up?

REICHERT: Uh, woke him up, yeah. Put him right on the floor. We had to call an ambulance to come and get him. . . . We got a lot in common.

RIDGWAY: Uh-huh. We do.

REICHERT: Yeah. Can you just give me the one thing? One thing? Share one thing that you haven't shared before.[4]

The sheriff seemed to be begging for just one revelation. Commonalities or not, Ridgway said he had revealed all that he knew.

Reichert's mood suddenly changed to a persistent, authoritative interrogator. The two men's chairs were almost side-by-side, and as Reichert pushed, he leaned forward, getting into Ridgway's comfort zone and forcing Ridgway to lean back. In a low voice, Reichert said

Tell me Gary. Tell me Gary. Don't say you don't remember. The next words that come out of your mouth need to be all about what happened on the last one you killed. The last time you killed somebody. Think about it. I know you. I know you're smart. I know you're organized. I know you have an opinion and I know that you care somewhere deep down and inside. Tell me about the last person you killed. . . . Do it Gary. Do it. Do it. You can do it. It's there. You can do it. You're this close. You can do it. (Pause). Don't. Don't. I want to help but you've got to be able to trust me. We are in this together. You can call me anytime. You leave here and you go away. You can always call me. If you need something wherever you're gonna be. You can always call me. I will help you but you need to help me help you. The only way you can do that is to begin to tell your story today. Right now. It's you and me here in this room. Who was the last person? Tell me about the last person you killed. It's okay. It's okay. It's okay. (Pause). Don't shake your head. Come on. You can do this. You can do it. Right? Yes. The answer's yes. All you have to do is (unintell). You can do it, right? Gary, you can do this. The answer's yes. The answer is yes. You want to. I can tell you want to. You want to. The answer is yes. Tell me about the last person you've killed. Don't shake your head. I won't let you do that.[5]

But Ridgway couldn't or wouldn't offer any new information.

At one point, Reichert informed Ridgway that he was not leaving the room until Ridgway was more forthcoming. Reichert sat peering at Ridgway, eyeball-to-eyeball, silent for several minutes. Reichert resembled a stern father trying to stare down a teenage son. Ridgway stared back,

silent. Trying to stare down a man who had nothing to lose—Ridgway had
already successfully bartered for his life—turned out to be a psychological
mistake. It seemed imprudent for Reichert to use such an adolescent approach with a hardened criminal. Ridgway had nothing else to do: He had
all day and all night and into the following week and year. In fact, he had
the rest of his life. Ridgway just sat there, able to get lost in his thought, like
he had done for years with his horrid secrets. Reichert had no option but to
blink first and ask more questions.

REICHERT: So you got some stuff (jewelry). Easy to tell the truth. You've
    got some stuff, I know you do. Yes, you do. YES, you do.
RIDGWAY: I don't . . .
REICHERT: GARY, GARY, GARY . . .
RIDGWAY: I don't have anything.
REICHERT: Yes, you do have. You have something. You do. Stop. Stop.
RIDGWAY: The only thing I have is memories.
REICHERT: No.
RIDGWAY: Don't have, no. . . .
REICHERT: No.
RIDGWAY: . . . no possessions.
REICHERT: Yes, you do. You do. You, you can't, you can't . . .
RIDGWAY: I can't (cross-talk unintell.)
REICHERT: . . . you can't convince . . .
RIDGWAY: . . . I can't give it to you because there isn't any.
REICHERT: Yes, there is.
RIDGWAY: There isn't.
REICHERT: There is. There is.[6]

Round and round they went like two incorrigible kids in the elementary school playground. Finally, Reichert proclaimed:

And you're not being honest right now, so you, what you've done is you
just *sentenced yourself to eternal life in hell.* Your ass is just gonna burn the
rest 'a your life . . . have you read Revelation? . . . You ought'a read the
Book a' Revelation. Not only will you be on fire, but you're gonna have
sores and stuff happenin' all over your body . . . and you can never stop it.
It'll never heal. You'll be in constant pain and torture, That's what it says.
. . . The only way you can stop that is by tellin' the truth.[7]

Later, Reichert would say, "You better not offend me. I'm the guy in
charge, right? . . . You don't want to piss me off.[8] How would you like to go
with me and visit the families? Maybe I ought to just take you to one of the
families. I know one I could take you to and leave you there, and guess
what?"[9]

That didn't scare Ridgway, or he did not show his fear. So, the sheriff decided to try a different tactic, the low road. Reichert's strategy seemed dubious since he opted for wallowing in the gutter with a killer who was set in his denial. The victims' families would not have appreciated how the two men laughed over the murder of their daughters and wives:

- REICHERT: Is that something you ever thought about doing? Being a cop?
  RIDGWAY: I thought about being a doctor and a cop.
  REICHERT: Yeah. What kind of doctor?
  RIDGWAY: Just a doctor. You know when you're young you . . .
  REICHERT: Not a gynecologist?
  RIDGWAY: No. Not a gynecologist.
  REICHERT: (Laughing). Just a doctor.[10]

- REICHERT: Did you ever play doctor when you were a little boy? . . . The neighborhood girls?
  RIDGWAY: A cousin. I gave her a—a penny to see what her, uh, vagina looked like.
  REICHERT: Big—big spender.
  RIDGWAY: And of course I got caught and got whipped, you know.
  REICHERT: You should've given her a dollar instead of a penny.[11]

- In trying to find out how a dead dog came to be next to one of the Green River victims at a dump site in area called Star Lake, Reichert asked: "Was it around the neighbor—, did it happen to kind of wander down and just bark or something when you were trying to get rid of the body? Now that would make sense, see . . . you don't choke the dog doggie style. . . . Like your favorite style (laughs)."
  RIDGWAY: Yeah, (unintelligible) doggie style, yeah, doggie.[12]
  REICHERT: Pretty good for a sheriff, huh (laughs)?

- REICHERT: Did you ever think about somehow trying to figure out a way to keep it?
  RIDGWAY: Never, uh, never, never thought about cutting them off or anything like that.
  REICHERT: Maybe keep, you know, in the, in the freezer or something?
  RIDGWAY: I never thought about it. Never thought about that or, or anything that, uh, uh, from a woman's body, to keep it someplace, it never, uh, thought of cutting anything off like, like a breast or something like that.
  REICHERT: How come?
  RIDGWAY: I don't know . . .
  REICHERT: Plus, your wife when, uh, open up a freezer and see a boob in there. . . . Wouldn't be good?
  RIDGWAY: Or a, or a clitoris in there, a couple of them, you know.
  REICHERT: You'd have a lot of explaining to do?

RIDGWAY: Uh-huh.

REICHERT: (laughs).

RIDGWAY: Or girlfriend, uh, come over, hey, I need to get some ice out of the refrigerator.

REICHERT: Yeah.

RIDGWAY: What's this?

REICHERT: (laughs) Exactly. Well, and then what would you say?

RIDGWAY: Uh, I don't know what I would say. Uh, maybe, uh, those are, uh, oysters.

REICHERT: Think she'd buy that?[13]

RIDGWAY: Uh, (unintelligible) she cook it up.[14]

In attempting to convince Ridgway the two were simply having "a good 'old time'" "sittin' in a bar," the sheriff desecrated the victims. To the sheriff the end justified the means.[15] In return Reichert obtained nothing new. And he unleashed his displeasure, again: "They're pissed. They're tired of your crap. They're tired of your bullshit. They're tired of your lies. They're tired of your attitude now since the plea because you've not been cooperative."[16]

Reichert made it a point to be the last King County Police officer to speak with Ridgway on December 16, 2003. On that day he took a moment to call Ridgway a coward for choosing to kill women and choking them from behind. And he emphasized that nobody was going to feel sorry for him.

The plethora of interrogation techniques and persuasive strategies employed by investigators for six months were successful in some ways. The remains of several missing women were found, and society learned the fate of most of the women who disappeared during the long running murder mystery known as the Green River Murders case. In the end, though, King County Police felt cheated. They believed Ridgway failed to divulge many secrets. Ridgway's efforts to hide specific facts was obvious throughout the confession. Not so obvious was his subtle attempt to reinvent himself amid the acrimony. In his own simple, unsophisticated way, he had an agenda. Ridgway regularly served up vignettes that were intended to humanize him. He told of occasionally buying the "ladies" on the street food, a jacket or a pair of boots.

RIDGWAY: That's what everybody calls me is monster.

DET. JENSEN: Well . . . I don't recall having [hearing] anybody around here say that.

RIDGWAY: Yeah, the news and stuff like that says it.

JENSEN: But you don't wanna be portrayed as a monster do you?

RIDGWAY: No. I wanted to be portrayed . . . did all the killings . . . but also the one that helped find the bodies.[17]

As early as the fifth day of the interrogation, Ridgway started spinning details of the murders to fit his personal psychological needs and influence what the world thought of him. His most elaborate concoction involved Carol Christensen, the young mother who took a job along the prostitution strip while separated from her husband. She was the victim found in Maple Valley with a paper bag over her head and fish about her body. Ridgway's initial story to his attorney and police included a lengthy description of how Ridgway cared for Christensen's body after he killed her in his house. According to Ridgway, Christensen was special so he kissed her, caressed her hair, cuddled her, spoke kind words to her, and redressed her. Ridgway did redress Christensen, but it was to throw the investigation off. Everything else was a lie.

Ridgway always sought to minimize his sexual behavior. The investigators and the psychologists asked Ridgway if he considered himself a child molester since he once convinced a cousin to show her pubic area. Ridgway characterized the incident as mere child's play, even though he was much older than the girl. It seemed to interrogators, too, that Ridgway was a rapist. Ridgway protested strongly, arguing that he paid for the women and they should produce. His interrogators pointed out that Ridgway always took his money back after killing them. In fact, they stated, he robbed his victims after the murder. He would rummage through their undergarments and the inside tips of their shoes. He then would use his victims' money to pay for gas to prey or to convince another victim to hop in his truck. Detective Sue Peters asked, Do you think you're a rapist?"

RIDGWAY: No.
PETERS: Why?
RIDGWAY: I'm a . . . I'm a killer. I killed 'em.
PETERS: You don't like that word, do you?
RIDGWAY: I don't like that word because I . . . uh, I don't fit in that category. I'm a killer.[18]

Perhaps Ridgway fought the labels *child molester* and *rapist*—and desired to label himself a killer with a heart—because he understood the stigma society and prison places on such criminals. In prison, child molesters and rapists occupy the lowest social status and, often, are the targets of threats, sexual abuse, and death. All in all, Gary Leon Ridgway's repeated use of euphemisms to characterize himself and his behavior amounted to denial. Even after he had been apprehended and was about to be sent off to prison, he refused to acknowledge his hideous and repulsive deeds.

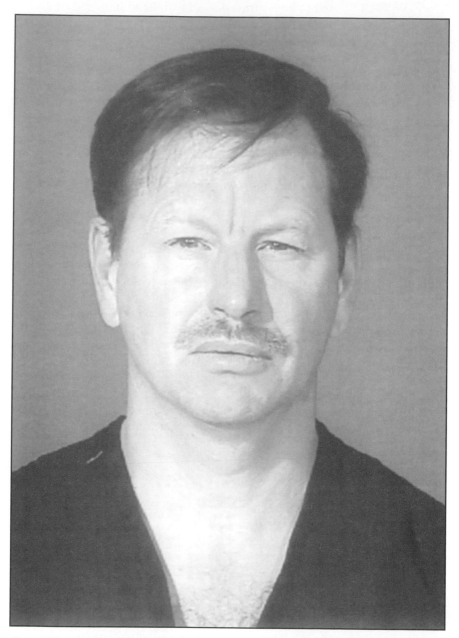

Green River Killer Gary Leon Ridgway after his arrest. *(Courtesy of King County Police.)*

CHAPTER

Evolution of a Serial Killer

10

I just had no release point for my rage other than to kill a person. . . . They meant less than a dog did.

Gary Leon Ridgway
Green River Killer[1,2]

Why did Gary Leon Ridgway kill?

For years that question tore at everyone even remotely familiar with the Green River Murders case. Theories abound as to why serial killers kill. Perhaps Ridgway was born with a psychological propensity to take lives, as some pundits who study serial killers would have everyone believe. Or did he suffer blunt head trauma as an infant or youth, causing neurological damage and making him more prone to violent behavior? There is no doubt Ridgway suffered from some level of cognitive dysfunctionalism, which at times manifested itself in learning and articulation problems. No one is certain whether Ridgway possessed his initial urge to kill from birth or whether he acquired it after a hard knock on the head. What does appear evident is that Ridgway *evolved* into the serial killer he eventually became. His environment played a powerful role.

In his specific serial case, people wondered, Why did he select women to murder? Why prostitutes? Why did he choke them from behind? Why was blood not shed in the killings? Why did he insert rocks in their vaginas? Why did he visit his victims days after death? Why did he kill so many so effortlessly? Why was there no contrition?

The extensive investigation into the turbulent life of Ridgway provided the answers to the questions most relevant to his murderous habits. And with the persistence of the psychologists and investigators involved in the confession, Ridgway revealed the psychological triggers that help explain how he evolved from human to monster. His evolution began when he was a boy living in South King County in Washington and continued until the day investigators took him into custody in 2001. His complex transformation was rooted in many disciplines, among them sociology, psychology, theology, and criminology.

While most people felt relieved to finally get answers to the nagging questions, few were prepared for the graphic scheming and the unnatural rage toward women. The answers, when they came, brought renewed anguish and more perplexing questions.

A MOTHER'S TOUCH

Gary Leon Ridgway was born on February 18, 1949, in Salt Lake City, Utah, to Thomas and Mary Ridgway. The family moved to Washington state when Gary was a young boy. In all, the couple raised three sons: Gregory Lee, who was two years older than Gary, and Thomas Edward, who was two years younger than Gary. Both of Gary's parents worked long hours: his father as a bus driver and his mother as a salesperson in the men's clothing section of a department store. His father died in 1998, and his mother passed away three months before Gary's arrest in 2001.

The behavior that initiated prolonged psychological consternation began at a very early age. As a boy Gary Leon Ridgway had a tendency to wet the bed. Usually it was Ridgway's mother who discovered the accidents in the morning as her son slept. She would awaken Ridgway and hurry him into the bathtub. It became a routine that Ridgway would come to deplore. The constant bedwetting and bathing caused Ridgway much embarrassment in the family since his mother belittled him. After the bath, his mother dried his entire body.[3] His mother's practice may have been acceptable when Ridgway was a small boy, but it seemed inappropriate when Ridgway reached the age of 12 and became sexually aroused. Making matters worse was his mother's habit of wearing a bathrobe while bathing and drying Ridgway. At times, the robe opened, revealing her body. The regular episodes caused much sexual confusion for Ridgway. On the one hand, Ridgway became sexually attracted to his mother; on the other hand, Ridgway grew to dislike his mother for belittling him over bedwetting and his inability to learn. Two powerful opposites—love and hate—commingled deviantly in Ridgway's mind well before the age of 14.

On the love side, Ridgway fantasized about his mother. Ridgway told FBI Agent Dr. Mary Ellen O'Toole: "Just a fantasy of wanting to uh, have sex—to touch her, feel her body, um, to have her show me how to have sex, um, 'cause mothers teach you a lot a' things, you know."[4] Ridgway's mother "loved her body"[5] and often sunbathed outside. It was during those sunbathing sessions that Ridgway looked out a window from his home to fantasize sexually about his mother.

On the hate side, Ridgway contemplated hurting or killing his mother. One of his schemes called for setting the house on fire with his mother in it. In another plot, Ridgway would take a knife and slash his mother to deform her body since it was her body that she cherished. Or, Ridgway said to Dr. O'Toole, ". . . cut her throat just so she wouldn't, wouldn't, uh . . . stop uh, uh, uh, degrading me. . . . I couldn't remember things and that was the only way I could think of hurting her to get her to stop."[6]

Dr. O'Toole summed up Ridgway's familial revelations this way: "At some point we know that sex becomes uh, violence, and violent sex becomes erotic for a serial killer. That's a given. That's profiling 101 for us . . . at some point violence was erotic for you."[7]

Over and over again during Ridgway's lengthy interrogation the psychologists zeroed in on how his mother dressed and behaved. One psychologist characterized her dress habits as provocative, while another called it "dressed very provocatively whorish."[8] Several times the psychologists asked about the mother's flirtatious manners, especially while working in the men's clothing department, where she measured men's inseam to size pants and brought home stories of men getting "hard."

Ridgway agreed that his mother liked to dress very well, but downplayed any flirtatious habits. Primarily, Ridgway characterized his mother as a "clean freak"[9] whose bossy, temperamental behavior earned her the nickname "the warden"[10] among her sons. His mother was always in control of her boys' emotions, which Ridgway detested.

It was the love-hate tempest in Ridgway's mind that created and fostered his annihilation thinking. By the time Ridgway was in his mid-teens, he'd put a cat in a container and let it suffocate, set a structure fire, broken windows at a school with rocks, considered drowning a boy who splashed him while swimming, stabbed and seriously injured a 6-year-old boy, and desired to kill or disfigure his mother.

REJECTION

As Ridgway became a young adult, his mind was filled with anger, and he could brag of no meaningful interpersonal relationship with anyone except the family dog. The dog was the only living being he confided in. Perhaps some psychological intervention could have helped him deal with his troubled feelings, but he shared none of his frustrations with his mother, father, or brothers. No one knew of his pent-up hate and desire to strike out at women, not even the women he married or dated in subsequent years. And they would not be aware, until several decades later, that their treatment of Ridgway helped direct his vengeance toward women and, specifically, prostitutes.

Ridgway's first serious relationship in the late 1960s and early 1970s involved a woman named Claudia. While married, Ridgway was in the U.S. Navy, which sent him to the Philippines. While in the Philippines, Ridgway paid for his first prostitutes. And it was there he became fascinated with women in bars inserting bottle of beers in their vagina. That fascination would prompt him to insert rocks in his victims' vaginas. Ironically, Ridgway later would claim that his wife moved in with another man while Ridgway served in the military. It was Ridgway who filed for a divorce after only one year of marriage. At the time, he was in his early 20s. He cited "mental cruelty" and to get back at his wife he spread rumors that she was a whore. Ridgway liked to explain: "It was my way of degrading her in my mind. If anybody asked, that's what I would say."[11]

Ridgway's next marriage came a couple of years after his divorce. He married a woman named Marcia, who was two years younger than him. In 1975, the couple had a son, and they named him Matthew Leon Ridgway. Ridgway eventually decided that Marcia was "a little bit too much overweight"[12] and not pretty enough. It did not help the relationship that Ridgway felt Marcia always wanted to be in charge, like his mother. The two could not communicate to resolve problems. When she was ready to talk about a marital problem, Ridgway was not. And when Ridgway seemed ready, she was not. That unproductive interplay led one day in 1979 to Ridgway experimenting with getting his wife's attention. He came up behind her and began choking her. Ridgway told his interrogators: "I was angry at her for not answering me and that was my way of getting her to answering me and I didn't know how . . . without hitting her, slapping her or anything like that which I didn't wanna do."[13] The next day Marcia told her father of the incident, who warned Ridgway never to assault his daughter again. Ridgway never did, but he learned that choking Marcia sexually aroused him. That discovery—erotic violence—prompted him to begin sneaking up on his wife from behind. And, eventually, the choking episode would be the beginning of Ridgway choking his Green River victims from behind.

It was after divorcing Marcia in 1981 and buying a house near the prostitution strip that Ridgway began regularly frequenting prostitutes. Several times he maneuvered behind prostitutes and began choking them, but he let go before killing them. To Ridgway, picking up hookers was "like candy in a dish."[14] And they all seemed to be attractive with nice figures, unlike his former wife. Very quickly, Ridgway learned the ways of the street and how to avoid protective, bad-tempered pimps. To his chagrin, though, he ended up the victim of shrewd streetwalkers. Several times Ridgway was fleeced of his wallet and money. Once a cunning prostitute somehow removed a chain from around his neck while they had sexual intercourse. The jewelry piece had been given to him by a girlfriend, and Ridgway would never forget the theft. It could be argued that his loss of his chain was the impetus for him taking the Green River victims' jewelry after murdering them.

Between marriages and prostitutes, Ridgway spent time with half a dozen girlfriends. Some he met at Parents Without Partners meetings and dances. Although the relationships were sexually satisfying, they led nowhere. In the end, he felt they all dumped him.

All in all, Ridgway saw himself as a failure when it came to women. He had gone through two failed marriages and several unfruitful relationships. Rejection best described his attempts to forge a meaningful union with a woman. He felt like a loser, and that angered him. With every unsuccessful relationship, Ridgway became angrier at women. He could not live without them emotionally or physically. He yearned to love and be loved. And his sexual drive demanded he have sex three or four times a week. Slowly, his anger turned to rage when he reflected on how much women controlled his emotions, like his mother used to do. He began to detest every aspect of femininity, especially a woman's vagina, which Ridgway considered the source of all his problems. It possessed too much power and control over men.

His rage was exacerbated by all his other concerns and pressures.

- He felt cheated when he bought his home off Military Road. The roof leaked, it smelled like dog urine, and birds had taken to inhabiting the attic.
- He felt cheated in the divorce with Marcia. He did not like the custody arrangement or support payments.
- He felt cheated by the women at his work at Kenworth. To Ridgway, the women would "manipulate people to get the easy jobs."[15]

Schemes to hurt or annihilate surfaced continuously in Ridgway's mind during the early 1980s. At one store he put a scoop of plaster in flour. At another supermarket he sprinkled rat poison on birdseed. He also put rat poison on croutons at a fast-food restaurant.

The angrier Ridgway became, the more frequent were his visits to the street to sexually release the pressures of life. Caught up in his life with the prostitutes, he became enmeshed in events that enraged him. The streetwalkers showed no respect for Ridgway in the cat-and-mouse game over money and several times infected him with a venereal disease. Ultimately, Ridgway suffered public humiliation when he was arrested in a police sting operation involving an undercover female officer posing as a hooker. Adding insult to injury, it was a woman who "duped" him.

> My self respect for myself just went down the tube . . . that's when I started killin'. There was just problem and problem after problem, and no way of releasing, nobody to talk to anybody about it.[16] I just got fed up . . . I choked a person every month after that, and then hit the Green Rivers and I had what five in a month.[17]

RAGE

It was in the beginning of summer 1982 that all the psychological compo-
nents came together to create the mind-set that made Ridgway a serial
killer. All his thoughts gravitated to an invisible spot in his brain to shape a
mood to kill: his childhood bedwetting, his sexual fascination for his
mother, his frustration of women controlling his emotions, his voracious
appetite for sex, his endless blunders, his hate of women, his refusal to seek
counseling; his learning deficiencies, his habit of stammering and stuttering
when trying to articulate his frustration, and his inability to fit in society.
The mood justified the anger, and the anger ignited the rage that triggered
the urge to kill.

When Ridgway developed his mood to kill, it appears that he, himself,
did not completely understand his reasons for killing, who he had evolved
into. Somehow he thought external forces—bossy women, lazy coworkers,
conniving hookers—triggered his desire to murder. In the initial stages of
the Green River serial killings, Ridgway thought he was deciding which
woman to kill as the proposition and sex act progressed. He believed he
would kill the woman if:

- She did not talk dirty to him.
- She did not perform as he expected her to.
- She refused to do the sex acts he desired.
- She did not touch him in the right places.
- She asked him to hurry up.
- She only wanted the money and did not care about the sex act.
- She lied to him.
- The sound of a truck passing by or plane flying over head interrupted
  his concentration.
- Ridgway could not have a climax.

For a while, Ridgway even believed that his rage surfaced because he
could not experience ideal lovemaking with the prostitutes: showering in a
comfortable room, foreplay, having romantic sex, and falling asleep in each
other's arms until morning.

In fact, Ridgway was in denial. He wanted to believe that outside
forces triggered a kill. He wanted to believe that he was not responsible for
his murderous acts. The truth was, he picked up women to kill, whether
they performed well or not. They were as good as dead once they climbed
into his old pickup truck and fixed their eyes on his wad of money. By the
time Ridgway's killing mood crystalized, he hated women so much he
blamed them for all of his troubles, including their own deaths. "Why did I
hate 'em?" Ridgway was asked during his interrogation. "Because . . .

women had control over me and don't like being controlled . . . I didn't care anything about 'em."[18] "They're the cause of my problems, women. The divorces. The lies they told me."[19]

DET. SUE PETERS: So you took your rage out on these girls?
RIDGWAY: Yes, I did.
PETERS: They didn't mean anything to you. You weren't goin' home to 'em every day.
RIDGWAY: No.
PETERS: So basically, they were . . . they were like garbage. It didn't matter. That's kinda what you're telling me, correct?
RIDGWAY: Yes.[20]

Later in the interrogation Ridgway would add:

> I took . . . took the towel and wrapped around their neck and pulled 'em and killed 'em. Some I used, ah, ah, a tie . . . I pulled 'em back and I put my legs in the back of her back on some of the women, and just pulled as hard as I could to kill 'em. I, ah, I did it because I hated them. And I had . . . and after I killed 'em I mighta screwed a few of 'em but I didn't give a shit, they were just pieces of trash to me. They were . . . *they were garbage.*[21] . . . I don't give a shit. Ah, sorry, but that's just the way I feel about those women. I had control and that's what it . . . what it all comes down to is control of those bitches. I told 'em to . . . to shut up and don't yell and I'll let you go, but I kept on choking and didn't. . . . I didn't give a shit about givin' 'em . . . givin' 'em . . . getting 'em up to . . . I didn't wanna get caught. I didn't have no love and I didn't . . . nobody loved me so fuck 'em all.[22]

Sometimes Ridgway was so upset he would stand on a victim's throat to kill her. And as he murdered many of the women, he called them names and blamed them for him having to kill them. Ridgway evolved into such a coldhearted killer that he murdered even the women who begged to live so they could go home to care for their children.

Nothing seemed to faze Ridgway at the height of his erotic rage.

He took to visiting his dead victims in the woods to have sex. Why? The idea was planted in his mind as a boy. According to Ridgway, he once overheard his father telling other adults about working at a mortuary and seeing a male employee having sex with a dead woman. That image stuck in Ridgway's mind and apparently prompted him to practice necrophilia with many of his victims.

Ridgway's many years of success without being caught emboldened him to think of evolving into another murderous phase: savagery. He fantasized about hurting women while they were still alive. He dreamed of gouging out their eyes and cutting off their tongue, burning their pubic hair, inserting footballs and fireworks in their vaginas, and inserting a pole

up the vagina and setting it upright. Most of all, Ridgway thought of tortur-
ing their vaginas to make women realize how they psychologically tortured
men with their sexuality. Said Ridgway to investigators:

> That part of her body is what the woman is trappin' the . . . the man with,
> you know, a man will do anything to . . . to have sex with a woman. . . .[23]
> Pleasure in killing is to uh, get s . . . you know, be control . . . to ha-have sex
> with 'em if I wanted afterwards, and to uh, take away uh, uh, another
> woman that, so she won't hurt anybody else.[24]

At times, Ridgway contemplated shocking the community by leaving
body parts at a schoolyard or putting a head in a shoebox and leaving it on
top of a police car.

THE JUDITH FACTOR

After several years of flaunting his macabre proclivities with impunity,
Ridgway sought to halt, if not reverse, his morbid psychological evolution.
Why? In 1985, he met a woman he liked, a woman that needed him more
than he needed her. Her name was Judith, and she was five years older
than him. She depended on him, especially since she had a bad back. To
Ridgway, she was worth trying to do what other serial killers historically
had failed to do: stop killing. The couple met in 1985 at Parents Without
Partners and lived together before getting married in 1988.

Unbeknownst to Judith, she became a restraint to Ridgway's serial
killing. She influenced his mood toward women enough where he thought
of the good times he could have with a woman instead of focusing on the
bad times and seeking vengeance. She changed his daily routine to such an
extent that he found it difficult to find time to kill. And that came to pass
only because he allowed a woman to influence his daily thinking. Life with
Judith meant attending church and reading the Bible regularly. And it required Ridgway to help care for the family pets. Ridgway and Judith gar-
dened and frequented swap meets. Judith even convinced Ridgway to sell
Amway products and attend a seminar out of town. By the late 1980s,
Ridgway had evolved into a traditional family man.

During his interrogation, Ridgway tried convincing Green River investigators that he had not killed a woman since he met Judith. Ridgway said

> And then I stopped, cold turkey after that, and that was, that's the way it
> happened, 'cause it's just got to, it's got to stop. I caring more about Judith
> than killing the women. . . . And that, that made me feel better. I had
> somebody to care for, cared for Judith, and uh, my, I was coming down off
> 'a that hate I had. I got busy doin' other things. . . .[25] I didn't kill any more.
> Judith was worth more to me than killin', that's why I stopped.[26]

When Ridgway offered that explanation, Detective Randy Mullinax exploded:

> So havin' a fucking dog or Peaches the Poodle or some fucking thing like that is suppose to suddenly cause you to be cured of killin' prostitutes. We're suppose to sit here and believe that you're able to just bam, stop that urge! 'Cause you got Peaches ridin' around in your lap, and you go the motor home, you got Judith, you got a life.[27]

In eventually admitting he killed after meeting Judith, Ridgway explained that he lied to keep Judith from knowing he murdered women during their relationship. In truth, Ridgway did change his behavior dramatically while with Judith and that, arguably, saved the lives of countless women. Judith acted as a deterrent in keeping Ridgway on a short leash. She expected him home promptly after work, kept close track of the family money, and insisted on doing most things together. However, Ridgway managed to find ways to fulfill his deviant behavior. He lied to Judith about visiting his parents' home on his way home from work, and he skimmed change from their yard sales. Short on time and cash, Ridgway picked up fewer prostitutes and was forced to satisfy his sexual cravings in urban areas not conducive to killing. When Ridgway did kill, the slayings were less planned since he was in a hurry and the emphasis was on sex, not vengeance. Less planning meant more mistakes. Still, Ridgway went undetected on the strip.

As incredulous as it seems, Ridgway made a strong effort to undo his killing mood, which had taken decades to create through a complex evolutionary process. During the Judith years, Ridgway wrote these initials inside his work locker: "NK and DK." They stood for "No Kill. Don't Kill." Ridgway told interrogators: "I had it written on my hand and stuff, and that helped me stop. . . . Plus also I loved Judith."[28]

DET. MULLINAX: You get real emotional every time you talk about Judith.
RIDGWAY: Um-hm. (yes)
MULLINAX: Like you are right now.
RIDGWAY: Yeah. Yes, I do.
MULLINAX: Why.
RIDGWAY: 'Cause I screwed up. . . . Screwed her bad.[29]

WARNING: THE FOLLOWING SUMMARY CONTAINS GRAPHIC AND DISTURBING DESCRIPTIONS OF VIOLENT CRIMINAL ACTS AND MAY NOT BE SUITABLE FOR ALL READERS. IN PARTICULAR, FAMILY MEMBERS AND FRIENDS OF VICTIMS ARE CAUTIONED THAT THIS DOCUMENT DESCRIBES HIGHLY DISTURBING ELEMENTS OF THE CRIMES IN GRAPHIC DETAILS.

CHAPTER

In Search of Closure

11

I then drove down to the Green River. I hadn't been there in over 20 years. There were two fishermen standing on the bank where Opal was found. Families and a couple in love were walking, laughing, being happy, perhaps talking about their dreams and future plans. I sat on the bank and cried.

Garrett Mills, brother of Green River victim Opal C. Mills[1]

Green River Killer Gary Leon Ridgway's confession was supposed to bring "closure" for Seattle and the many people touched by the historic Green River Murders case. At least that was what officials promised when they allowed Ridgway to live in exchange for revealing his deadly secrets. But no one ever specified what exactly closure meant or included or how one reached it. Everyone simply seemed to accept the notion that the confession would make everything okay and everyone involved in the case could get back to living and creating new relationships. The confession did *legally* close the book on the Green River investigation, but the vast majority of the people enmeshed in the case have not found closure to the decades of emotional distress. In actuality, the confession exacerbated everyone's despair since Ridgway provided countless raw, disturbing vignettes of his abduction and murder of over sixty women. While the confession may have helped unravel the 20-year mystery, it failed to offer peace of mind and probably prolonged emotional healing.

An analysis of the involvement of the various participants in the tragic case revealed who found closure and who will be mired in grief or a dysfunctional life for years to come. The analysis also identified the many and varied obstacles and traumas that have hindered the attainment of closure. It is evident from examining the lives and comments of the participants that closure—an emotional reconciliation with the loss of an individual or relationship—had to come from within the individual and did not automatically surface when Ridgway confessed. The confession's role in closure depended on how each participant processed it and how they responded.

GARY LEON RIDGWAY

Arguably, Ridgway found overall closure upon his capture. Confessing, he told interrogators, lifted a heavy burden from his shoulders. He had never experienced nightmares over his killings, but he had always felt a pressure on his chest. Confessing gave him relief, and he felt relieved that he no longer had to worry about his wife discovering he was still paying for sex and killing women. Revealing that he was the Green River Killer also gave Ridgway the ability to sleep easier at night, more than two hours a night. Ridgway lost his freedom, forever, but that did not trouble him. His life revolved so much around his thoughts—independent of interpersonal relationships and external happenings—that he planned to simply adapt to his new environment. The following exchange with King County Sheriff David G. Reichert showed Ridgway's nonchalance toward ending up in prison:

REICHERT: And you're gonna need to take somebody there.
RIDGWAY: Gonna take, you know, God there to help me out.
REICHERT: Um-hm. (yes) He's not gonna go. Does that surprise ya?
RIDGWAY: I'll prob'ly be alone then.
REICHERT: You'll be alone?
RIDGWAY: Um-hm. (yes)[2]
REICHERT: He's not gonna go with you. Does that bother you?
RIDGWAY: It bothers me, but been alone most a my life anyway, so . . .[3]

Judith, Ridgway's wife, did not fair as well at the end of the ordeal. She had lost her husband, privacy, and reputation. Her sexual preferences were detailed in confession transcripts made available to anyone who wished to read them. Ridgway's arrest assured that she always would be known as the wife of the Green River Killer. The shame of being lied to and publicly humiliated prevented her from achieving her closure, an end to her hiding and living a normal life. Ridgway's two other former wives also were forced to keep a low profile in life, always in fear of having their past revealed. Their sexual desires were described in legal records, too. Ridgway's numerous in-laws hid from the news media, and some moved out of Washington State. Some shuddered when recalling family social functions in which they greeted Ridgway with a hug. Matthew, Ridgway's adult son, considered changing his name to distance himself from his infamous father and his link to one of the country's most horrific serial murder cases. By the time Ridgway was arrested, his parents had died.

INVESTIGATORS

For over two decades investigators lived amid the trauma that Ridgway inflicted. Hour after hour, week after week, month after month, year after year, they interviewed grieving parents and crawled on their knees through dirt and leaves recovering flesh and bones. Often, they worked into the night and weekends trying to come up with the clues that would solve the case, that would bring closure. Eventually the stress would get to every investigator in one fashion or another. And on at least one occasion the King County sheriff sent a psychologist to the Green River Task Force to coax detectives into discussing their emotions.

The pressure affected investigators at home and at work. During the height of the discovery of skeletal remains, David Reichert was still a detective, and he began questioning human compassion. He asked his wife, Julie, to stop telling him she loved him. His wife complied.[4] King County Police Detective Tom Jensen invested almost as many years on the Green River serial murders as Reichert, the first detective on the case. More than any other investigator, Jensen intimately knew the suffering the murders caused the victims' relatives. Once while interrogating Ridgway, Jensen broke down and cried. Often, too, he became very angry at Ridgway when the killer was less then forthcoming in giving up details that would help everyone learn what happened to specific women.

For the most part, investigators achieved professional closure. They experienced bouts of depression and grief triggered by the human loss, but they, personally, did not lose a loved one. Therefore, it was easier for them to find closure after the arrest and confession. They were a step removed from bereavement. In the end, investigators failed to achieve complete professional and person closure. They were convinced Ridgway retained some of the victims' jewelry and other personal possessions, but they were unable to persuade him to give them up. Investigators also felt a sense of failure in not recovering the remains of several missing Green River victims.

It could be said that some investigators found it difficult to feel a sense of professional closure even with the resolution of the case. King County Police Major Richard Kraske believed King County Sheriff Bernard Winskoski and politicians denied him the resources to search for the Green River Killer in the initial months of the serial murders in 1982. He felt shunned by other administrative officers, and he retired with haunting thoughts that he failed to capture Ted Bundy in the 1970s and Ridgway in the 1980s. King County Police Detective John Blake was given the job of analyzing information when the Green River Task Force was formed in 1984. He was certain a Kent attorney was the Green River Killer and for months battled with other investigators to convince them of his theory. When fellow detectives and the FBI failed to support his investigative obsession, he denounced everyone related to the hunt and took a medical leave. Eventually he left the department with a stress disability. For years he attempted to convince non–law enforcement officials that he was right and had even staked his career on his hunch. He was wrong, but was unable to realize it until Ridgway offered information that only the killer could have known.

FAMILIES OF GREEN RIVER VICTIMS

Over the course of almost two decades—beginning in 1982 and ending in 2001 when the Green River case was solved—nearly 100 young women were murdered in and around the Seattle area. Many of those women were abducted and murdered in a way that strongly resembled the killing behavior of Ridgway. With each murder, investigators struggled to ascertain if the victim was related to the Green River Murders. The process was less than scientific and, often, arbitrary. When all was said and done, however, it was physical evidence and Ridgway's confession that dictated the final roll call. The 48 women named during the sentencing phase of the death penalty plea agreement on December 18, 2003, forever will be known as the official Green River victims. A look at the lives of the extended families of these specific victims illustrated the varied ways they have suffered grief and how multiple traumas have hindered or delayed closure. All experienced some form of prolonged mental anguish, inability to do their job, trouble concentrating, images of death, marital problems, sleeplessness, fear, loneliness, and a lack of hope. Year after year, with each new investigative development, the grief and bereavement became deeper and more complex. It was not surprising that most of the extended families were far from closure when they attended and spoke at Ridgway's sentencing.

A few relatives spoke of finding closure. One of them was Robert Rule, father of victim Linda Rule. At the time of Rule's death, her parents were divorced and she was living on the street.

> Mr. Ridgway. There are people that hate you. I'm not one of them. I forgive you for what you've done . . . you've made it difficult to live up to what I believe and that is what God says to do. And that's to forgive. And he doesn't say to forgive just certain people. He says to forgive all. So you are forgiven sir.[5]

For Robert Rule, the confession helped find closure: "I appreciate that you said you killed our daughter. There's definitely closure when you know who did it. And you did. And I am sorry for you."[6] The confession helped Kathy Mills find closure, too. She told the packed courtroom during the sentencing:

> I first of all would like to thank Mr. Ridgway for there being no trial. That would be hard to take. This is enough. . . . You have held us in bondage all these years because we have hated you. We wanted to see you die, but it's all over now. And that is, providing we can forgive you. Gary Leon Ridgway, I forgive you. I forgive you. You can't hold me anymore. I'm through with you. I have a peace that is beyond human understanding. My life now is to live to one day be with little Opal. . . . And I also have to forgive you because that is what the word of God says. I have to forgive you so I can be forgiven my sins.[7]

Clearly, spirituality played a major role in Rule and Mills forgiving Ridgway and finding closure. The majority of the extended families offered no forgiveness and showed little signs of closure. Instead, they spoke of being trapped in a cycle of hurt, grief, anger, hate, and loathing. Day in and day out their lives had revolved around playing and replaying in their minds happier days and lamenting what might have been.

Mills' son, Garrett, keeps visualizing the childhood habits that characterized his sister, Opal. He recalls her love of braided pigtails, a bear lunch box, and swings. He nicknamed her "Little Peanut." The two siblings were inseparable, and Opal planned to name her children Garrett and Opal. One specific conversation still haunted Garrett: "I promised her that I would never leave her and I would never let anyone hurt her."[8]

Ridgway's inability to recall victim Debra Estes' face tormented Virginia Graham the most:

> You made the statement that you did not know Debbie or remembered her face or name. I will take this time to tell you about her. . . . I am a patient and hopeful person. You are going to die of something. It is then that I will have closure in my life. Not because you are dead, but because the evil you chose to become has left this earth and gone back to hell from where it came.[9]

Others wished Ridgway a painful death. Said Tim Meehan angrily:

> Now it's my turn. I'm done with you Gary. Finished. It's my turn to put you with garbage. . . . It's garbage like you, not these victims, that you took their lives that doesn't deserve to live on. But now I can only hope that someday, someone gets the opportunity to choke you unconscious 48 times. So you can live through the horror that you put our daughters, our sisters, our mothers through. And then, sometime after that, whether it be the 51st or the 60th or the 64th or whatever, you won't know when it's

coming. That they choke you till your dead . . . and stand on your throat. To me, you are already dead. . . . May God have no mercy on your soul.[10]

Closure for a great number of relatives seemed especially impossible because the deaths deeply affected several generations in an extended family. The relatives who testified at the sentencing spoke of emotional distress to four generations: grandparents, parents, siblings, and children of the victims. One victim left behind five children.

The death of Sandra K. Gabbert, 17, traumatized her grandmother, mother, and sister. Sandra's mother, Nancy Gabbert, tearfully recounted how the murder destroyed the life of Sandra's older sister:

> The disappearance of her sister caused inexpressible emotional trauma . . . (she) began to suffer periods of anxiety, denial, guilt, and period of depression . . . (she) lost her job. She lost her apartment.[11] After Sandra's remains were found, her sister's periods of depression became longer, increasingly overwhelming and debilitating. Her behavior became erratic and sometimes very reckless. She started drinking, using street drugs, and carousing with vagrants and criminals. Eventually she met a good hearted man and fell in love. They had two beautiful daughters.[12]

But Sandra's sister was "haunted by grief and plagued with depression," and eventually "she put an end to her own pain and suffering."

The trauma and grief affected some relatives so profoundly that they were rendered dysfunctional for life.

Jose Malvar, Jr., brother of Marie M. Malvar, gritted his teeth when he spoke, "I'm angry, I will always be angry. I will never have closure. I will never have my sister back in my life . . . you broke my family apart 20 years. For 20 long years . . . a lot of Christmasses and a lot of birthday parties were missed 'cause of you."[13]

"There isn't any life for me anymore," cried Carol Estes, mother of Debra Estes. "I just go through life day by day. And trying to hold myself together."[14]

Victim Tracy Winston's brother, Kevin Winston, still had tremendous trouble dealing with his sister's murder in 1983:

> I was 12 years old and a classmate came up to me and said: "I heard your sister is missing. She's on the Green River Killer's list. And I said. You don't know what you're talking about. Get out of my face. Went home that night. And I asked my mom where Tracy was. And she said she didn't know. And from that day this is what I get. Every day, every day. There is not one day that doesn't go by that I don't feel like shit. You don't understand what you've done. I'm a grown man and I can't help but cry, snot coming out of my nose. . . . You ruined my family.[15]

In an attempt to deal with her death, Winston tattooed his sister's birthday on his left arm. On his right arm, he tattooed eight angels. Seven list the evidence that was going to be used against Ridgway before he decided to confess. The eighth angel represents his sister.

Winston has promised to never let Ridgway forget Tracy. Every year on her birthday Winston plans to mail Ridgway a picture of his sister.

UNOFFICIAL GREEN RIVER VICTIMS

Bewildered—that is how the families of six murdered women felt when the Green River Murders investigation came to a close in 2003. For years their daughters had been on the list of Green River victims. The young women were missing and presumed dead since they had not been heard from for years and their bodies had not been found. Investigators felt certain the women were murdered by the man known as the Green River Killer. And with each new development, investigators included the womens' names and photographs with information distributed to the public. Investigators still think the women were victims of the Green River Killer, but the six were not included in final charges against Ridgway for one or more of several reasons: (1) Their remains have never been found; (2) There exists no physical evidence linking their disappearance with Ridgway; and (3) Ridgway cannot recall abducting and killing them.

There may never be closure for those extended families.

Ridgway told interrogators he remembers specifically murdering one of the women on the Green River missing list, Kace A. Lee, and depositing her body near a drive-in theater off the prostitution strip. Her body has never been found.

There may never be closure, too, for the families of two dozen or so women killed in the 1990s. The abduction and murder of several of the women fit Ridgway's murderous behavior pattern, but Ridgway denied killing them.

Ridgway was adamant he killed a teenage girl shortly after King County Police unsuccessfully searched his home for evidence in 1987. But investigators refused to charge him with that slaying, partly since Ridgway was unable to explain what specifically had been done to the victim's sexual organs. Again, no closure for that family.

CHILDREN OF THE DEAD

The littlest victims of the Green River Murders case turned out to be the many children orphaned by the serial killings. Almost two decades later, they, too, sought answers to put the tragedy behind them, if that was possible. Their trauma began as children, when their minds were the most vulnerable. And they still felt the loss of their mother when Ridgway was sentenced. Of the dozen or so children born to the victims, two expressed their grief publicly. Said Sarah King, daughter of victim Carol Christensen, who was found dead with the fish and wine bottle about her:

> Never in my years did I ever think that I would be standing up here facing the man who killed my mother. I was only five when my mother died, when my dad told me that she was never coming home. I found out on Mother's Day. There's nothing anybody can say or ever do for me that will bring my mother back. . . . The one thing I want you, Gary Ridgway, to know . . . I was that daughter at home . . . waiting for my mom to come home. And I tried to grow up for the last twenty years. This has been my life. I didn't have a life before this. I was so young. . . . I had to defend my mother. She wasn't a prostitute. She was a mother. She was a wife. She was a sister. And we miss her. . . . And no matter what you say, I will never, ever, ever forgive you. I will never forgive you.[16]

Daryle Imburgia also felt compelled to describe his loss. His mother was Delise L. Plager, who vanished in October 1983 near a bus stop in Seattle. At the time, he was two years old. Imburgia said

> I never got to be with her. My sisters have never got to be with her. We don't have any memories of her. The grandchildren will never meet her. I have two beautiful sons that will never know her. . . . And I think its amazing you sit here and stare back at me not having any feelings at all.[17]

The only relationship he has ever had with his mother has been vicariously through a tattoo.

"I got her name tattooed to my neck," Imburgia explained. "That is the only thing I'll ever have of hers. That is the only thing I'll have to remember her by."[18]

Relatives of Becky Marrero were invited to the sentencing to express what effect the serial murders had on their lives, but they did not respond to the invitation. Marrero disappeared in December 1982 after getting a phone call at home. Ridgway was not charged with her probable death since her remains had not been found and Ridgway could not recall killing her. Although Marrero's family was not represented at the sentencing, her daughter, Shawnte Marie Fashaw, spoke about her life shortly after Ridgway's arrest in 2001. In her interview Fashaw minced no words in describing a chaotic existence since her mother's disappearance. At the time Fashaw was almost three years old. Before and after Fashaw's birth, Marrero lived and associated with boyfriends who physically and mentally abused her. Once, one of her boyfriends kicked her in the crotch so hard she required hospitalization to repair the damage. After Marrero disappeared, Fashaw lived with her grandmother, who believed her daughter was being held captive and one day would escape and walk in the front door.

Unfortunately, Fashaw's life mirrored that of her mother. She became involved with the proverbial wrong crowd, drank alcohol heavily, dropped out of school, and became pregnant and gave birth to a little girl out of wedlock.

"I was evil. I ran away a lot," said Fashaw, who began leaving home at 13.[19]

In 1999, Fashaw began having the same nightmare. She dreamed of someone raping and killing her. Just as she was about to be killed, she woke up.

For as long as she can remember, Fashaw has been paranoid of people. And for as long as she can recall, she has been aggressive, violent, toward men she dates. She says she can't help it.

Multiple traumatic events since childhood had a powerful effect on Fashaw's psyche. That trauma seems to have spawned some of her aggressive behavior.

Try as they might, it is unlikely Fashaw and most of the other relatives of Green River victims will find closure. They will grieve the loss of their loved one and, to some extent, be driven by emotions and behavior fostered by the death of their daughter, sister, mother, or wife.

Closure, also, will prove elusive to the parents of five women who disappeared years ago. The women walked out of their homes one day and never came back. Someone has been waiting for them to return home since. The emptiness has caused pain for probably longer than the women lived. The families may have no idea if their loved one is among five skeletal remains discovered years ago by Green River investigators in Washington or Oregon.

Perhaps one day new forensic technology specific to identifying skeletal remains will unite the families with those remains to allow some closure. Even that may be an impossibility for one set of remains found in a suburb of Portland, Oregon, in April 1985. Those remains were lost while under care of the medical examiner's office in Portland.

CHASING THE DEVIL

GREEN RIVER, RUNNING RED

Through A Mother's Eyes

Through A Mother's Eyes

GARY RIDGWAY:THE GREEN RIVER KILLER

The Riverman

My Life Among the Serial Killers

RIVER

CHAPTER

Pop Culture 12

> I think I will write a book.... Maybe we should do it together ... Gary, man, that'd be history. No other case that I know of where the case detective and the killer worked together on a book. It'd be shocking.
>
> *David G. Reichert*
> *King County Sheriff*[1]

Dirt head—in police lingo, that is what investigators considered Green River Killer Gary Leon Ridgway. To them, he brought to mind a dirt clod, worthless and ready to disintegrate with the slightest Seattle drizzle. Here one moment, gone the next. Nothing lost. But to get Ridgway to cooperate, investigators sometimes had to make him feel like a diamond in the rough that everyone would want to examine and admire. Investigators appealed to his ego and the legacy he could create for himself as the most prolific serial killer in the country. Why should Ridgway believe them? The public reveled in such a paradox: They deplored evil and condemned the preying on young women, yet they bought the books, music, and films that glorified serial killers. Pop culture demanded that people love Jack the Ripper, the Boston Strangler, Son of Sam, the Zodiac, John Wayne Gacy, and *Silence of the Lambs*. And it would require that people fall in love with Gary Leon Ridgway as the antagonist in the historic Green River Murders drama. So it was that investigators decided to use the public's obsession with serial murder to try to trick Ridgway into divulging more secrets in his mind. That was part of the strategy when King County Sheriff David G. Reichert sat down to talk with Ridgway in 2003. Reichert already knew Ridgway enjoyed reading true crime magazines and dabbled in true crime books. It was Reichert's job to engage Ridgway and warm him to the idea of a mass market venture to build him up.

REICHERT: Maybe I'll write a book. What do you think I should title it?

Ridgway suggested a title that belittled investigative efforts to catch him: "You could title uh, uh, 'Technology Caught the Green River Killer.'"[2]

Reichert ignored the jab to promote interaction. Together, they came up with: *Catching the Green River Killer; Solving the Worst Murder Cases;* and *Green River Killer Case Solved.* None seemed sensational enough to fit the bill. When their conversation touched on Reichert possibly running for governor, which would put Reichert in a position to sign Ridgway's death warrant if sentenced to death, they came up with the title: *From Search Warrant to Death Warrant.*

As the two natural enemies talked nonchalantly, Reichert produced the book *Killers Next Door* to appeal to Ridgway's ego. Reichert pointed out that the book only dedicated a page and a half to Ridgway. Not very much. If Ridgway was completely forthcoming with details of his murders, Reichert argued, it was likely future books would give him the respect and fame he deserved. Moreover, Ridgway could control how he was characterized by supplying every detail and not giving true crime writers room to fictionalize his killings.

"If you and I, uh, did one together . . . you know what that means?" asked Reichert. Ridgway responded: "That means I got to get this cloudiness out of my head and bring everything out."[3]

Reichert continued:

> That's how we can start doing this book thing together. This is our, your chance to start to tell your story. You know, so we can get it down and get it right, otherwise you're going to end up with a page and half and all these other guys are going to get, you know, full page books written about them. And they're going to make a lot of money. Does Judith need money? She's got no income. No way to survive.[4] She had a house, she had a nice house. She doesn't have shit anymore . . . and that's because of you. But are you going to help her?[5] You can make a lot of money off this book and a movie, you'll have enough to give, pay all the victims' families and give some to Judith, too.[6]

Movie? Ridgway thought actor Tom Cruise would play him. Reichert threw out the name Leslie Nielsen for his part.

When Ridgway claimed he could not provide additional details, Reichert tried another tack:

> I'm thinking maybe I just . . . I write it with Judith. Do you think she'd like me? She might have a lot of things to tell.[7] What I could do is get Judith and maybe all your wives and girlfriends. . . . That would be a good one. Lead detective sheriff and Ridgway's girlfriends and wives. . . . Forget you

and me.[8] Maybe she and I together could be . . . on the back (cover of the book). And my arm could be around her or something like that, like good buddies.

Reichert was attempting to goad Ridgway with jealousy. Ridgway did not bite. He said: "That'd probably sell a lot of books."[9]

"I don't know if I'd give her very much, though. I, 'cause I had more role than she did, really," Reichert said. "I'd probably be . . . probably be a 75/25 split for me. Yeah, but then you wouldn't get any."[10]

When Ridgway indicated he didn't need money in jail, Reichert opined, "Well, you're going to need some money in jail. . . . To keep yourself out of trouble. . . . If you had big money, and you know you could say, 'Hey, I need you for protection.' You know, I'd give you a couple hundred bucks here, you know, to keep safe."[11]

Clearly, Reichert seemed desperate in suggesting such an outrageous scenario. Or he never intended to keep his promise.

There was one thing Reichert did not lie about in his interrogation of Ridgway: writing a book. His would not be the first on the infamous serial murders, though. The case would produce several books, each with its positive perspective, along with controversies. To the families of the victims, books on the murders—no matter how authoritative or insightful—added insult to injury. To Helen Dexter, mother of Green River victim Constance Naon, all the authors would be "blood writers" out to "make tons of money from our suffering."[12]

The first book came out in 1990 with the title *The Search for the Green River Killer.* It chronicled the meandering investigation and documented why investigators had been unable to catch the Green River Killer. Although the authors did not name Ridgway in the book, they detailed the evidence against him and reasons why he could be the killer. On the negative side, the book revealed confidential investigative information valuable to ascertaining if a specific individual was the killer. Ridgway possessed a copy of the book in his Auburn, Washington, home when arrested in 2001.[13]

During the 1970s, King County Police Detective Robert Keppel was the lead investigator on the Ted Bundy murders of Western Washington. When the Green River Task Force was formed in 1984, Keppel was working for the Washington State Attorney General's Office as an investigator. In an effort to help solve the case, the state allowed Keppel to work with the task force as a consultant. It was while working in that capacity that he received a letter from Bundy, on death row in a Florida prison. To try to avoid the electric chair, Bundy offered to help investigators get inside the mind of the elusive Green River Killer. Bundy called him "Riverman." Having nothing to lose, Keppel and Reichert flew to Florida to interview

Bundy. When Keppel decided to write his long-awaited book on Bundy in 1995, he used the Green River case to draw attention to his work. He and his publishers titled the publication *The Riverman: How Ted Bundy and I Hunted the Green River Killer.* Keppel briefly discussed the Green River case in the book. Most of the book delved into the history of the Bundy investigation. The book drew even more controversy when Ridgway was arrested. Long before any trial, death-penalty deal, or confession, the photograph of Bundy on the cover of the book was replaced with Ridgway's photograph. In short, the book convicted Ridgway publicly before any adjudication. Several years later A&E produced a film based on the book. The film was dubbed *The Riverman* and aired in 2004. It followed the same story line as the book and received the same criticism as the book; it pretended to be about the Green River murders but it was not.[14]

The next book on the case turned out to be a fictionalized account by Roderick Thorp. It's title was *River: A Novel of the Green River Killings.* Although fiction, the author claimed in prepublication promotions that the primary suspect in the book was the killer and that suspect represented William J. Stevens III, a real Spokane, Washington, law student once investigated by the Green River Task Force. History proved the author wrong.[15]

Kathy Mills, mother of Green River victim Opal C. Mills, wrote a short book on how special her daughter had been and the factors that led the teenager to the streets. That 2002 book was published under the title *Through a Mother's Eyes: The Untold Story of Opal Charmaine Mills, Fifth Victim of the Green River Murders.*[16]

As soon as Ridgway pled guilty and was sentenced, the King County Journal of King County rushed to compile many of its news stories on the case and bound them into a book it called *The Green River Killer.* The book came out in 2003 and offered little beyond what the rest of the news media was reporting.[17]

The year 2004 brought a bumper crop of books on the Green River Murders.

Psychiatrist Helen Morrison authored *My Life among the Serial Killers: Inside the Minds of the World's Most Notorious Murderers.* She, like Keppel, exploited the Green River case. The front and back cover of the book highlight a photograph of Ridgway's face, insinuating that the book contains substantial material on the Green River Killer. It does not. Six and a half pages were dedicated to the investigation, and much of the superficial information could have been read in any one of hundreds of news stories on the case.[18]

A ghost writer assisted Reichert in penning his book titled *Chasing The Devil: My Twenty-Year Quest to Capture the Green River Killer.* The book revolved around Reichert rather than the investigation, and it minimized the vast contribution of dozens of investigators and law enforcement agencies. Most people viewed the book primarily as a tool to help Reichert get elected to the U.S. Congress.[19]

His memoir was succeeded by a book written by true-crime writer Ann Rule. It was titled *Green River Running Red: The Real Story of the Green River Killer—America's Deadliest Serial Murderer.* Odd the title contained the word "Red" since the murders involved little bloodshed, if any at all. Ridgway despised the sight of blood and avoided it. The method of death was asphyxia. This book's strength centered on showing the victims' human side, their lives before they ventured into the seedy streets.[20] In several of her books, Rule tended to create a personal link to the case she wrote about. Long before the publication of *Green River Running Red,* Rule claimed Ridgway attended some of her book signings and appeared to be stalking her. Ridgway debunked that claim in his interrogation. "I hear that she says I stalked her, but I didn't," said Ridgway.[21] "There's no reason for me to stalk her. . . . She's just not my type."[22] Ridgway's denial rang true. That was not his modus operandi.

Media critics were especially harsh on Rule and Reichert. *Seattle Post-Intelligencer* book critic John Marshall called Rule's book a disappointment and described it as a rambling chronicle of the case. Marshall thought Reichert's book focused too much on Reichert.[23]

No doubt more true-crime narratives will be written on the Green River Murders, some by the victims' relatives and some by those charged with legally defending the killer. There will never be a shortage of mass market books, songs, and films to anoint serial killers and give them notoriety worldwide. There is a shortage, however, of books that support the intellectual study of the serial killer phenomenon in an academic setting. Only during the mid-1980s did serious academic research begin surfacing to help affirm or negate the content in mass market publications. Perhaps it was that lack of research that motivated FBI Agent Dr. Mary Ellen O'Toole and Dr. Judith Becker to participate in the interrogation of Ridgway. Their first responsibility called for them to get into Ridgway's mind to convince him to give a complete, detailed picture of his murders so investigators could ascertain exactly how many women he killed and when. They did that, but somewhere during the interrogation each decided they wanted special or exclusive access to Ridgway in the future, after the adjudication of the case. Their efforts appeared dubious. They should not have been allowed to use their privileged access to try to horde knowledge about the Green River case. Each jockeyed for position to elbow out the other and any expert interested in questioning Ridgway to better understand his behavior.

O'Toole attempted to persuade Ridgway to work with her by telling him that the FBI's profiling unit was probably the world's best in understanding serial killers and Ridgway would be treated like an expert in serial killer matters. She explained that "you have control over it and you do it in an academic way and you do it in a way that is going to help educate or train law enforcement, maybe even mental health professionals."[24] Then she sought to record his permission. "I know you know we are on tape, but actually look into that camera and kind of let people know that you are committed to this process of seeing how . . . whether or not you would be in a position, based on your insights, to work with our unit."[25] Obediently, Ridgway said: "I would like to help the FBI . . . uh . . . to help educate them on what I was at that time when I was killing people and to see if it can help change somebody early in their development. That they won't turn out like me."[26]

Toward the end of the interrogation sessions, Defense Attorney Mark Prothero told Ridgway that after the sentencing all types of experts and researchers would be asking for interviews. Prothero discouraged Ridgway from giving any and asked him to refer all requests to him. Prothero then encouraged Ridgway to work with Becker, a psychologist working with the defense team:

> In your way you can contribute to the body of science out there about what we know about serial killers and potentially help society and that way if we can learn something more from you. . . . I sense that you have a pretty good relationship with Judith Becker. . . . Would you agree to have her come up and be that psychologist to delve into that, maybe write the book?[27]

Ridgway said yes. When Becker joined the two men in the interrogation room, she said: "I would be happy to do that . . . to work with you to, tell your story if that's something that you would like to do."[28]

At a later session, Becker came prepared to get Ridgway's commitment in writing:

> I put together a release so that, you know, um, I have a document indicating that you've given your consent for that. . . . And you might wanna read along with me. It says, 'I . . .' and then if you would read . . . if you put your name in there . . ., um, '. . . do hereby give permission to Judith V. Becker, PhD . . .,' that's me . . . to record information that I have, um, related, and will relate to her during a series of interviews. I further give her permission to make use of that information for educational lectures, presentations and publications with the purpose of assisting mental health professionals and the public at large in understanding my behaviors. Permission is granted for use of this information for the ultimate aim of prevention of similar behaviors by others in our society.[29]

As soon as Ridgway signed, Prothero warned Ridgway not to sign similar requests from anyone. Then he added

I'm going to take the opportunity to tell the world, and the press at least that's gathered, that that is your request, that any contacts made through you by people who wanna talk to you, whether they be law enforcement, academia, you know, professors, researchers, um, psychologists, authors, whatever, that any contacts with you should be . . . be . . . be initiated through Todd (Defense Attorney Todd Gruenhagen) or I.[30]

It could be argued that Ridgway was coerced into giving video permission to O'Toole and written permission to Becker. The agreements came under duress, during months of intense interrogation that would determine whether Ridgway lived or died. Ridgway had not been sentenced and still was beholden to O'Toole and Becker. He needed to keep everyone happy.

Just a few months before in his King County Jail, Ridgway wanted no part of any scheme to sell his life story to feed the world's popular culture. All the notes he took while in his cell he tore up and flushed down the toilet out of fear they would end up on Ebay. Ridgway told Detective Tom Jensen: "I didn't want anybody to find 'em . . . that would be worth a million bucks to somebody. . . . I don't want anybody makin' money off this."[31]

Endnotes

CHAPTER 1: MARGINALIZING THE MISSING

[1] Carol Estes (mother of Green River victim Debra Estes), in discussion with author, 1988. Seattle, Washington.

[2] King County Department of Public Safety, Theft Report 82-132624 on Debra Estes, July 4, 1982.

[3] Carol Estes, in discussion with author, 1984. Seattle, Washington.

[4] Tacoma Police Department, Missing Person Report 82-230-193 on Debra Bonner. August 18, 1982.

[5] Carol Estes, in discussion with author, 1988. Seattle, Washington.

[6] Green River Task Force Commander Capt. Bob Evans, in discussion with author, 1989. Seattle, Washington.

[7] Proverbs 7:10–14 (New International Version. Reference Edition).

[8] King County Superior Courthouse, *State v. Ridgway* Case No. 01-1-10270-9 Sentencing Hearing, December 18, 2003. Seattle, Washington.

[9] *Ibid.*

[10] *Ibid.*

[11] Tomás Guillén, "Missing Persons: Lost in the Shuffle," *Seattle Times,* June 7, 1993, A-1.

[12] Lewis Kamb, "People Go Missing, Killers Go Free," *Seattle Post-Intelligencer,* February 17, 2003, A-1.

[13] King County Police Confession Tape 81, Page 24. *State v. Ridgway* Case No. 01-1-10270-9. Seattle, Washington. June 26, 2003. King County Police Detective Randy Mullinax and Detective Jon Mattsen.

[14] King County Police Confession Tape 99, Page 9. *State v. Ridgway* Case No. 01-1-10270-9. Seattle, Washington. June 30, 2003. Dr. Robert Wheeler.

CHAPTER 2: SCIENCE OF PREYING

[1] King County Prosecutor's Office, State v. Ridgway Case No. 01-1-10270-9 Summary of Evidence, November 2003, Seattle, Washington.

[2] King County Department of Public Safety, Missing Person Report 82-204879 on Denise D. Bush, October 10, 1982.

[3] Seattle Police Department, Missing Person Report 83-889470 on Sue Feeney, September 30, 1983.

[4] King County Prosecutor's Office, *State v. Ridgway* Case No. 01-1-10270-9 Summary of Evidence, November 2003, Seattle, Washington.

[5] King County Police Confession Tape 306, Page 27. *State v. Ridgway* Case No. 01-1-10270-9. Seattle, Washington. November 17, 2003. Dr. Mary Ellen O'Toole.

[6] King County Police Confession Tape 166, Page 40. *State v. Ridgway* Case No. 01-1-10270-9. Seattle, Washington. July 28, 2003. Dr. Robert Wheeler.

[7] King County Police Confession Tape 166, Page 41. *State v. Ridgway* Case No. 01-1-10270-9. Seattle, Washington. July 28, 2003. Dr. Robert Wheeler.

[8] King County Police Confession Tape 166, Page 42. *State v. Ridgway* Case No. 01-1-10270-9. Seattle, Washington. July 28, 2003. Dr. Robert Wheeler.

[9] King County Police Confession Tape 141, Page 16. *State v. Ridgway* Case No. 01-1-10270-9. Seattle, Washington. July 18, 2003. Detective Tom Jensen and Dr. Mary Ellen O'Toole.

[10] King County Police Confession Tape 305, Page 33. *State v. Ridgway* Case No. 01-1-10270-9. Seattle, Washington. November 17, 2003. Dr. Mary Ellen O'Toole.

[11] King County Police Confession Tape 305, Page 34. *State v. Ridgway* Case No. 01-1-10270-9. Seattle, Washington. November 17, 2003. Dr. Mary Ellen O'Toole.

[12] King County Police Confession Tape 161, Page 15. *State v. Ridgway* Case No. 01-1-10270-9. Seattle, Washington. July 25, 2003. Detective Randy Mullinax, Detective Tom Jensen, Dr. Mary Ellen O'Toole.

[13] King County Police Confession Tape 170, Page 17. *State v. Ridgway* Case No. 01-1-10270-9. Seattle, Washington. July 29, 2003. Dr. Robert Wheeler, Detective Tom Jensen, Detective Randy Mullinax.

[14] King County Police Confession Tape 166, Page 3. *State v. Ridgway* Case No. 01-1-10270-9. Seattle, Washington. July 28, 2003. Dr. Robert Wheeler.

[15] King County Police Confession Tape 145, Page 19. *State v. Ridgway* Case No. 01-1-10270-9. Seattle, Washington. July 19, 2003. Dr. Mary Ellen O'Toole.

[16] King County Police Confession Tape 31, Page 9. *State v. Ridgway* Case No. 01-1-10270-9. Seattle, Washington. June 18, 2003. Detective Jon Mattsen, Detective Tom Jensen.

[17] King County Police Confession Tape 31, Page 9. *State v. Ridgway* Case No. 01-1-10270-9. Seattle, Washington. June 18, 2003. Detective Jon Mattsen, Detective Tom Jensen.

[18] King County Police Confession Tape 144, Page 15. *State v. Ridgway* Case No. 01-1-10270-9. Seattle, Washington. July 19, 2003. Dr. Mary Ellen O'Toole.

[19] King County Police Confession Tape 144, Page 28. *State v. Ridgway* Case No. 01-1-10270-9. Seattle, Washington. July 19, 2003. Dr. Mary Ellen O'Toole.

[20] King County Police Confession Tape 23, Page 6. *State v. Ridgway* Case No. 01-1-10270-9. Seattle, Washington. June 16, 2003. Detective Randy Mullinax, Detective Sue Peters.

[21] King County Police Confession Tape 24, Page 11. *State v. Ridgway* Case No. 01-1-10270-9. Seattle, Washington. June 16, 2003. Detective Jon Mattsen, Detective Tom Jensen.

[22] King County Police Confession Tape 139, Page 16. *State v. Ridgway* Case No. 01-1-10270-9. Seattle, Washington. July 17, 2003. Dr. Mary Ellen O'Toole, Detective Sue Peters, Detective Randy Mullinax.

[23] King County Police Confession Tape 144, Page 10. *State v. Ridgway* Case No. 01-1-10270-9. Seattle, Washington. July 19, 2003. Dr. Mary Ellen O'Toole.

[24] King County Police Confession Tape 144, Page 12. *State v. Ridgway* Case No. 01-1-10270-9. Seattle, Washington. July 19, 2003. Dr. Mary Ellen O'Toole.

[25] King County Police Confession Tape 144, Page 9. *State v. Ridgway* Case No. 01-1-10270-9. Seattle, Washington. July 19, 2003. Dr. Mary Ellen O'Toole.

[26] King County Police Confession Tape 144, Page 16. *State v. Ridgway* Case No. 01-1-10270-9. Seattle, Washington. July 19, 2003. Dr. Mary Ellen O'Toole.

[27] King County Police Confession Tape 38, Page 2. *State v. Ridgway* Case No. 01-1-10270-9. Seattle, Washington. June 19, 2003. Detective Randy Mullinax, Detective Jon Mattsen.

[28] King County Police Confession Tape 189, Page 38. *State v. Ridgway* Case No. 01-1-10270-9. Seattle, Washington. August 6, 2003. Detective Tom

Jensen, Detective Sue Peters, Detective Randy Mullinax, Attorney. Todd Gruenhagen.

[29] King County Police Confession Tape 145, Page 19. *State v. Ridgway* Case No. 01-1-10270-9. Seattle, Washington. July 19, 2003. Dr. Mary Ellen O'Toole.

[30] King County Police Confession Tape 2, Page 30. *State v. Ridgway* Case No. 01-1-10270-9. Seattle, Washington. June 13, 2003. Detective Randy Mullinax, Detective Tom Jensen, Detective Jon Mattsen, Detective Sue Peters.

[31] King County Police Confession Tape 145, Page 6. *State v. Ridgway* Case No. 01-1-10270-9. Seattle, Washington. July 19, 2003. Dr. Mary Ellen O'Toole.

[32] King County Police Confession Tape 145, Page 2. *State v. Ridgway* Case No. 01-1-10270-9. Seattle, Washington. July 19, 2003. Dr. Mary Ellen O'Toole.

[33] King County Police Confession Tape 145, Page 1. *State v. Ridgway* Case No. 01-1-10270-9. Seattle, Washington. July 19, 2003. Dr. Mary Ellen O'Toole.

[34] King County Police Confession Tape 144, Page 21. *State v. Ridgway* Case No. 01-1-10270-9. Seattle, Washington. July 19, 2003. Dr. Mary Ellen O'Toole.

[35] King County Police Confession Tape 139, Page 115. *State v. Ridgway* Case No. 01-1-10270-9. Seattle, Washington. July 17, 2003. Dr. Mary Ellen O'Toole, Detective Sue Peters, Detective Randy Mullinax.

[36] King County Police Confession Tape 134, Page 29. *State v. Ridgway* Case No. 01-1-10270-9. Seattle, Washington. July 16, 2003. Detective Tom Jensen, Detective Randy Mullinax, Detective Jon Mattsen.

[37] King County Police Confession Tape 157, Page 27. *State v. Ridgway* Case No. 01-1-10270-9. Seattle, Washington. July 24, 2003. Dr. Mary Ellen O'Toole.

[38] King County Police Confession Tape 204, Page 20. *State v. Ridgway* Case No. 01-1-10270-9. Seattle, Washington. Aug. 15, 2003. Detective Sue Peters, Detective Randy Mullinax.

[39] King County Police Confession Tape 40, Page 7. *State v. Ridgway* Case No. 01-1-10270-9. Seattle, Washington. June 19, 2003. Detective Jon Mattsen, Detective Tom Jensen.

[40] King County Police Confession Tape 173, Page 48. *State v. Ridgway* Case No. 01-1-10270-9. Seattle, Washington. July 30, 2003. Dr. Robert Wheeler.

[41] King County Police Confession Tape 40, Page 7. *State v. Ridgway* Case No. 01-1-10270-9. Seattle, Washington. June 19, 2003. Detective Jon Mattsen, Detective Tom Jensen.

42 King County Police Confession Tape 203, Page 16. *State v. Ridgway* Case No. 01-1-10270-9. Seattle, Washington. August 14, 2003. Dr. Mary Ellen O'Toole.

43 King County Police Confession Tape 330, Page 34. *State v. Ridgway* Case No. 01-1-10270-9. Seattle, Washington. December 8, 2003. Detective Sue Peters, Detective Randy Mullinax, Dr. Judith Becker.

44 King County Police Confession Tape 203, Page 17. *State v. Ridgway* Case No. 01-1-10270-9. Seattle, Washington. August 14, 2003. Dr. Mary Ellen O'Toole.

45 King County Police Confession Tape 313, Page 34. *State v. Ridgway* Case No. 01-1-10270-9. Seattle, Washington. November 19, 2003. Dr. Robert Wheeler.

46 King County Police Confession Tape 202, Page 13. *State v. Ridgway* Case No. 01-1-10270-9. Seattle, Washington. August 14, 2003. Dr. Mary Ellen O'Toole.

47 King County Police Confession Tape 203, Page 7. *State v. Ridgway* Case No. 01-1-10270-9. Seattle, Washington. August 14, 2003. Dr. Mary Ellen O'Toole.

48 *Ibid.*

49 King County Police Confession Tape 153, Page 24. *State v. Ridgway* Case No. 01-1-10270-9. Seattle, Washington. July 23, 2003. Detective Randy Mullinax, Detective Jon Mattsen.

50 King County Police Confession Tape 154, Page 12. *State v. Ridgway* Case No. 01-1-10270-9. July 23, 2003. Detective Randy Mullinax, Detective Jon Mattsen, Detective Tom Jensen, DPA Jeff Baird, Dr. Mary Ellen O'Toole.

CHAPTER 3: PRIVACY AMID THE MEDIA

1 King County Superior Courthouse, *State v. Ridgway* Case No. 01-1-10270-9 Sentencing Hearing, December 18, 2003, Seattle, Washington.

2 Alex Tizon, "A Mother's Pain Returns," *Seattle Times,* December 8, 1988, A1.

3 Nancy Gabbert (mother of Green River victim Sandra Gabbert), in discussion with author, 1990. Seattle, Washington.

4 Carol and Tom Estes (parents of Green River victim Debra Estes), in discussion with author, 1990, Seattle, Washington.

5 Linda Barker (victim rights advocate), in discussion with author, 1990, Seattle, Washington.

6 *Ibid.*

7 George Foster, "Funeral of Opal Mills Inspires a Message to Other Young Girls," *Seattle Post-Intelligencer,* August 28, 1982, A5.

[8] Seattle Police Department, Missing Person Report 83-176443 on Kimi Kai Pitsor, May 3, 1983.

[9] King County Superior Courthouse, *State v. Ridgway* Case No. 01-1-10270-9 Sentencing Hearing, December 18, 2003.

[10] Linda Barker, in discussion with author, 1990, Seattle, Washington.

[11] Carlton Smith and Tomás Guillén, *The Search for the Green River Killer* (New York: New American Library, 1990).

[12] Linda Barker, in discussion with author, 1990, Seattle, Washington.

[13] M. Barber and J. Hessburg, " Grisly Twist in Green River Case, Remains Found near Tukwila Match Skull Discovered Five Years Ago in Oregon. *Seattle Post-Intelligencer* (February 17, 1990): A-1.

[14] Roderick Thorp, *River: A Novel of the Green River Killings* (New York: Fawcett Columbine, 1995).

[15] Linda Barker, in discussion with author, 1990, Seattle, Washington.

[16] Lou Gorfain (Producer of Green River Murders case docudrama), in discussion with author, 1989. Seattle, Washington.

[17] Robert D. Keppel, *The Riverman: Ted Bundy and I Hunt for the Green River Killer* (New York: Pocket Books, 1995), 23.

[18] Robert D. Keppel, *The Riverman: Ted Bundy and I Hunt for the Green River Killer* (New York: Pocket Books, 1995), 15.

[19] King County Prosecutor's Office, *State v. Gary Leon Ridgway* No. 01-1-10270-9 Summary of Evidence, November 2001. Seattle, Washington.

[20] L. Mauro, "Seattle's River of Strangled Whores," *True Police,* April 1983, 6-11, 63.

[21] Linda Barker, in discussion with author, 1990, Seattle, Washington.

[22] King County Superior Courthouse, *State v. Ridgway* Case No. 01-1-10270-9 Sentencing Hearing, Dec. 18, 2003. Seattle, Washington.

[23] Carol and Tom Estes (Parents of Green River victim Debra Estes), in discussion with author, 1990, Seattle, Washington.

[24] Nancy Gabbert, in discussion with author, 1990. Seattle, Washington.

[25] *Ibid.*

[26] Phil Sturholm, letter to the editor, *The Seattle Times,* January 8, 1990.

CHAPTER 4: THE INVESTIGATION . . . I

[1] Green River Task Force Commander Captain Bob Evans, in discussion with author, 1989. Seattle, Washington.

[2] Federal Bureau of Investigation, Behavior Science Unit, Psychological Profile by John Douglas.

[3] Carlton Smith and Tomás Guillén, *The Search for the Green River Killer* (New York: New American Library, 1990).

[4] Sheriff David Reichert, *Chasing the Devil: My Twenty-Year Quest to Capture the Green River Killer* (New York: Little Brown and Company, 2004).

[5] *Ibid.*

[6] King County Department of Public Safety, Criminal Investigation Division Expenditure Receipts, 1982, 1983, and 1984.

[7] King County Department of Public Safety, Criminal Investigation Division Expenditure Receipt for "Trudy's Tavern, 150th & PHS," Case No. 82-244386, January 27, 1983.

[8] *Ibid.*

[9] King County Police Confession Tape 68, Page 30. *State v. Ridgway* Case No. 01-1-10270-9. Seattle, Washington. June 24, 2003. Detective Tom Jensen, Detective Sue Peters.

[10] King County Department of Public Safety, Criminal Investigation Division Expenditure Receipt for "White Shutters," April 6, 1983.

[11] King County Police Confession Tape 72, Page 30. *State v. Ridgway* Case No. 01-1-10270-9. Seattle, Washington. June 25, 2003. Detective Tom Jensen, Detective Jim Doyon.

[12] *Ibid.*

[13] King County Department of Public Safety, Criminal Investigation Division Expenditure Receipt for "Denny's (Lounge) So. 188 & PHS," May 3, 1983.

[14] King County Department of Public Safety, Criminal Investigation Division Expenditure Receipt for "Red Lion (Peppins Lounge) 188 & PHS," May 3, 1983.

[15] King County Department of Public Safety, Criminal Investigation Division Expenditure Receipt for "Red Lion (Maxis Lounge) So. 188 & PHS," May 3, 1983.

[16] King County Department of Public Safety, Criminal Investigation Division Expenditure Receipt for "French Quarter Massage Parlor," May 3, 1983.

[17] King County Department of Public Safety, Criminal Investigation Division Expenditure Receipt for "North City Adult Book Store," May 3, 1983.

[18] King County Executive, *Green River Task Force Report, Sept. 6, 1984.* By King County Executive Staff Assistant Shelly Sutton for King County Executive Randy Revelle.

[19] King County Police Green River Task Force Organizational Chart. 1984.

[20] King County Executive, *Green River Task Force Report, Sept. 6, 1984.* By King County Executive Staff Assistant Shelly Sutton for King County Executive Randy Revelle.

[21] *Ibid.*

[22] Carlton Smith and Tomás Guillén, *The Search for the Green River Killer* (New York; New American Library, 1990).

[23] Green River Task Force Commander Captain Frank Adamson, in discussion with author, 1986. Seattle, Washington.

[24] Green River Task Force Pro-Active Unit 1986 Report to King County Police Commanders.

[25] Carlton Smith and Tomás Guillén, *The Search for the Green River Killer* (New York; New American Library, 1990).

[26] *Ibid.*

[27] Tomás Guillén, "Green River Killer Back?—New Murders Show Some Similarities," *The Seattle Times,* November 21, 1991, A-1.

[28] *Ibid.*

CHAPTER 5: . . . THE INVESTIGATION II

[1] King County Police Confession Tape 166, Page 3. *State v. Ridgway* Case No. 01-1-10270-9. Seattle, Washington. June 28, 2003. Dr. Robert Wheeler.

[2] King County Police Confession Tape 99, Page 34. *State v. Ridgway* Case No. 01-1-10270-9. Seattle, Washington. June 30, 2003. Dr. Robert Wheeler.

[3] King County Police Confession Tape 99, Page 35. *State v. Ridgway* Case No. 01-1-10270-9. Seattle, Washington. June 30, 2003. Dr. Robert Wheeler.

[4] *Ibid.*

[5] King County Police Confession Tape 68, Page 13. *State v. Ridgway* Case No. 01-1-10270-9. Seattle, Washington. June 24, 2003. Detective Tom Jensen, Detective Sue Peters.

[6] King County Police Confession Tape 100, Page 8. *State v. Ridgway* Case No. 01-1-10270-9. Seattle, Washington. June 30, 2003. Dr. Robert Wheeler.

[7] King County Police Confession Tape 189, Page 44. *State v. Ridgway* Case No. 01-1-10270-9. Seattle, Washington. Aug. 6, 2003. Detective Tom Jensen, Detective Sue Peters, Detective Randy Mullinax, Attorney Todd Gruenhagen.

[8] King County Police Confession Tape 209, Page 44. *State v. Ridgway* Case No. 01-1-10270-9. Seattle, Washington. August 18, 2003. King County Sheriff Dave Reichert.

[9] King County Police Confession Tape 61, Page 26. *State v. Ridgway* Case No. 01-1-10270-9. Seattle, Washington. June 23, 2003. Detective Jon Mattsen, Detective Randy Mullinax.

[10] King County Police Confession Tape 61, Page 31. *State v. Ridgway* Case No. 01-1-10270-9. Seattle, Washington. June 23, 2003. Detective Jon Mattsen, Detective Randy Mullinax.

[11] *Ibid.*

[12] King County Police Confession Tape 61, Page 32. *State v. Ridgway* Case No. 01-1-10270-9. Seattle, Washington. June 23, 2003. Detective Jon Mattsen, Detective Randy Mullinax.

[13] King County Prosecutor's Office "Statement of Probable Cause," by King County Detective Tom Jensen, November 30, 2001.

[14] King County Police Confession Tape 61, Page 30. *State v. Ridgway* Case No. 01-1-10270-9. Seattle, Washington. June 23, 2003. Detective Jon Mattsen, Detective Randy Mullinax.

[15] King County Police Confession Tape 60, Page 21. *State v. Ridgway* Case No. 01-1-10270-9. Seattle, Washington. June 23, 2003. Detective Jon Mattsen, Detective Randy Mullinax.

[16] King County Police Confession Tape 60, Page 22. *State v. Ridgway* Case No. 01-1-10270-9. Seattle, Washington. June 23, 2003. Detective Jon Mattsen, Detective Randy Mullinax.

[17] King County Police Confession Tape 29, Page 10. *State v. Ridgway* Case No. 01-1-10270-9. Seattle, Washington. June 17, 2003. Detective Sue Peters, Detective Randy Mullinax.

[18] King County Police Confession Tape 150, Page 11. *State v. Ridgway* Case No. 01-1-10270-9. Seattle, Washington. July 22, 2003. Dr. Mary Ellen O'Toole.

[19] King County Police Confession Tape 26, Page 18. *State v. Ridgway* Case No. 01-1-10270-9. Seattle, Washington. June 17, 2003. Detective Jon Mattsen, Detective Tom Jensen.

[20] King County Police Confession Tape 214, Page 37. *State v. Ridgway* Case No. 01-1-10270-9. Seattle, Washington. August 19, 2003. Sheriff David G. Reichert.

[21] King County Police Confession Tape 38, Page 34. *State v. Ridgway* Case No. 01-1-10270-9. Seattle, Washington. June 19, 2003. Detective Randy Mullinax, Detective Jon Mattsen.

[22] King County Police Confession Tape 35, Page 9. *State v. Ridgway* Case No. 01-1-10270-9. Seattle, Washington. June 18, 2003. Detective Tom Jensen, Detective Sue Peters.

[23] King County Police Confession Tape 35, Page 21. *State v. Ridgway* Case No. 01-1-10270-9. Seattle, Washington. June 18, 2003. Detective Tom Jensen, Detective Sue Peters.

[24] King County Police Confession Tape 198, Page 22. *State v. Ridgway* Case No. 01-1-10270-9. Seattle, Washington. Aug. 12, 2003. Detective Tom Jensen, Detective Sue Peters.

[25] King County Police Confession Tape 198, Page 23. *State v. Ridgway* Case No. 01-1-10270-9. Seattle, Washington. Aug. 12, 2003. Detective Tom Jensen, Detective Sue Peters.

[26] Tomás Guillén, "We Thought It Was the Green River Killer: Prostitute and Her Husband Believe She Met Serial Murderer," *Seattle Times,* May 13, 1987, A-1.

[27] King County Police Confession Tape 38, Page 31. *State v. Ridgway* Case No. 01-1-10270-9. Seattle, Washington. June 19, 2003. Detective Randy Mullinax, Detective Jon Mattsen.

[28] King County Police Confession Tape 62, Page 24. *State v. Ridgway* Case No. 01-1-10270-9. Seattle, Washington. June 23, 2003. Detective Tom Jensen, Detective Sue Peters.

[29] King County Police Confession Tape 332, Page 28. *State v. Ridgway* Case No. 01-1-10270-9. Seattle, Washington. December 8, 2003. Dr. Judith Becker, Attorney Mark Prothero, Attorney Todd Gruenhagen.

[30] King County Police Confession Tape 332, Page 25. *State v. Ridgway* Case No. 01-1-10270-9. Seattle, Washington. December 8, 2003. Dr. Judith Becker, Attorney Mark Prothero, Attorney Todd Gruenhagen.

[31] King County Police Confession Tape 99, Page 8. *State v. Ridgway* Case No. 01-1-10270-9. Seattle, Washington. June 30, 2003. Dr. Robert Wheeler.

[32] King County Police Confession Tape 104, Page 4. *State v. Ridgway* Case No. 01-1-10270-9. Seattle, Washington. June 30, 2003. Dr. Robert Wheeler.

[33] King County Police Confession Tape 40, Page 16. *State v. Ridgway* Case No. 01-1-10270-9. Seattle, Washington. June 19, 2003. Detective Jon Mattsen, Detective Tom Jensen.

[34] King County Police Confession Tape 145, Page 21. *State v. Ridgway* Case No. 01-1-10270-9. Seattle, Washington. July 19, 2003. Dr. Mary Ellen O'Toole.

[35] King County Police Confession Tape 149, Page 37. *State v. Ridgway* Case No. 01-1-10270-9. Seattle, Washington. July 22, 2003. Detective Kevin O'Keefe, Dr. Mary Ellen O'Toole.

[36] King County Police Confession Tape 150, Page 1. *State v. Ridgway* Case No. 01-1-10270-9. Seattle, Washington. July 22, 2003. Dr. Mary Ellen O'Toole.

[37] King County Police Confession Tape 210, Page 34. *State v. Ridgway* Case No. 01-1-10270-9. Seattle, Washington. August 18, 2003. King County Sheriff David Reichert.

[38] King County Police Confession Tape 32, Page 11. *State v. Ridgway* Case No. 01-1-10270-9. Seattle, Washington. June 19, 2003. Detective Tom Jensen.

39 King County Police Confession Tape 32, Page 12 . *State v. Ridgway* Case No. 01-1-10270-9. Seattle, Washington. June 18, 2003. Detective Tom Jensen.

40 King County Police Confession Tape 82, Page 3 . *State v. Ridgway* Case No. 01-1-10270-9. Seattle, Washington. June 26, 2003. Detective Randy Mullinax, Detective Jon Mattsen.

41 King County Police Confession Tape 82, Page 4. *State v. Ridgway* Case No. 01-1-10270-9. Seattle, Washington. June 26, 2003. Detective Randy Mullinax, Detective Jon Mattsen.

42 King County Police Confession Tape 82, Page 3. *State v. Ridgway* Case No. 01-1-10270-9. Seattle, Washington. June 26, 2003. Detective Randy Mullinax, Detective Jon Mattsen.

43 King County Police Confession Tape 331, Page 9. *State v. Ridgway* Case No. 01-1-10270-9. Seattle, Washington. December 8, 2003. Detective Sue Peters, Detective Randy Mullinax, Dr. Judith Becker.

44 King County Police Confession Tape 82, Page 4. *State v. Ridgway* Case No. 01-1-10270-9. Seattle, Washington. June 26, 2003. Detective Randy Mullinax, Detective Jon Mattsen.

45 King County Police Confession Tape 98, Page 9. *State v. Ridgway* Case No. 01-1-10270-9. Seattle, Washington. June 30, 2003. Dr. Robert Wheeler.

CHAPTER 6: COMMUNIQUÉ

1 U.S. Department of Justice Federal of Investigation Criminal Profilist John E. Douglas letter to Detective Bruce Kalin of the Department of Public Safety, King County, August 24, 1984.

2 Green River Killer Gary Leon Ridgway letter to the *Seattle Post-Intelligencer,* February 20, 1984.

3 Mike Barber, "Letter from a Serial Killer: 19 Years Ago, Ridgway Offered Tantalizing Clues," *Seattle Post-Intelligencer,* November 7, 2003, A-1.

4 Green River Killer Gary Leon Ridgway letter to the *Seattle Post-Intelligencer,* February 20, 1984.

5 *Ibid.*

6 Mike Barber, "Letter from a Serial Killer: 19 Years Ago, Ridgway Offered Tantalizing Clues," *Seattle Post-Intelligencer,* November 7, 2003, A-1

7 King County Department of Public Safety, Latent Lab Work Sheet: Lab # 82-1163, Case # 82-162398.

8 King County Department of Public Safety Latent Print Examiner Tonya Yzaguirre, letter to U.S. Department of Justice Federal Bureau of Investigation Identification Division, July 19, 1984.

[9] U.S. Department of Justice Federal Bureau of Investigation Laboratory File No. 40720052 D QJ letter to King County Department of Public Safety Sheriff Vernon Thomas, August 3, 1984.

[10] U.S. Department of Justice Federal Bureau of Investigation Latent Fingerprint Section Identification Division Case No. C-33489 letter to King County Department of Public Safety Sheriff Vern Thomas of the King County Department of Public Safety.

[11] U.S. Department of Justice Federal Bureau of Investigation Criminal Profilist John E. Douglas letter to King County Department of Public Safety Detective Bruce Kalin, August 24, 1984.

[12] Green River Killer Gary Leon Ridgway letter to the *Seattle Post-Intelligencer,* February 20, 1984.

[13] Orchid Cellmark Margaret A. Terril, M.S.F.S., DNA Analyst III, and Charlotte J. Word, PhD, Laboratory Director Case No. F021304 letter to King County Department of Public Safety Detective Jake Pavlovich of King County Police, July 17, 2003.

[14] King County Police Confession Tape 275, Page 28. *State v. Ridgway* Case No. 01-1-10270-9. Seattle, Washington. October 9, 2003. Detective Randy Mullinax, Detective Tom Jensen, Detective Jon Mattsen, Attorney Mark Prothero.

[15] King County Police Confession Tape 275, Page 47. *State v. Ridgway* Case No. 01-1-10270-9. Seattle, Washington. October 9, 2003. Detective Randy Mullinax, Detective Tom Jensen, Detective Jon Mattsen, Attorney Mark Prothero.

[16] King County Police Confession Tape 276, Page 13. *State v. Ridgway* Case No. 01-1-10270-9. Seattle, Washington. October 9, 2003. Detective Tom Jensen, Detective Jon Mattsen, Attorney Mark Prothero.

[17] King County Police Confession Tape 285, Page 4. *State v. Ridgway* Case No. 01-1-10270-9. Seattle, Washington. October 16, 2003. Detective Tom Jensen, Detective Sue Peters.

[18] King County Police Confession Tape 40, Page 24. *State v. Ridgway* Case No. 01-1-10270-9. Seattle, Washington. June 19, 2003. Detective Jon Mattsen, Detective Tom Jensen.

[19] King County Police Confession Tape 338, Page 20. *State v. Ridgway* Case No. 01-1-10270-9. Seattle, Washington. December 10, 2003. Detective Randy Mullinax, Detective Tom Jensen, Dr. Judith Becker.

[20] King County Police Confession Tape 338, Page 26. *State v. Ridgway* Case No. 01-1-10270-9. Seattle, Washington. December 9, 2003. Dr. Judith Becker.

[21] King County Police Confession Tape 348, Page 13. *State v. Ridgway* Case No. 01-1-10270-9. Seattle, Washington. December 16, 2003. Sheriff David G. Reichert.

22 King County Police Confession Tape 348, Page 14. *State v. Ridgway* Case No. 01-1-10270-9. Seattle, Washington. December 16, 2003. Sheriff David G. Reichert.

23 Mike Barber and Venessa Ho, "Ex-FBI Profiler Admits Missing Clues on Ridgway Letter," *Seattle Post-Intelligencer,* November 27, 2003, B-1.

CHAPTER 7: INVESTIGATION AND MEDIA CONFLICTS

1 Green River Task Force Commander Captain Bob Evans, in discussion with author, 1989. Seattle, Washington.

2 King County Police Confession Tape 212, Page 24. *State v. Ridgway* Case No. 01-1-10270-9. Seattle, Washington. August 18, 2003. King County Sheriff David G. Reichert.

3 Brian Basset, "Freeze Dog-Breath! Green River Task-Force!" *Seattle Times* February 13, 1986.

4 Carlton Smith, "Truth or Death, *Seattle Weekly,* November 20, 2002, A-1.

5 KIRO Television Executive John Lippman, letter to King County Executive Randy Revelle, August 17, 1984.

6 KIRO Television Executive John Lippman letter to King County Sheriff Vern Thomas, June 18, 1986.

7 KINGTV 5 Journalist Jack Hamann, in discussion with author, 1988. Seattle, Washington.

8 King County Executive Office Staff Assistant Sam Sperry memo King County Executive Randy Revelle, 1984.

9 H. E. McLean, "The News Media: Friend or Foe?" *Law and Order* (July 1985): 52, 54.

10 KOMO Radio Journalist Ken Kohl letter to King County Executive Randy Revelle, July 14, 1984.

11 King County Executive Randy Revelle letter to KOMO Radio Journalist Ken Kohl, October 2, 1984.

12 Green River Task Force Commander Captain Bob Evans, in discussion with author, 1989. Seattle, Washington.

13 Carlton Smith and Tomás Guillén, "Is the Green River Killer Now in San Diego?" *Seattle Times,* June 19, 1988, A-1.

14 King County Police Department of Public Safety, News Conference on "Manhunt Live: A Chance to End the Nightmare," December 6, 1988. Seattle, Washington.

CHAPTER 8: CONFESSION OR DECEPTION? . . . I

[1] King County Police Confession Tape 65, Page 1. *State v. Ridgway* Case No. 01-1-10270-9. Seattle, Washington. June 24, 2003. Detective Randy Mullinax, Detective Tom Jensen.

[2] Office of the Prosecuting Attorney, King County, Washington, "Statement of Norm Maleng on Ridgway Plea," news release, November 5, 2003.

[3] King County Sheriff Office, "Green River Homicides Investigation," news release, August 16, 2003.

[4] King County Police Confession Tape 22, Page 1. *State v. Ridgway* Case No. 01-1-10270-9. Seattle, Washington. June 16, 2003. Detective Randy Mullinax, Detective Sue Peters.

[5] King County Police Confession Tape 26, Page 1. *State v. Ridgway* Case No. 01-1-10270-9. Seattle, Washington. June 17, 2003. Detective Jon Mattsen, Detective Tom Jensen.

[6] King County Police Confession Tape 4, Page 36. *State v. Ridgway* Case No. 01-1-10270-9. Seattle, Washington. June 13, 2003. Detective Randy Mullinax, Detective Tom Jensen, Detective Jon Mattsen, Detective Sue Peters.

[7] King County Police Confession Tape 17, Page 19. *State v. Ridgway* Case No. 01-1-10270-9. Seattle, Washington. June 15, 2003. Detective Sue Peters, Detective Tom Jensen.

[8] King County Police Confession Tape 15, Page 19. *State v. Ridgway* Case No. 01-1-10270-9. Seattle, Washington. June 15, 2003. Detective Sue Peters, Detective Tom Jensen.

[9] King County Police Confession Tape 17, Page 6. *State v. Ridgway* Case No. 01-1-10270-9. Seattle, Washington. June 15, 2003. Detective Sue Peters, Detective Tom Jensen.

[10] King County Police Confession Tape 17, Page 8. *State v. Ridgway* Case No. 01-1-10270-9. Seattle, Washington. June 15, 2003. Detective Sue Peters, Detective Tom Jensen.

[11] King County Police Confession Tape 20, Page 3. *State v. Ridgway* Case No. 01-1-10270-9. Seattle, Washington. June 15, 2003. Detective Jon Mattsen, Detective Tom Jensen.

[12] King County Police Confession Tape 22, Page 18. *State v. Ridgway* Case No. 01-1-10270-9. Seattle, Washington. June 16, 2003. Detective Randy Mullinax, Detective Sue Peters.

[13] King County Police Confession Tape 22, Page 19. *State v. Ridgway* Case No. 01-1-10270-9. Seattle, Washington. June 16, 2003. Detective Randy Mullinax, Detective Sue Peters.

[14] King County Police Confession Tape 22, Page 34. *State v. Ridgway* Case No. 01-1-10270-9. Seattle, Washington. June 16, 2003. Detective Randy Mullinax, Detective Sue Peters.

[15] King County Police Confession Tape 22, Page 38. *State v. Ridgway* Case No. 01-1-10270-9. Seattle, Washington. June 16, 2003. Detective Randy Mullinax, Detective Sue Peters.

[16] King County Police Confession Tape 26, Page 2. *State v. Ridgway* Case No. 01-1-10270-9. Seattle, Washington. June 17, 2003. Detective Jon Mattsen, Detective Tom Jensen.

[17] King County Police Confession Tape 26, Page 3. *State v. Ridgway* Case No. 01-1-10270-9. Seattle, Washington. June 17, 2003. Detective Jon Mattsen, Detective Tom Jensen.

[18] King County Police Confession Tape 26, Page 4. *State v. Ridgway* Case No. 01-1-10270-9. Seattle, Washington. June 17, 2003. Detective Jon Mattsen, Detective Tom Jensen.

[19] King County Police Confession Tape 27, Page 1. *State v. Ridgway* Case No. 01-1-10270-9. Seattle, Washington. June 17, 2003. Detective Randy Mullinax, Detective Jon Mattsen.

[20] King County Police Confession Tape 27, Page 2. *State v. Ridgway* Case No. 01-1-10270-9. Seattle, Washington. June 17, 2003. Detective Randy Mullinax, Detective Jon Mattsen.

[21] King County Police Confession Tape 27, Page 3. *State v. Ridgway* Case No. 01-1-10270-9. Seattle, Washington. June 17, 2003. Detective Randy Mullinax, Detective Jon Mattsen.

[22] King County Police Confession Tape 31, Page 1. *State v. Ridgway* Case No. 01-1-10270-9. Seattle, Washington. June 18, 2003. Detective Jon Mattsen, Detective Tom Jensen.

[23] King County Police Confession Tape 31, Page 3. *State v. Ridgway* Case No. 01-1-10270-9. Seattle, Washington. June 18, 2003. Detective Jon Mattsen, Detective Tom Jensen.

[24] King County Police Confession Tape 32, Page 6. *State v. Ridgway* Case No. 01-1-10270-9. Seattle, Washington. June 18, 2003. Detective Jon Mattsen, Detective Tom Jensen.

[25] King County Police Confession Tape 32, Page 6. *State v. Ridgway* Case No. 01-1-10270-9. Seattle, Washington. June 18, 2003. Detective Jon Mattsen, Detective Tom Jensen.

[26] King County Police Confession Tape 32, Page 9. *State v. Ridgway* Case No. 01-1-10270-9. Seattle, Washington. June 18, 2003. Detective Jon Mattsen, Detective Tom Jensen.

[27] King County Police Confession Tape 65, Page 1. *State v. Ridgway* Case No. 01-1-10270-9. Seattle, Washington. June 24, 2003. Detective Randy Mullinax, Detective Jon Mattsen.

[28] King County Police Confession Tape 65, Page 2. *State v. Ridgway* Case No. 01-1-10270-9. Seattle, Washington. June 24, 2003. Detective Randy Mullinax, Detective Jon Mattsen.

[29] King County Police Confession Tape 65, Page 5. *State v. Ridgway* Case No. 01-1-10270-9. Seattle, Washington. June 24, 2003. Detective Randy Mullinax, Detective Jon Mattsen.

[30] King County Police Confession Tape 213, Page 40. *State v. Ridgway* Case No. 01-1-10270-9. Seattle, Washington. Aug. 19, 2003. Detective Tom Jensen, Detective Randy Mullinax, Detective Jon Mattsen.

[31] King County Police Confession Tape 106, Page 3. *State v. Ridgway* Case No. 01-1-10270-9. Seattle, Washington. July 1, 2003. Detective Raphael Crenshaw.

[32] King County Police Confession Tape 119, Page 21. *State v. Ridgway* Case No. 01-1-10270-9. Seattle, Washington. July 7, 2003. Detective Tom Jensen, Detective Sue Peters.

[33] King County Police Confession Tape 199, Page 29. *State v. Ridgway* Case No. 01-1-10270-9. Seattle, Washington. Aug. 12, 2003. Detective Sue Peters, Detective Jon Mattsen, Detective Tom Jensen.

[34] King County Police Confession Tape 65, Page 5. *State v. Ridgway* Case No. 01-1-10270-9. Seattle, Washington. June 24, 2003. Detective Randy Mullinax, Detective Jon Mattsen.

[35] King County Police Confession Tape 65, Page 6. *State v. Ridgway* Case No. 01-1-10270-9. Seattle, Washington. June 24, 2003. Detective Randy Mullinax, Detective Jon Mattsen.

[36] King County Police Confession Tape 135, Page 25. *State v. Ridgway* Case No. 01-1-10270-9. Seattle, Washington. July 16, 2003. Detective Jon Mattsen, Detective Randy Mullinax, Detective Sue Peters.

[37] King County Police Confession Tape 98, Page 29. *State v. Ridgway* Case No. 01-1-10270-9. Seattle, Washington. June 30, 2003. Dr. Robert Wheeler.

[38] King County Police Confession Tape 103, Page 21. *State v. Ridgway* Case No. 01-1-10270-9. Seattle, Washington. June 30, 2003. Dr. Robert Wheeler.

[39] King County Police Confession Tape 130, Page 25. *State v. Ridgway* Case No. 01-1-10270-9. Seattle, Washington. July 12, 2003. Dr. Christian Harris.

[40] King County Police Confession Tape 143, Page 15. *State v. Ridgway* Case No. 01-1-10270-9. Seattle, Washington. July 18, 2003. Dr. Mary Ellen O'Toole.

[41] *Ibid.*

[42] King County Police Confession Tape 166, Page 14. *State v. Ridgway* Case No. 01-1-10270-9. Seattle, Washington. July 28, 2003. Dr. Robert Wheeler.

[43] King County Police Confession Tape 166, Page 20. *State v. Ridgway* Case No. 01-1-10270-9. Seattle, Washington. July 28, 2003. Dr. Robert Wheeler.

[44] King County Police Confession Tape 166, Page 11. *State v. Ridgway* Case No. 01-1-10270-9. Seattle, Washington. July 28, 2003. Dr. Robert Wheeler.

[45] King County Police Confession Tape 166, Page 12. *State v. Ridgway* Case No. 01-1-10270-9. Seattle, Washington. July 28, 2003. Dr. Robert Wheeler.

[46] King County Police Confession Tape 166, Page 13. *State v. Ridgway* Case No. 01-1-10270-9. Seattle, Washington. July 28, 2003. Dr. Robert Wheeler.

[47] King County Police Confession Tape 162, Page 16. *State v. Ridgway* Case No. 01-1-10270-9. Seattle, Washington. July 25, 2003. Dr. Mary Ellen O'Toole.

[48] King County Police Confession Tape 162, Page 17. *State v. Ridgway* Case No. 01-1-10270-9. Seattle, Washington. July 25, 2003. Detective Randy Mullinax, Detective Tom Jensen, Dr. Mary Ellen O'Toole.

[49] King County Police Confession Tape 162, Page 18. *State v. Ridgway* Case No. 01-1-10270-9. Seattle, Washington. July 25, 2003. Detective Randy Mullinax, Detective Tom Jensen, Dr. Mary Ellen O'Toole.

[50] King County Police Confession Tape 162, Page 19. *State v. Ridgway* Case No. 01-1-10270-9. Seattle, Washington. July 25, 2003. Detective Randy Mullinax, Detective Tom Jensen, Dr. Mary Ellen O'Toole.

[51] King County Police Confession Tape 37, Page 22. *State v. Ridgway* Case No. 01-1-10270-9. Seattle, Washington. June 19, 2003. Detective Randy Mullinax Detective Jon Mattsen.

[52] King County Police Confession Tape 239, Page 1. *State v. Ridgway* Case No. 01-1-10270-9. Seattle, Washington. September 3, 2003. Detective Tom Jensen, Detective Jon Mattsen, Detective Sue Peters.

[53] King County Police Confession Tape 239, Page 28. *State v. Ridgway* Case No. 01-1-10270-9. Seattle, Washington. September 3, 2003. Detective Tom Jensen, Detective Jon Mattsen, Detective Sue Peters.

[54] King County Police Confession Tape 274, Page 21. *State v. Ridgway* Case No. 01-1-10270-9. Seattle, Washington. October 7, 2003. Detective Randy Mullinax, Detective Tom Jensen.

[55] King County Police Confession Tape 281, Page 33. *State v. Ridgway* Case No. 01-1-10270-9. Seattle, Washington. October 13, 2003. Detective Tom Jensen, Detective Jon Mattsen, Detective Sue Peters, Detective Raphael Crenshaw.

[56] King County Police Confession Tape 281, Page 34. *State v. Ridgway* Case No. 01-1-10270-9. Seattle, Washington. October 13, 2003. Detective Tom Jensen, Detective Jon Mattsen, Detective Sue Peters, Detective Raphael Crenshaw.

[57] King County Police Confession Tape 281, Page 42. *State v. Ridgway* Case No. 01-1-10270-9. Seattle, Washington. October 13, 2003. Detective Tom Jensen, Detective Jon Mattsen, Detective Sue Peters, Detective Raphael Crenshaw.

[58] King County Police Confession Tape 347, Page 11. *State v. Ridgway* Case No. 01-1-10270-9. Seattle, Washington. December 15, 2003. Detective Randy Mullinax, Detective Tom Jensen, Detective Jon Mattsen, Attorney Mark Prothero.

CHAPTER 9: . . . CONFESSION OR DECEPTION? II

[1] King County Police Confession Tape 219, Page 6. *State v. Ridgway* Case No. 01-1-10270-9. Seattle, Washington. August 20, 2003. Detective Randy Mullinax, Detective Sue Peters, King County Sheriff David G. Reichert.

[2] King County Police Confession Tape 208, Page 27. *State v. Ridgway* Case No. 01-1-10270-9. Seattle, Washington. August 18, 2003. King County Sheriff David G. Reichert.

[3] King County Police Confession Tape 208, Page 23. *State v. Ridgway* Case No. 01-1-10270-9. Seattle, Washington. August 18, 2003. King County Sheriff David G. Reichert.

[4] King County Police Confession Tape 210, Page 17. *State v. Ridgway* Case No. 01-1-10270-9. Seattle, Washington. August 18, 2003. King County Sheriff David G. Reichert.

[5] King County Police Confession Tape 208, Page 39. *State v. Ridgway* Case No. 01-1-10270-9. Seattle, Washington. August 18, 2003. King County Sheriff David G. Reichert.

[6] King County Police Confession Tape 209, Page 16. *State v. Ridgway* Case No. 01-1-10270-9. Seattle, Washington. August 18, 2003. King County Sheriff David G. Reichert.

[7] King County Police Confession Tape 209, Page 18. *State v. Ridgway* Case No. 01-1-10270-9. Seattle, Washington. August 18, 2003. King County Sheriff David G. Reichert.

[8] King County Police Confession Tape 211, Page 24. *State v. Ridgway* Case No. 01-1-10270-9. Seattle, Washington. August 18, 2003. King County Sheriff David G. Reichert.

[9] King County Police Confession Tape 211, Page 33. *State v. Ridgway* Case No. 01-1-10270-9. Seattle, Washington. August 18, 2003. King County Sheriff David G. Reichert.

[10] King County Police Confession Tape 208, Page 11. *State v. Ridgway* Case No. 01-1-10270-9. Seattle, Washington. August 18, 2003. King County Sheriff David G. Reichert.

[11] King County Police Confession Tape 213, Page 28. *State v. Ridgway* Case No. 01-1-10270-9. Seattle, Washington. August 19, 2003. King County Sheriff David G. Reichert.

[12] King County Police Confession Tape 210, Page 15. *State v. Ridgway* Case No. 01-1-10270-9. Seattle, Washington. August 18, 2003. King County Sheriff David G. Reichert.

[13] King County Police Confession Tape 214, Page 18. *State v. Ridgway* Case No. 01-1-10270-9. Seattle, Washington. August 19, 2003. King County Sheriff David G. Reichert.

[14] King County Police Confession Tape 214, Page 19. *State v. Ridgway* Case No. 01-1-10270-9. Seattle, Washington. August 19, 2003. King County Sheriff David G. Reichert.

[15] King County Police Confession Tape 219, Page 6. *State v. Ridgway* Case No. 01-1-10270-9. Seattle, Washington. August 20, 2003. Detective Randy Mullinax, Detective Sue Peters, King County Sheriff David G. Reichert.

[16] King County Police Confession Tape 348, Page 45. *State v. Ridgway* Case No. 01-1-10270-9. Seattle, Washington. December 16, 2003. Detective Randy Mullinax, Detective Kevin O'Keefe, King County Sheriff David G. Reichert.

[17] King County Police Confession Tape 241, Page 45. *State v. Ridgway* Case No. 01-1-10270-9. Seattle, Washington. September 4, 2003. Detective Tom Jensen, Detective Jon Mattsen, Detective Randy Mullinax.

[18] King County Police Confession Tape 330, Page 6. *State v. Ridgway* Case No. 01-1-10270-9. Seattle, Washington. December 8, 2003. Detective Sue Peters, Detective Randy Mullinax, Dr. Judith Becker.

CHAPTER 10: EVOLUTION OF A SERIAL KILLER

[1] King County Police Confession Tape 21, Page 28. *State v. Ridgway* Case No. 01-1-10270-9. Seattle, Washington. June 15, 2003. Detective Randy Mullinax, Detective Sue Peters.

[2] King County Police Confession Tape 65, Page 14. *State v. Ridgway* Case No. 01-1-10270-9. Seattle, Washington. June 24, 2003. Detective Randy Mullinax, Detective Jon Mattsen.

[3] King County Prosecutor's Office, Summary of Evidence *State v. Gary Leon Ridgway* Case No. 01-1-102700-9, November 2001. Seattle, Washington.

[4] King County Police Confession Tape 141, Page 19. *State v. Ridgway* Case No. 01-1-10270-9. Seattle, Washington. July 18, 2003. Detective Tom Jensen, Dr. Mary Ellen O'Toole.

[5] King County Police Confession Tape 141, Page 23. *State v. Ridgway* Case No. 01-1-10270-9. Seattle, Washington. July 18, 2003. Detective Tom Jensen, Dr. Mary Ellen O'Toole.

[6] King County Police Confession Tape 141, Page 18. *State v. Ridgway* Case No. 01-1-10270-9. Seattle, Washington. July 18, 2003. Detective Tom Jensen, Dr. Mary Ellen O'Toole.

[7] King County Police Confession Tape 141, Page 22. *State v. Ridgway* Case No. 01-1-10270-9. Seattle, Washington. July 18, 2003. Detective Tom Jensen, Dr. Mary Ellen O'Toole.

[8] King County Police Confession Tape 133, Page 14. *State v. Ridgway* Case No. 01-1-10270-9. Seattle, Washington. July 12, 2003. Dr. Christian Harris.

[9] King County Police Confession Tape 133, Page 14. *State v. Ridgway* Case No. 01-1-10270-9. Seattle, Washington. July 12, 2003. Dr. Christian Harris.

[10] King County Police Confession Tape 131, Page 32. *State v. Ridgway* Case No. 01-1-10270-9. Seattle, Washington. July 12, 2003. Dr. Christian Harris.

[11] King County Police Confession Tape 65, Page 16. *State v. Ridgway* Case No. 01-1-10270-9. Seattle, Washington. June 24, 2003. Detective Randy Mullinax, Detective Jon Mattsen.

[12] King County Police Confession Tape 21, Page 28. *State v. Ridgway* Case No. 01-1-10270-9. Seattle, Washington. June 15, 2003. Detective Randy Mullinax, Detective Jon Mattsen.

[13] King County Police Confession Tape 68, Page 19. *State v. Ridgway* Case No. 01-1-10270-9. Seattle, Washington. June 24, 2003. Detective Tom Jensen, Detective Sue Peters.

[14] King County Police Confession Tape 103, Page 2. *State v. Ridgway* Case No. 01-1-10270-9. Seattle, Washington. June 30, 2003. Dr. Robert Wheeler.

[15] King County Police Confession Tape 22, Page 20. *State v. Ridgway* Case No. 01-1-10270-9. Seattle, Washington. June 15, 2003. Detective Randy Mullinax, Detective Jon Mattsen.

[16] King County Police Confession Tape 68, Page 23. *State v. Ridgway* Case No. 01-1-10270-9. Seattle, Washington. June 24, 2003. Detective Det. Tom Jensen, Detective Sue Peters.

[17] King County Police Confession Tape 338, Page 9. *State v. Ridgway* Case No. 01-1-10270-9. Seattle, Washington. December 10, 2003. Detective Randy Mullinax, Detective Jon Mattsen, Dr. Judith Becker.

[18] King County Police Confession Tape 31, Page 4. *State v. Ridgway* Case No. 01-1-10270-9. Seattle, Washington. June 18, 2003. Detective Jon Mattsen, Detective Tom Jensen.

[19] King County Police Confession Tape 66, Page 10. *State v. Ridgway* Case No. 01-1-10270-9. Seattle, Washington. June 24, 2003. Detective Randy Mullinax, Detective Jon Mattsen.

[20] King County Police Confession Tape 22, Page 21. *State v. Ridgway* Case No. 01-1-10270-9. Seattle, Washington. June 16, 2003. Detective Randy Mullinax, Detective Sue Peters.

[21] King County Police Confession Tape 31, Page 4. *State v. Ridgway* Case No. 01-1-10270-9. Seattle, Washington. June 18, 2003. Detective Jon Mattsen, Detective Tom Jensen.

[22] King County Police Confession Tape 31, Page 5. *State v. Ridgway* Case No. 01-1-10270-9. Seattle, Washington. June 18, 2003. Detective Jon Mattsen, Detective Tom Jensen.

[23] King County Police Confession Tape 343, Page 9. *State v. Ridgway* Case No. 01-1-10270-9. Seattle, Washington. December 11, 2003. Dr. Judith Becker, Attorney Mark Prothero, Attorney Todd Gruenhagen.

[24] King County Police Confession Tape 103, Page 24. *State v. Ridgway* Case No. 01-1-10270-9. Seattle, Washington. June 30, 2003. Dr. Robert Wheeler.

[25] King County Police Confession Tape 69, Page 2. *State v. Ridgway* Case No. 01-1-10270-9. Seattle, Washington. June 24, 2003. Detective Tom Jensen, Detective Sue Peters.

[26] King County Police Confession Tape 69, Page 10. *State v. Ridgway* Case No. 01-1-10270-9. Seattle, Washington. June 24, 2003. Detective Tom Jensen, Detective Sue Peters.

[27] King County Police Interrogation Tape 82, Page 3. *State v. Ridgway* Case No. 01-1-10270-9. Seattle, Washington. June 26, 2003. Detective Randy Mullinax and Detective Jon Mattsen.

[28] King County Police Confession Tape 57, Page 2. *State v. Ridgway* Case No. 01-1-10270-9. Seattle, Washington. June 21, 2003. Detective Jon Mattsen, Detective Randy Mullinax.

[29] King County Police Confession Tape 46, Page 7. *State v. Ridgway* Case No. 01-1-10270-9. Seattle, Washington. June 20, 2003. Detective Randy Mullinax, Detective Tom Jensen.

CHAPTER 11: IN SEARCH OF CLOSURE

[1] King County Courthouse, *State v. Ridgway* Case No. 01-1-10270-9 Sentencing Hearing, December 18, 2003. Seattle, Washington.

[2] King County Police Confession Tape 209, Page 4. *State v. Ridgway* Case No. 01-1-10270-9. Seattle, Washington. August 18, 2003. Sheriff David G. Reichert.

[3] King County Police Confession Tape 209, Page 5. *State v. Ridgway* Case No. 01-1-10270-9. Seattle, Washington. August 18, 2003. Sheriff David G. Reichert.

[4] Sheriff David Reichert, *Chasing the Devil: My Twenty-Year Quest to Capture the Green River Killer* (New York: Little Brown and Company, 2004).

[5] King County Courthouse, *State v. Ridgway* Case No. 01-1-10270-9 Sentencing Hearing, December 18, 2003. Seattle, Washington.

[6] *Ibid.*

[7] *Ibid.*

[8] *Ibid.*

[9] *Ibid.*

[10] *Ibid.*

[11] *Ibid.*

[12] *Ibid.*

[13] *Ibid.*

[14] *Ibid.*

[15] *Ibid.*

[16] *Ibid.*

[17] *Ibid.*

[18] *Ibid.*

[19] Shawnte Marie Fashaw (daughter of suspected Green River victim Becky Marrero), in discussion with author, 2001. Seattle, Washington.

CHAPTER 12: POP CULTURE

[1] King County Police Confession Tape 211, Page 13. *State v. Ridgway* Case No. 01-1-10270-9. Seattle, Washington. August 18, 2003. King County Sheriff David G. Reichert.

[2] King County Police Confession Tape 209, Page 35. *State v. Ridgway* Case No. 01-1-10270-9. Seattle, Washington. August 18, 2003. King County Sheriff David G. Reichert.

[3] King County Police Confession Tape 211, Page 14. *State v. Ridgway* Case No. 01-1-10270-9. Seattle, Washington. August 18, 2003. King County Sheriff David G. Reichert.

[4] King County Police Confession Tape 211, Page 16. *State v. Ridgway* Case No. 01-1-10270-9. Seattle, Washington. August 18, 2003. King County Sheriff David G. Reichert.

[5] King County Police Confession Tape 211, Page 17. *State v. Ridgway* Case No. 01-1-10270-9. Seattle, Washington. August 18, 2003. King County Sheriff David G. Reichert.

[6] *Ibid.*

[7] King County Police Confession Tape 220, Page 3. *State v. Ridgway* Case No. 01-1-10270-9. Seattle, Washington. August 20, 2003. King County Sheriff David G. Reichert.

[8] King County Police Confession Tape 220, Page 4. *State v. Ridgway* Case No. 01-1-10270-9. Seattle, Washington. August 20, 2003. King County Sheriff David G. Reichert.

[9] King County Police Confession Tape 220, Page 5. *State v. Ridgway* Case No. 01-1-10270-9. Seattle, Washington. August 20, 2003. King County Sheriff David G. Reichert.

[10] *Ibid.*

[11] *Ibid.*

[12] King County Superior Courthouse, *State v. Ridgway* Case No. 01-1-10270-9 Sentencing Hearing, December 18, 2003, Seattle, Washington.

[13] Carlton Smith and Tomás Guillén, *The Search for the Green River Killer* (New York: New American Library, 1990).

[14] Robert D. Keppel, *The Riverman: Ted Bundy and I Hunt for the Green River Killer* (New York: Pocket Books, 1995).

[15] Roderick Thorp, *River: A Novel of the Green River Killings* (New York: Fawcett Columbine, 1995).

[16] Kathy Mills, *Through a Mother's Eyes: The Untold Story of Opal Charmaine Mills, Fifth Victim of the Green River Murders* (Washington: Theresa Thomas Books, 2002).

[17] King County Journal Staff, *The Green River Killer* (Washington: King County Journal, 2003).

[18] H. Morrison and H. Goldberg, *My Life among the Serial Killers: Inside the Minds of the World's Most Notorious Murderers* (New York: William Morrow, 2004).

[19] David Reichert, *Chasing the Devil: My Twenty-Year Quest to Capture the Green River Killer* (New York: Little, Brown and Company, 2004).

[20] Ann Rule, *Green River, Running Red: The Real Story of the Green River Killer—America's Deadliest Serial Murderer* (New York: Free Press, 2004).

[21] King County Police Confession Tape 298, Page 10. *State v. Ridgway* Case No. 01-1-10270-9. Seattle, Washington. November 11, 2003. Detective Tom Jensen, Detective Randy Mullinax, Detective Sue Peters, Detective Jon Mattsen.

[22] King County Police Confession Tape 298, Page 12. *State v. Ridgway* Case No. 01-1-10270-9. Seattle, Washington. November 11, 2003. Detective Tom Jensen, Detective Randy Mullinax, Detective Sue Peters, Detective Jon Mattsen.

[23] John Marshall, "Reading Ridgway," *Seattle Post-Intelligencer,* October 18, 2004, E-1.

[24] King County Police Confession Tape 157, Page 2. *State v. Ridgway* Case No. 01-1-10270-9. Seattle, Washington. July 24, 2003. Dr. Mary Ellen O'Toole.

[25] *Ibid.*

[26] *Ibid.*

[27] King County Police Confession Tape 296, Page 2. *State v. Ridgway* Case No. 01-1-10270-9. Seattle, Washington. October 28, 2003. Dr. Judith V. Becker, Attorney Mark Prothero, Attorney Todd Gruenhagen.

[28] King County Police Confession Tape 296, Page 4. *State v. Ridgway* Case No. 01-1-10270-9. Seattle, Washington. October 28, 2003. Dr. Judith V. Becker, Attorney Mark Prothero, Attorney Todd Gruenhagen.

[29] King County Police Confession Tape 339, Page 22. *State v. Ridgway* Case No. 01-1-10270-9. Seattle, Washington. December 10, 2003. Dr. Judith V. Becker, Attorney Mark Prothero, Attorney Todd Gruenhagen.

[30] King County Police Confession Tape 339, Page 24. *State v. Ridgway* Case No. 01-1-10270-9. Seattle, Washington. December 10, 2003. Dr. Judith V. Becker, Attorney Mark Prothero, Attorney Todd Gruenhagen.

[31] King County Police Confession Tape 20, Page 36. *State v. Ridgway* Case No. 01-1-10270-9. Seattle, Washington. June 15, 2003. Detective Jon Mattsen, Detective Tom Jensen.

INDEX